SECOND EDITION

SOCIAL STUDIES CONTENT FOR ELEMENTARY AND MIDDLE SCHOOL TEACHERS

SECOND EDITION

SOCIAL STUDIES CONTENT FOR ELEMENTARY AND MIDDLE SCHOOL TEACHERS

Penelope Joan Fritzer
Florida Atlantic University

Ernest Andrew Brewer
Florida Atlantic University

Allyn & Bacon

Boston   New York   San Francisco
Mexico City   Montreal   Toronto   London   Madrid   Munich   Paris
Hong Kong   Singapore   Tokyo   Cape Town   Sydney

Series Editor: Kelly Villella Canton
Editorial Assistant: Annalea Manalili
Senior Marketing Manager: Darcy Betts Prybella
Production Manager: Kathy Sleys
Creative Director: Jayne Conte
Cover Design: Lisbeth Axell
Cover Illustration/Photo: Getty Images
Full Service Project Management/Composition: Saraswathi Muralidhar/
   GGS Higher Education Resources, A Division of Premedia Global, Inc.
Printer/Binder: Bind-Rite, Robbinsville/Command Web

For related titles and support materials, visit our online catalog at www.pearsonhighered.com.

Between the time website information is gathered and then published, it is not unusual for some sites to have closed. Also, the transcription of URLs can result in typographical errors. The publisher would appreciate notification where these errors occur so that they may be corrected in subsequent editions.

Library of Congress Cataloging-in-Publication Data

Fritzer, Penelope Joan
  Social studies content for elementary and middle school teachers/Penelope Joan Fritzer,
Ernest Andrew Brewer.—2nd ed.
    p. cm.
  Includes bibliographical references and index.
  ISBN-13: 978-0-13-701125-4 (alk. paper)
  ISBN-10: 0-13-701125-3 (alk. paper)
  1. Social sciences—Study and teaching (Elementary)—United States. 2. Social sciences—Study and teaching (Middle school)—United States. I. Brewer, Ernest Andrew. II. Title.
  LB1584.F75 2010
  372.3'5—dc22

                                                                                   2009000480

Printed in the United States of America
10 9 8 7 6 5 4 3 2   13 12 11 10 09

Allyn & Bacon
is an imprint of

www.pearsonhighered.com

ISBN-13: 978-0-13-701125-4
ISBN-10:   0-13-701125-3

To my mother Louise Kelly, who encouraged all my scholarly efforts, to my dear wife Heather, who is always supportive and loving, and to our son Drew, who will be the beneficiary of this and all other educational endeavors.

(from Ernest Andrew Brewer)

and

To all the men in the family who have served their country in wartime:
Thomas Gannon, Union Army, the War Between the States
George Oren Burns, Canadian Expeditionary Force, France and Belgium, World War I
John Harold Burns, Canadian Expeditionary Force, France and Belgium, World War I
Frederick Charles Hillier, (British) Royal Air Force, World War I
Charles Henry Fritzer, United States Navy, World War I
Charles Ross Fritzer, United States Navy, Pacific Theater, World War II
Thomas Albert Fritzer, United States Navy, Pacific Theater, World War II
Alan George Burns, United States Army, Philippines, World War II
Frederick Raymond Bland, United States Coast Guard, Atlantic, World War II
Joseph Gannon Bland, United States Army /Air Force, Korea, Korean War
Richard Stephen Burns, United States Air Force, Korea, Korean War
Thomas Albert Fritzer, Jr., United States Army, killed in Vietnam War

(from Penelope Joan Fritzer)

CONTENTS

Preface: A Word to the Reader   xi
About the Authors   xiii

Chapter 1   Why Study Social Studies?   1

Chapter 2   History   3
   Early Humans   3
   Europe   4
      The Greeks   4
      The Romans   4
      The Middle Ages   5
      The Renaissance and the Reformation   7
      The Enlightenment Period   9
      The Age of Revolution and the Industrial Revolution   12
   Asia   13
      The Byzantine Empire, the Ottoman Empire, and the Middle East   13
      India   15
      China   16
      Japan   18
   Africa   19
      Western Africa   19
      Eastern Africa   19
      Outside Influences   20
   The Americas   21
      Native Americans   21
      European Exploration   23
      Colonial Life   26
      Revolutionary War   32
      The 1800s   36
   The Twentieth and Early Twenty-First Centuries Around the World   39
      World War I   40
      World Between the Wars   43
      World War II   47

Cold War   50

Independence Movements   51

Cultural Change   53

History Resources   58

History Websites   63

Chapter 3   Geography   65

Basic Ideas   65

Water and Land   66

Reading Maps   68

The Physical Movement of the Earth and Its Effects   70

Continents   72

Asia   72

Africa   74

North America   76

South America   79

Antarctica   80

Europe   82

Australia   84

Geography Resources   85

Geography Websites   86

Chapter 4   Economics   89

The Basic Premises   89

The History of Economics   90

Government Involvement in Economics   93

Consumer Choices Related to Needs and Wants   96

Entrepreneurs and Wage-Earners   97

Supply and Demand   97

Economics Recourses   100

Economics Websites   101

Chapter 5   Government   103

The Purpose of Government   103

Values of American Democracy   105

Constitutional Governments   105

The U.S. Constitution   106

State and Local Government in the United States   108

The United States in the World   110

Resources on Government   111

Government Websites   112

A Final Word   115

General Resources for the Teacher   117

Index   119

PREFACE: A WORD
TO THE READER

This book is a short primer in content to be used by the hard-pressed elementary or middle school teachers as a quick reference to social studies chronology, events, and concepts. It does not claim to be everything they need to know in depth, and it contains some information beyond the scope of primary grades, where much of the social studies content concerns self, family, and neighborhood. Nevertheless, it is relevant for any teacher wishing to be better prepared to teach social studies and includes often-overlooked contributions of women and minorities. If teachers come from states that are strengthening their social studies content in the younger grades as part of the standards movement, this book will help them gain the confidence to keep up with and integrate newly required content.

For reasons of space, this book does not detail each state individually (home state makes up most 4th grade curricula), but gives teachers enough general historical and geographical information for them to fit their particular states into social context. It also gives a broad enough overview of both American and World History (grades 5–8) for teachers to find information on important events and people, see where significant moments in human history fit chronologically, and improve their own understanding of historical events and geography, economics, and government/civics concepts.

This is not a methods book; there are many good social studies methods books already on the market that address, for example, interesting ways students may learn about life as a U.S. Revolutionary War soldier, or a slave, or a pioneer. Rather, this book is aimed at raising teachers' content knowledge, often a problem with elementary education majors because the many pedagogy courses they must take frequently crowd out content courses. Social studies is often neglected at the elementary level, especially with the current emphasis on standardized testing of reading and math; but experience indicates that lack of teacher knowledge is also a major factor in the weakness of elementary social studies teaching. This work is intended to address that lack of knowledge and help teacher candidates pass state content licensure exams.

The book is organized into chapters on History, Geography, Economics, and Government, with the History chapters arranged chronologically by parts of the world, going through Europe, Asia, Africa and the Americas, and finishing with an overview of the twentieth and early twenty-first centuries, in which, because of advances in travel and communications, world events have been intricately entwined. The biggest emphasis is on American History and the twentieth century, which will be most relevant to many teachers. A substantial index as well as lists of content resources will help teachers further improve their social studies content knowledge and teaching.

ABOUT THE AUTHORS

Penelope Joan Fritzer is a former public school teacher who is a Professor in the Department of Teaching and Learning at the Davie Campus of Florida Atlantic University. She earned her B.A. in History at Connecticut College, a B.A. in Education and an M.A. in English at Florida Atlantic at Florida Atlantic University, and her Ph.D. in English from the University of Miami. Her research interests include various aspects of English and social studies education, literature as social history, and nineteenth-century British literature. She is the author of numerous articles on education and of *Jane Austen and Eighteenth Century Courtesy Books, Ethnicity and Gender in the Barsetshire Novels of Angela Thirkell, Aesthetics and Nostalgia in the Barsetshire Novels of Angela Thirkell*. She is the co-author of *Merry Wives: A History of Domestic Humor Writing, Science Content for Elementary and Middle School Teachers, Mathematics Content for Elementary and Middle School Teachers,* and is the editor of *Character and Concept in the Barsetshire Novels of Angela Thirkell*.

Ernest Andrew Brewer is a former public school teacher who is an Assistant Professor in the Department of Teaching and Learning at the Jupiter Campus of Florida Atlantic University. He earned his B.A. in Elementary Education and his M.Ed. in Elementary Education from the University of Florida, and his Ed.D. in Curriculum and Instruction from the University of Central Florida. His research interests include social studies in the elementary school, civic education, classroom management, character education, bullying, and social studies integration. He is the author of numerous articles on education.

CHAPTER 1

Why Study Social Studies?

Many people are interested in their or their families' own personal histories, since it is often difficult to understand people or their actions without knowing what shaped those people and caused those actions. History is an expansion of that desire for knowledge, extended to local, national, or international cultural groups and movements. Although many people are familiar with George Santayana's reason to study history, that "Those who do not know history are condemned to repeat it" (the Holocaust and religious persecutions spring to mind), many more are unfamiliar with Friedrich Nietzsche's idea of the "**historical man**" or, in today's more inclusive atmosphere, the "historical person." Nietzsche's point was that knowledge and memory of the human past and condition and ideas about where humans as a whole are going are what set people apart from animals (who live only in the present), and make them truly and uniquely human. The importance of knowledge of their past, and control and dissemination of that knowledge, to individuals and to groups, has driven the expansion of more inclusive curricula in recent years and resulted in struggles over whose version of history will prevail. Since **prehistory** has been generally designated as the time before written records, while history has usually implied a written record, and in the Americas, as in Africa, most early cultures did not have writing, it is only in recent years that more has been learned about the early cultures in those areas. Therefore, it is now possible to have at least a passing familiarity with them, as well as with the more traditional written histories of Europe and Asia.

Similarly, geography is inseparable from humankind's activities, since the vagaries of climate and the importance of place, particularly in relation to other humans, have shaped and continue to shape people's experiences, knowledge, conflicts, diversions, diet, housing, and, indeed, every aspect of life, and the reader would do well to keep an atlas close at hand when reading about history, since geography is crucial in making meaning out of historical events. Just as geography shapes those many aspects for humans, government is also affected by economics, and much of the history of humankind is the history of dealing with people's wants and needs and with the way they, individually and in groups, fill their desires for goods and services. Finally, from the time of the first permanent settlements, people's lives have been and are inextricably intertwined with the forms of their governments: whether those shall be benevolent or militaristic, helpful or hindering, guarding the people's rights or those of the governors, they have affected the quality of life of their citizens. These four most important social studies permeate most aspects of life for nearly every human being.

CHAPTER 2

History

EARLY HUMANS

It is thought by anthropologists and archaeologists that early forms of human life first appeared in the country that is now Tanzania in Africa (and possibly in the south China part of Asia) nearly four million years ago. As the population grew and spread out, people developed basic tools, the ability to use fire and the wheel, and the ability to domesticate animals. Over thousands of years, as they learned to grow food, they gradually developed from hunting-and-gathering societies to farming societies, which allowed them to stay in permanent towns, probably starting about 7,000 years ago. Civilizations sprang up, especially along rivers, often based on the need to irrigate and cooperate in farming. Most civilizations developed governments, religions, and the ability to write. Early major river valley civilizations were the Tigris–Euphrates in the Middle East, the Nile in Africa, the Indus in India, and the Yellow River in China.

Archaeology is the study of human history and culture through material evidence, using artifacts as a basis for both theory and proof. One of the most helpful tools in the field of archaeology has been the twentieth-century development of carbon dating, which helps roughly measure the age of a once-living entity by measuring its amount of carbon. **Anthropology** is the study of human culture both in context and in cross-cultural comparisons, and the two disciplines sometimes overlap. Much research on early humans has been done in Africa, in the Great Rift Valley. One of the most prominent researchers was Louis Leakey in the mid-twentieth century. Leakey's discoveries, and those of some of his family members, helped establish archaeology and anthropology as important fields of study.

The earliest known civilization is that of the Sumerians, located in the valley between the Tigris and Euphrates rivers in the area that is now Iraq. The Sumerians, and the Mesopotamians who followed them, built thriving societies that included irrigation, writing, religion, mathematics, and law. Other significant civilizations in the Middle East included the Phoenicians, who made glass and created an alphabet; the Hittites, who worked with iron; the Hyksos, who first used the horse; and the Hebrews, who created the first permanent monotheistic religion (Judaism), including the Ten Commandments. Eventually, the Persians conquered much of the Middle East.

3

The great Egyptian civilization arose in northern Africa around the Nile River almost 5,000 years ago. The Egyptians are famous for their elaborate polytheistic religion, their glorification of the dead with pyramids and mummification, their system of irrigation, and their advances in medicine and astronomy, many of which later influenced the Greeks.

EUROPE

The Greeks

Greek civilization, often considered a peak of human achievement, began with the Minoans and the Mycenaeans, then spread through much of the Middle East, culminating in the Greek "**Golden Age**," of approximately 450 B.C. The Greeks, organized by small city-states, originated philosophy, drama, the Olympics, an elaborate religion based on myth, many forms of mathematics, and democracy, although they also held slaves and denied rights to women and most of their foreign-born inhabitants. They originated beautiful building styles based on balance and proportion (known as the "Golden Mean"), as well as idealized sculptures of the human body based on the same principles. The two most important Greek city-states were Athens, known for culture and intellect, and Sparta, known for athletics and military prowess. Some important Greek figures were the philosophers Socrates, Plato, and Aristotle; the political leader Pericles; the dramatists Aeschylus, Sophocles, Euripides, and Aristophanes; the poet Sappho; the mathematician Pythagoras; and the doctor Hippocrates. It is thought that about 800 B.C., the poet Homer wrote the epic poems *The Odyssey* and *The Iliad* about the much earlier Trojan War, won by the Greeks. Several hundred years later, the long-lasting Peloponnesian Wars between the city-states weakened the Greeks, and they were taken over by Philip of Macedonia and his son, Alexander the Great. Alexander was a fervent admirer of Greek culture, and spread it widely throughout all the areas he conquered, including most of the Middle East and North Africa. Beginning with Alexander in the 300s B.C., the Egyptian city of Alexandria became a great center of learning with its famous library, botanical gardens, and zoo. Some great scholars who worked there included Archimedes, Euclid, Eratosthenes, and Aristarchus. Alexander died young and eventually the Greeks were taken over by the Romans.

The Romans

The earliest Roman civilization was that of the Etruscans, who mixed with other peoples to become the Romans. Rome became the capital city of a republic with two consuls and a senate instead of a king. The upper-class patricians ran most things and the lower-class plebians had little influence. The Romans battled the North Africans of Carthage in the Punic Wars, burning the city of Carthage after the Carthaginian general, Hannibal, invaded Italy by taking elephants through Spain and across the Alps to win the Battle of Cannae. Later in the republic, there were tremendous power struggles, and political assassination became common. After Julius Caesar, who had conquered Gaul (France), was assassinated for taking too much power, the senate was weakened. Rome, as it conquered its neighbors and spread its influence, ceased to be a representative republic and became a mighty empire under Augustus Caesar and the emperors who followed him. Rome was known for its well-organized, powerful army, and the Romans for their administrative abilities, including tax-collecting, road-building, and governing. They copied much of Greek civilization, including academics, religion, and building styles, although they originated the arch, the dome, and waterworks. The Romans eventually took over much of Europe as far north as England and as far east as the Danube River, most of north Africa, and a great deal of the Middle East. But as the empire got larger and harder to administer, the lower classes (including many slaves) grew in numbers and rebelliousness; the upper classes fell into decadence; and the army became more unruly and less willing to follow orders. In addition, the influx of foreigners further weakened the power of the government. Chariot-racing, animal fights, gladiator battles, and other spectacles were held frequently to give the restless population entertainment.

Christianity, the second monotheistic religion, grew out of Judaism in the Roman Empire, but Christ, himself a Jew viewed as a threat to the government, was killed by Roman soldiers about 30 A.D. (meaning Anno Domini or "in the year of our Lord." Another designation of the passage of historical time is "Common Era," using B.C.E., "Before Common Era" for B.C., and C.E. in place of A.D. The CE usage is considered sensitive to those uncomfortable using explicitly Christian references). In the ensuing years, Christianity grew and spread, especially through the efforts of the missionary, Paul, and later when Emperor Constantine converted to Christianity in 312 A.D. That was the fourth century, as the 1900s are the twentieth century, since the first century is expressed by only two-digit numbers.

During all this time, Rome was under increasing attack in northern Europe by Germanic tribes such as the Visigoths, the Vandals, and the Huns trying to get into the Empire, and it split into two parts as its leaders struggled for power. Eventually Rome fell in 476 A.D., sacked by barbarians, the western portion becoming increasingly chaotic and the eastern portion continuing as the Byzantine Empire.

The Middle Ages

As the government of Rome fell apart, taxes went uncollected, the roads went unrepaired, the army disappeared, travel became unsafe, and learning declined. Western Europe went into a period of small, local lords building strongholds (castles) to protect themselves and the local people became vassals and serfs tied to the land, since they owed the lords allegiance in return for that protection. Thus, the system of **feudalism** developed in Europe. This period was called the Middle Ages and lasted for approximately a thousand years. The early part of this period used to be called the "Dark Ages," from the fall of Rome until roughly the 1400s. This is the period in which the stories of King Arthur and of Robin Hood are set, and it included not only castles, lords, and serfs, but knights in armor, legends of dragons, and the building of great Gothic cathedrals with stained glass and flying buttresses, since the Church was the only important institution, and the only institution of learning, left after the fall of the Roman Empire. Most of the northern European barbarians were converted to Christianity, notably by the force of the Frankish (French/German) ruler Charlemagne. The Pope became very powerful, crowning Charlemagne "Emperor of the Romans" in 800 A.D. Additionally, many convents and monasteries were founded for nuns and monks, and religion played a large part in most people's lives. In the 900s, Vikings from

Scandinavia invaded Europe repeatedly, looting and killing, as did the Magyars of Asia and the Muslims of the Middle East. North African and Arabic Muslims swept through Spain into central France, and were defeated by Charles Martel at the Battle of Tours, reversing the Islamic advance, although Muslims retained control of some areas, including parts of Spain. Albania in southeastern Europe is still Islamic today.

Gradually the economies improved and banking, guilds, apprentices, trade, and towns developed and grew. In the late Middle Ages, noblemen expanded their holdings, becoming kings and consolidating power and land. In 1066, William the Conqueror of France invaded England successfully, which blended Anglo-Saxon (Germanic-based) and French (Latin-based) culture and speech. In England, a system of common law and jury trials evolved, reinforced by the Magna Carta of 1215, in which King John reluctantly agreed to limits to his power, trial-by-peer jury for the barons, and representation for taxation, all of which contributed toward a limited monarchy in England. The English monarchy controlled much of France in this period, notably from land gained through marriage with the great heiress Eleanor of Aquitaine.

Eventually French kings gained control as "absolute monarchs," with few checks on the royal powers in spite of the Estates General, the assembly of nobles and clergy, since the kings rarely called them together. Otto the Great had himself crowned "Emperor of the Romans," in the Holy Roman Empire (today's Germany), made up of many small German states. Italy remained divided into city-states, with the Pope in control of those owned by the Church. Throughout the Middle Ages and well into the Renaissance and Enlightenment, the power struggles went on between European royalty and the Roman Catholic Church. They joined forces to defeat the Muslims and regain Spain, and to sponsor the Crusades, Christian attempts from 1095 to 1291 to liberate the Holy Land and put Jerusalem in Christian hands.

The Crusades, which eventually failed, caused terrible hardship in Europe and the Middle East, and were marked by atrocities on both sides. Many thousands of people were killed, enslaved, died of hunger or exposure, or turned into looters, causing much criticism of the Church and a decline in stability, but a great increase in trade and knowledge from increased contact with the East.

One of the consequences of that increased contact, however, was the arrival of the **bubonic plague**, also known as the Black Death, carried by fleas on ship rats, from Asia in 1348. It killed about one-third to one-half of the European population and led to mass hysteria, black magic, and increased persecution of the Jews by the terrified survivors (some of whom thought the plague was punishment for not trying harder to convert the Jews). The decline in the population led to an increase in both wages (fewer workers) and taxes (fewer payers), which in turn led to peasant rebellions across Europe, as workers resisted the taxes but were crushed in their revolts. Gradually, however, over the centuries they began to win slightly more freedoms and rights.

Learning increased as contact with the Byzantine Empire and Muslim world (Marco Polo also went from Italy to China in the 1200s) led to the establishment of European universities and new interest in the intellectual life. Scholarship was still centered around theology and the Church. Albertus Magnus and Roger Bacon promoted science, but the main subjects of interest for most people were still astrology and alchemy (the attempt to change lead into gold). Additionally, local languages had developed, some from Latin, and literature began using them in various epics, songs, and poems by troubadours and noble men and women.

There were also great changes in the way wars were conducted: the Hundred Years' War (1337–1453), fought over French territory by France and England, was marked by three major battles, in which it became clear that foot soldiers using long-bows were superior in battle to mounted, armored knights, ending the medieval form of warfare. In spite of their temporary wins, the English ultimately lost most of the land they had captured when the French were rallied by the young peasant girl, Joan of Arc, who led them to victorious battle. The French victory contributed to the power of the king, but in England, strong nobles fought for the throne among themselves for thirty-five years in the Wars of the Roses. It was finally won by Henry VII, who founded the Tudor dynasty.

The Renaissance and the Reformation

The Middle Ages drew to a close as Europe went into the period known as the **Renaissance**, for the rebirth of interest in knowledge and learning, often based on the culture of the Greeks and Romans. The dates of the Renaissance are approximately late 1300s–1600s. It encompasses great changes in art, literature, exploration, and science, which led to changes in government and religion, and to an emphasis on human life and achievement as opposed to the medieval emphasis on God and the afterlife. Religion was still a major issue, however, and the Reformation, the birth of Protestantism as a branch of Christianity, changed the face of Europe.

Johannes Gutenberg helped promote learning and literature with his invention of the moveable type printing press in 1454. Other important literary figures were the poet Petrarch, the political advisor Niccolò Machiavelli, the scholars Thomas More and Erasmus, and the poet and playwright William Shakespeare. Oil painting, perspective, and proportion were all discovered or invented, and although much painting still dealt with religious subjects, there was a new interest in humanizing them as individuals and in painting secular subjects, including portraits of great art patrons such as the Medici and d'Este families of Italy and of royalty around Europe. Some great Italian painters were Raphael Santi, Michelangelo Buonarroti, and Leonardo da Vinci, who was also a scientist and inventor, while in northern Europe, Jan van Eyck, Hans Holbein, Peter Bruegel, and Jan Vermeer were significant (all of them the so-called "**Old Masters**"). In architecture, too, styles shifted from the medieval and elaborate Gothic to the simple, balanced Greek and Roman styles promoted by the Italian architect Andrea Palladio.

The spirit of inquiry extended to religion. In the late 1300s John Wycliffe was condemned by the Catholic Church for translating the Bible (from Latin) into English for the first time. William Tyndale made the first translations of the Bible from Greek and Hebrew into English and was burnt at the stake in 1535. In the early 1400s, John Huss was executed for heresy for criticizing the Church, which was also in an internal battle known as The Great Schism, a power struggle over who would be Pope, at one dismal point, there were three, each claiming to be the one true Pope. German monk Martin Luther began the **Protestant Reformation** by nailing his 95 Theses on the church door at Wittenburg in 1517, objecting to the Church's sale of indulgences, or forgiveness, to raise money, in part to build St. Peter's Cathedral in Rome. To weaken the political power of the Church, some German princes defended Luther, whose main idea was that people could read the Bible for themselves and could achieve salvation without the Church's intervention. Europe plunged into a series of religious wars, with most of northern Europe following Luther or other Protestant reformers such as John Calvin in France and Switzerland or John Knox in Scotland and Switzerland. Most of southern Europe, led by Charles V, the Holy Roman Emperor, and later by Philip II of Spain, defended Catholicism while making some Church reforms, known as the **Counter-Reformation**, on the sale of indulgences and the training of clergy. Major elements of the Counter-Reformation were the Inquisitions (in which the Church inquired into people's beliefs to make them pledge faithfulness to Catholicism), especially the Spanish, which were very hard on Jews throughout Europe and on Muslims in Spain, as well as on Protestants. At the same time, many atrocities were committed by Protestants as well, especially at Geneva, the militantly Protestant city in Switzerland. France remained a Catholic country that persecuted its Protestants called Huguenots, notably at the St. Bartholomew's Day Massacre of 1572, where thousands of Protestants gathered for a wedding were slaughtered. Henry of Navarre, a Protestant who converted to Catholicism to become king, granted the Edict of Nantes in 1598, a policy of religious toleration that helped bring peace to France after years of religious wars. Following Cardinal Richelieu's advice, Catholic France sometimes helped other European Protestant countries for political reasons, trying to weaken the Catholic Holy Roman Empire and Spain in the Thirty Years' War. Through this pragmatic policy, France became the major power in Europe in the 1600s.

England's religious situation was unique. In the 1520s, King Henry VIII had declared himself the head of the English Church and given himself a divorce so he could marry again, in the hopes that he would have a male heir. His first wife had had a daughter, Mary, and girls could inherit, but he thought a male would better secure the throne in case of challenges. Henry beheaded his second wife for treason (but really because she gave him a daughter, Elizabeth) and finally had a son, Edward, with his third wife. Henry went through three more marriages (including another beheading), causing much scandal in Europe and the Pope's excommunication of Henry and his followers. When Henry died, his Protestant son ascended the throne, but died young, so Henry's Catholic daughter Mary became Queen and tried to convert England back to Catholicism. When she died after a few years, her Protestant sister Elizabeth (Henry's only remaining child) got the throne and made England permanently Protestant as it headed into the great period of power, prestige, and accomplishment of the late 1500s known as the Elizabethan Age.

Another element of the Renaissance was the new interest people and governments had in geography and exploration, with the prospect of land, wealth, and converts. Europeans were looking for an ocean route to the East, where they could trade in spices, silk, and other exotic goods. In the 1400s, Prince Henry the Navigator of Portugal encouraged exploration along the coast of Africa; Bartholomeu Dias sailed around the Cape of Good Hope and up the east coast; Christopher Columbus sailing for Spain made three voyages to the New World; Vasco da Gama found the sea route to India around Africa; and the Portuguese established many trading posts and plantations. In the early 1520s, Ferdinand Magellan's crew sailed from Spain around the world, although he himself was killed by inhabitants of the Philippines. There were many other notable expeditions by Spain, the Netherlands, England, and France, as countries competed for supremacy at sea and for wealth, with the honors passing from Portugal to Spain to the Netherlands to the English (cemented with their victory over the Spanish Armada in 1588). The French, while never supreme at sea and ultimately defeated by the British in North America, found fur trading in North America and their sugar islands in the Caribbean very lucrative. Colonial holdings, joint-stock companies, and gold and silver mining, especially for the Spanish, all contributed to the power and wealth of European countries flowing from the New World and from trade with the East and Africa, including the newly invigorated slave trade.

The Enlightenment Period

The Enlightenment was named for great intellectual achievements in many fields. In the early 1500s, Copernicus had suggested a sun-centered (heliocentric) universe, and later Galileo refined the telescope and promoted Copernicus's theory. Galileo was condemned by the Church, nervous about a possible loss of power, and forced to recant. Building on Tycho Brahe's observations, Johannes Kepler discovered that the planets revolved in ellipses, rather than in circles. In 1687, Isaac Newton, who invented calculus simultaneously with the German mathematician, Leibniz, published a very significant book explaining the laws of gravity and motion (thereby establishing the basis of modern physics). In this same period, René Descartes invented analytic geometry and wrote a book about mathematical method.

In other areas, Andreas Vesalius studied the human body; William Harvey explained the circulation of blood; and Antoni van Leeuwenhoek used the microscope to identify microcosms. Francis Bacon promoted scientific methods of observation, and Carolus Linnaeus invented classification systems still in use for plants and animals. Music went from the elaborate, Baroque style of Bach to the simple but powerful classical style of Mozart and Beethoven, as did art and literature. Thomas Hobbes suggested in his book *Leviathan* that people act predictably out of self-interest, so that strong government is needed, with citizens trading freedom for order in a "social contract." John Locke disagreed, writing that the purpose of government is to protect the rights of its citizens and that if a government fails to do so, its people have a right to overthrow that government. Locke's philosophy was the foundation for many revolutions, including the American and French. Enlightened thinkers valued education and freedom and questioned religious authority.

With the new contacts in the rest of the world came a tremendous growth of knowledge, so the period of the 1600s and 1700s in Europe is known generally as the **Age of Reason** or the **Enlightenment**, although there is, of course, much overlap between the various periods of history. As rulers and countries became richer and stronger, they consolidated their power, feudalism faded, and the merchant class grew. But the wars, often mixing religion and power, continued.

The Thirty Years' War of 1618–1648 devastated the various German states of the Holy Roman Empire. The war was a power struggle between the Austrian Habsburg royal family and the French Bourbon royal family, with the Catholic French siding with the Protestant Czechs in the Habsburg empire to weaken Habsburg power. The Protestant Swedes under King Gustavus Adolphus also joined against the Catholic Spanish and Austrians. The war, fought largely on German territory, killed about one-third of the German population. The outcome recognized Protestantism as a legitimate religion, one that the rulers of German states could choose; Spain finally recognized the Protestant Netherlands' independence; and France had broken the power of the Habsburgs and the Holy Roman Empire to become the strongest power in Europe.

In the ensuing years, Louis XIV and his advisor, Cardinal Mazarin, made France the envy of Europe with its strong army, its magnificent public buildings, and its elaborate royal life and support for the arts. But the king further entrenched the ideas of **absolute monarchy** and **"divine right"** of kings. In 1685, Louis XIV revoked the Edict of Nantes, which had granted toleration to Protestants, causing much of the middle class to flee and thereby weakening the economy. The economy was further hurt by Louis's many wars, especially the War of the Spanish Succession in the early 1700s, over the inheritance of the Spanish throne. France prevailed but had to make other concessions to Austria and England, so when Louis XIV died in 1715, the French economy was in bad condition.

Protestant England was also struggling with civil issues in the 1600s. James I of Scotland inherited the English crown, founding the Stuart dynasty, but he was often at odds with Parliament, many members of which were Puritan Protestants, rather than the established Anglican Protestants whose official Church retained many of the vestiges of Catholicism. The crowning of James I joined Scotland and England, but constant problems with money, taxes, and religion plagued him and his successor, Charles I. When the Scots revolted but Parliament refused to fund money to fight them, Civil War broke out in the 1640s. Led by the Puritan general Oliver Cromwell, Parliament reduced the king's power, made it illegal for him to raise taxes, and abolished the secret royal court called the Star Chamber. Cromwell eventually captured and beheaded Charles I and established a Puritan Republic, with an especially harsh treatment of Catholic Ireland. Cromwell's government became very unpopular by imposing Puritan ways on the country, so after Cromwell's death and his son Richard's attempt to run the country. Parliament gave the throne back to the Stuarts, crowning Charles II. But religion was still an issue. The Stuarts were sympathetic to Catholics, while England was officially Anglican again. When Charles died and his Catholic brother, James II, had a male heir, Parliament drove him out in the "Glorious Revolution" of 1688 and invited James's older, Protestant daughter, Mary, to take the throne with her Dutch husband William of Orange, "The Protestant Champion." Their invitation was conditional on them signing the English Bill of Rights limiting the powers of the monarchy, which they did. Parliament approved the **Act of Settlement**, stating that no Catholic could inherit the British throne, thus passing it in the early 1700s to the nearest Protestant relative, an obscure German prince (descendant of one of James I's daughters), who became George I of England. This disposition had major consequences, most notably a major growth of power on the part of Parliament, which was dealing with a foreign, non-English-speaking king, who appointed a series of ministers to help him rule. Out of that situation evolved a "prime minister," who effectively ran the government, establishing an important English tradition.

Inspired partly by the American Revolution of 1776, the French began a revolution that had long-lasting consequences and served as a beacon for many other countries. The French Revolution was begun in 1789 when the nobles pressed King Louis XVI to call a meeting of the Estates General, made up of nobles, clergy, and representatives of the Third Estate (the middle and lower classes combined). Quarrels broke out as the middle classes demanded better representation, and some clergy and nobles sided with them to form the National Assembly. Class differences were great in France, with most of the tax burden and social restrictions falling on the middle and lower classes, who were angry and resentful. France was in terrible condition financially, mostly as the result of Louis XIV's and Louis XV's previous wars and of an inequitable tax system. Louis XV himself, recognizing the problem and seeing no way to fix it, summed it up in the phrase "After me, the deluge!" The years 1788–1789 were also times of bad harvest, which drove up the price of food, and, on July 14, 1789, the masses stormed the Bastille prison and released the prisoners as an act of defiance.

The revolution ended feudalism in France and declared the "Rights of Man and Citizen," but not of women, in spite of demands by female revolutionaries such as Olympe de Gouges forced upon the king at Versailles by the "Bread March of the Women," which included men disguised as women. But in spite of a new constitution that limited the power of the king and the Church and expanded voting rights mostly for middle-class males, violence spread across France. Peasants, dismayed by years of bad treatment by the upper class, killed, looted, and burned. Their actions culminated in the "**Reign of Terror**," in which the revolutionaries, led by Robespierre's radical Jacobins, publicly beheaded thousands thought unsympathetic to the revolution. Two of the victims were King Louis XVI and his wife, Marie-Antoinette, who supposedly, upon being told the people had no bread, said "Let them eat cake!" showing her lack of understanding and empathy. Their deaths, and the death of their young son in prison, made France a republic. In the midst of all this internal upheaval, France went to war against Austria and Prussia, assembling a giant army that was eventually taken over by the young revolutionary general Napoleon Bonaparte when the Directory, a moderate group that replaced the Jacobins, failed. Napoleon quickly consolidated his power in France, seizing control in 1799 and crowning himself emperor in 1804.

Napoleon made many modern reforms, including imposing the metric system and the Code Napoleon, which promoted male equality and protected freedom of religion and property rights and is still used as the basis of law in France. The code also supported public education and a merit system in government and army promotions, and Napoleon finally made peace with the Catholic Church, which had disapproved of its loss of privilege in the revolution. He also carried on a series of wars, conquering much of Europe in spite of terrible losses as he tried and failed to take Russia, then losing his gains. He eventually was defeated at the Battle of the Nations in Leipzeig, Germany in 1814 after which he was exiled to the island of Elba in the Mediterranean. He was defeated again at Waterloo in Belgium in 1815 after escaping from Elba and raising another army. In the end, Napoleon was exiled to the British island of St. Helena in the South Atlantic, where he died six years later.

Eastern Europe continued to grow in this period: Russia first became a country in the 1400s under Czar Ivan the Great, who resisted the Mongols and gained much land. In the 1500s, Ivan the Terrible strengthened Russia but murdered thousands. On his death, Russia fell into a "Time of Troubles," that was only ended when the upper class elected Michael Romanov as Czar in 1613. The Romanovs unified the country, and in the late 1600s and early 1700s, Peter the Great modernized and strengthened it. That trend continued under Catherine the Great in the late 1700s, but in spite of her support as an "**enlightened despot**" for learning and culture, Russia, with its huge population of downtrodden serfs, lagged behind the other European countries. One of the changes Catherine made was to help partition Poland, which had been a strong empire in the 1500s and 1600s. By the late 1700s, Poland was unable to resist being swallowed by its neighbors Russia, Prussia, and Austria, much to the dismay of Polish patriots such as Tadeusz Kosciuszko. Similarly, Hungary was under constant attack from its neighbors, first Mongols, then Poles and Ottoman Turks, finally becoming part of the Austrian Empire. The Austrian throne was inherited in the 1740s by Maria Theresa, leading to the War of the Austrian Succession, which in turn led to the Seven Years' War in the 1750s. But Maria Theresa turned out to be a very astute ruler, who gained much land for Austria in the three Polish partitions. It was said of her that "She cried but she kept on taking."

The Age of Revolution and the Industrial Revolution

After the defeat of Napoleon in the early 1800s, the Congress of Vienna realigned European borders and put monarchs back on most thrones. However, the liberal ideas of equality and human rights persisted in revolutions throughout much of the century. There were revolutions in several countries in the early 1820s (Greece, Spain, Russia, and the Italian and German states of the Austrian empire), in 1830 (France, Italy, Belgium, and Poland), in 1848 (France, Austria, Bohemia, Hungary, and the small states in Germany and Italy) and in 1871 (France again). Most of the revolutions failed at their moment but their ideals eventually prevailed as most European countries became representative democracies (with the notable exception of Russia). In the 1860s and 1870s, Italy unified, through the efforts of the patriots Mazzini, Cavour, and Garibaldi, as did Germany, largely through Bismarck's policy of small strategic wars with Denmark, Austria, and France. The strength of Germany in the Franco-Prussian War of 1870–1871 shocked Europe and changed the balance of power, eventually leading to World War I. Europe was also involved in the Crimean War, fought largely in southern Russia. Britain and France supported the Turkish Ottoman Empire in order to limit Russia, and Florence Nightingale founded modern nursing during this war.

The main cultural movement of the first half of the 1800s in Europe was **Romanticism**, which stressed a reverence for nature, emotion over reason, imagination, the glorification of the individual, the uniqueness of nationality, and the glory of the past, especially the gothic/medieval period. Romanticism rejected the balanced Enlightenment ideas of order and reason, and in its glorification of nature and the past, it was a reaction against the Industrial Revolution. Mary Shelley's *Frankenstein* and Emily Brontë's *Wuthering Heights*, along with William Wordsworth's nature poetry, were notable in literature, as were the works of Frédéric Chopin, Richard Wagner, and Giuseppe Verdi (all glorifying nationalism) in music.

The **Industrial Revolution**, which had begun in England in the 1700s in the coal mining and textile industries, became increasingly important in the 1800s. The steam engine was first developed in 1702 to pump water out of coal mines. It was later improved and used for transportation, first for steamships, then for the newly invented locomotives. Some of the early inventions for textile production were the flying shuttle, the spinning jenny, the power loom, and the cotton gin. Because the size of some of the equipment meant it could not be used at home, in the 1800s factories grew up and people increasingly worked not on the land but in cities. Iron became more and more important for machinery, and several new processes were developed to make it more efficient and then to turn it into steel. Experiments with electricity led to the telegraph, electric lights, and the phonograph. Thomas Edison was particularly inventive in this area.

With the invention of the internal combustion engine, cars followed, and shortly after the turn of the century, the Wright brothers invented the airplane. The change in the traditional ways of life caused major social change, including the enclosure of many common lands in England, forcing people off the land and into the cities. England, soon followed by the United States, Germany, and France, became the world's first major industrial power.

In the first half of the 1800s, there had been little regulation of working and living conditions in the factories and cities, and life was very hard for people as they left their rural areas for the hardships of the new life. But as the century went on, governments, often pushed by unions or philanthropists, responded with safety and health reforms. By the end of the nineteenth century, some of the long-term benefits of the Industrial Revolution became apparent: cheaper goods, new opportunities, more education, and an increased standard of living. These reforms extended to politics as well, especially in England, where increased representation and broadened voting rights buffered England from the revolutions on the continent.

ASIA

The Byzantine Empire, the Ottoman Empire, and the Middle East

The eastern part of the Roman Empire, after the fall of Rome (see Europe), continued to exert influence, especially under Justinian and Theodora in the 500s A.D. In 1054, the Byzantine Empire, as it was called, broke with the Roman Catholic Church to become Eastern Orthodox Christian. The areas later converted to Christianity by Constantinople, such as Greece and Russia and other Slavic countries, also were Eastern Orthodox. The empire was under constant attacks from eastern neighbors and was finally taken by the Ottoman Turks in 1453. Throughout this period, the Mongols under Genghis Khan, Kublai Khan, and Tamerlane put together the largest empire ever known, dominating large chunks of Asia in the 1200s and 1300s, including Russia and India.

Islam (the third monotheistic religion, based on the holy book the Koran) arose around the prophet Mohammed in the early 600s A.D. in Arabia, with conversion as a major component. The Arabic language and culture spread with Islam west across North Africa, east into India, and even north into Europe, leaving Muslims defeated at Tours in France but ruling parts of eastern Europe and Spain for almost 500 years. In many ways, Muslim civilization was very sophisticated, encouraging scholarship and artistic advances. Suleiman I "the Magnificent" ruled the vast empire of the Ottoman Turks in the 1500s, including most of the Middle East. Although the Turks held their empire until after World War I, the Muslim world became more static due, in part, to a religious ruling that all essential and true knowledge was contained in the Koran, about the same time the West was heading into the Renaissance and Enlightenment. Consequently, the Muslim world started to fall behind in culture, education, and prosperity.

During World War I, the Ottoman Empire fought on the side of the Central Powers (Germany, Austria, and Bulgaria), but many of the Arabs within it fought on the Allied side, hoping for independence from the Turks. When the Ottoman Empire broke up after World War I, Britain and France were given mandates by the League of Nations to administer various countries, although the Arab nationalists saw this as a betrayal. Iraq, Palestine, Egypt, and Arabia fell under Britain's influence, while Syria and Lebanon came under France's. Turkey was greatly modernized by Mustafa Kemal, known as "Ataturk," into the first independent secular state in the Middle East. Iraq and Iran, known until 1935 as Persia, became independent nations, as did Egypt by 1936. Eventually so did the countries that made up Arabia, except for Palestine. Britain in the Balfour Declaration of World War I supported a Zionist (Jewish) homeland in Palestine, further enraging the Arabs, who considered it theirs. After World War II, Britain gave the Palestinian problem to the United Nations, which in 1948 created the Jewish state of Israel, claimed by the Jews as their ancient homeland, in the aftermath of the Holocaust. Arabs saw the move as unfair, since the Holocaust had been a European event. They refused to recognize Israel's legal existence, and six Arab countries immediately attacked it. The Israelis successfully resisted the attack, but several small wars were fought in the area over the next fifty years. These included incidents with Egypt over the Suez Canal in 1956, the Six Day War of 1967 (in which Israel picked up the Sinai Peninsula, the Golan Heights, and the West Bank of the Jordan River, including the Arab portion of Jerusalem), and the October War of 1973. Throughout, the Palestinian Arabs, many dislocated by the division of Palestine and by the fighting, suffered poverty in refugee camps. In 1964 they formed the Palestine Liberation Organization, headed by Yasir Arafat, to represent them, often through terrorist activities. In 1978–1979, Egypt and Israel made peace, but in the early 1980s, war broke out between Israel and Lebanon, and more unrest followed throughout the region. From the 1990s, the Arab Palestinians had some success with an uprising known as the Intifada, and are currently demanding more self-government within Israel.

Political unrest was common in the entire Middle East throughout the twentieth century, exacerbated by the development of the oil industry, which made influences and alliances, both internally and with other parts of the world, very important. The civil war in Lebanon, mostly among Palestinian Arabs, Christians, and Muslims, devastated the country in the 1970s and 1980s and drew in both Syria and Israel. Some nations, notably Saudi Arabia, Kuwait, Oman, Qatar, Bahrain, and the United Arab Emirates, became very wealthy from their oil reserves. Western culture began to influence many of these nations, but the latter part of the century saw a rise in religious fundamentalism in both rich and poor Arab countries and a rejection of Western values. This backlash was evidenced by the 1979 exile of the Shah of Iran by Muslim leaders, and the subsequent kidnapping of Americans at the embassy there. They were eventually released after more than a year's captivity. In the 1990s, the Taliban, a very fundamentalist rebel group, took over the government of Afghanistan, imposing tremendous limitations on women's rights in the name of religion, a view rejected by moderate Muslims.

On September 11, 2001, four passenger planes were hijacked by Islamic fundamentalist terrorists unhappy with U.S. influence and were used as weapons to bomb significant U.S. locations. The two World Trade Center towers in New York

City were each hit by a plane a few minutes apart, and the Pentagon in a Virginia suburb of Washington, D.C., was hit by a third plane. The fourth plane, United Flight 93, was heroically thwarted when some of its passengers, alerted by cell phone to those previous crashes, diverted the plane from its presumed White House or Capitol target, overpowering the hijackers but not able to stop its subsequent crash in a Pennsylvania field. Over 3,000 people on the ground and in the air were killed in those events. Despite the fact that most of the hijackers were Saudi nationals, attention turned to the Taliban in Afghanistan, which supported Al Qaeda, a Sunni Islamic fundamentalist terrorist group, one of whose leaders, Osama Bin Laden, located in Afghanistan, was the Saudi architect behind "9/11." Later in 2001, the Taliban was removed as Afghanistan's government by Afghans allied with the United States and other countries. When U.S. attention later turned to Iraq with the invasion and subsequent occupation there, the Taliban regrouped and continues to be an aggressive presence in Afghanistan at this writing.

The Middle East continues to be an area of unrest with sporadic fighting between the various traditional Middle Eastern countries, between Islamic countries and Israel, and between the Israelis and the Palestinians. There have been many efforts at peace, but thus far they have not been lasting.

India

From its earliest history until the present day, India has been an amalgamation of different peoples, cultures, religions, and languages. The early cities of Harappa and Mohenjo-Daro lasted until about 2000 B.C., then were supplanted in northwest India by a series of city-states established by the Aryanas. They created the Vedas and the Upanishads, books of elaborate religious knowledge interpreted by priests known as Brahmins out of which grew Hinduism and the caste system. About 500 B.C. Gautama Buddha founded Buddhism, based on the Four Noble Truths, stressing ethics and unselfishness, rather than ceremonies, but it became more successful in other Asian countries than in India.

After the defeats of the Persians in northwestern India, and just after Alexander the Great's forays in the 300s B.C., Chandragupta Maurya efficiently organized much of northern India. It passed to his son and then his grandson Asoka, a great ruler who rejected violence, worked hard for his people, and cared deeply for all living things. About 100 years after his death, the Gupta Empire, heavily influenced by Hinduism and Buddhism and very advanced in mathematics, united much of northern India again, until about 500 A.D., when northern India fell again into disarray. After a series of invasions over the course of the next several hundred years, the Muslims succeeded in setting up an unstable empire that became a center of learning and culture but was defeated by the Mongols in the 1300s and 1400s. They set up their own Mogul empire in India in the 1500s under Babur and his grandson Akbar, a skillful ruler and general. Akbar's descendants were good diplomatists and rulers who supported toleration, learning, and the arts, including the building of the Taj Mahal, until Aurangzeb, who ceased religious toleration. He concentrated on adding land through war and created many enemies and much disunity in the country in the process.

By the late 1400s, the Portuguese had started arriving in India, soon followed by other Europeans. The English prevailed there, mostly through the efforts of

Robert Clive and the East India (trading) Company. The English successfully pushed out the competitive French, eventually making India the "jewel in the crown" of the British Empire in 1876. Britain had set up a system of education and a civil service in India, but often offended the people by ignoring or changing traditional customs. In 1857 the Sepoy Rebellion broke out, challenging British rule and causing hardship and distrust on both sides. Under nationalists such as Surendranath Banerjea and the Englishman Allan O. Hume, an Indian National Congress was formed and established a major boycott to protest the heavy-handed division of Bengal that ignored religion and ethnicity. The protest was successful and Bengal was reunited, giving strength to the nationalist movement.

After World War I, the nationalist movement grew, led by Mohandas Gandhi, who advocated nonviolent acts of civil disobedience, and Jawaharlal Nehru. Gandhi had based his actions partly on those of Henry David Thoreau, whose work *Civil Disobedience* grew out of his resistance to the Mexican War, and Martin Luther King, Jr. was later to study and emulate both Thoreau and Gandhi. Many leaders of the Indian nationalist movement were jailed by the British during World War II, but the British agreed to Indian independence after the war. Muslims objected to being a minority in the country, so Britain agreed to a Muslim Pakistan and a Hindu India. In spite of a vicious civil war that broke out between the two religious groups, India and Pakistan gained their independence in 1947, just before Gandhi was assassinated by a religious fanatic. The new government of India became a democracy that tried to enforce equality among religious and social groups, tried to give the country a sense of unity, and made much progress in promoting education and a strong national defense. India, however, continued to have unrest and political assassination, and much illiteracy and poverty as well. East Pakistan, separated from West Pakistan by India, got its independence from West Pakistan as Bangladesh in 1971 after another devastating civil war, but neither government was democratic, both remaining under martial and/or Islamic law.

China

According to legend, the Hsia dynasty, which learned to control the Huang Ho (Yellow) River, first ruled part of China. From the earliest times, the Chinese made silk from silkworms. About 1600 B.C. came the Shang, who made bronze, and then the Chou, who made iron and lasted 900 years in central China, a period known as the **Middle Kingdom**. About 500 B.C. an elaborate bureaucracy evolved, staffed by scholars, teachers, and philosophers, whose written guides to society became known as "the classics," or guides for proper conduct in society. Most Chinese philosophers valued the family, including aged relatives and ancestors, as the most important social institution. Confucius, who exerted the most influence for the longest period of time, addressed ethics, morality, politeness, and civic duty. Mencius believed in the goodness of the individual and the people's right to overthrow an uncaring ruler. Conversely, Hsun-tzu felt that people were basically selfish and evil but could be forced into behaving better, a Legalist philosophy adopted by the Ch'in rulers. Lao-tse and the Taoists believed in harmony with nature.

In the 200s B.C., the Ch'in rulers established an empire, building the Great Wall and imposing better standards in education, measures, and roadbuilding, but crushing local governments and curtailing intellectual freedom. Rebellion brought the Han dynasty, which lasted about 400 years until 220 A.D. and expanded China tremendously (especially under Han Wu Ti), also developing trade with other countries and developing the first modern civil service system. Under the Han, scientists expanded studies in astronomy, navigation, and medicine, and inventors learned to make paper and china. When the Han empire fell apart, China went into the Age of Disunity, which lasted until unification under the Sui in 589 A.D. They rebuilt the Great Wall and created canals linking the country's rivers. Power soon passed to the T'ang dynasty which, between the 600s and the 900s became the envy of Asia (especially for its poets) and, under its only female empress, Wu Hou, expanded to take Korea. At this time, Buddhism achieved widespread influence. The T'ang fell to the Sung, under whom painting and printing flourished. By the 1200s, the Mongols ruled China, during the period of Marco Polo's visit from Italy. They lasted until the Ming dynasty took over in the late 1300s, emphasizing classical Chinese traditions and knowledge and promoting exploration and the payment of tribute by other countries. The Chinese also invented gunpowder, pasta, and an early form of the printing press.

The Manchus took over from the Ming in 1644, but followed their policy emphasizing internal China, limiting outside cultural contacts. European countries clashed with China over trade, tribute, and social conduct. The British especially were eager to promote trade to obtain silks and tea, but there was little demand in China for Western goods, so in the 1700s, the British began importing large quantities of opium. This dismayed the Chinese government, which by 1839 was treating British subjects in China harshly in an attempt to end the opium trade. The Opium War was won by the British, who expanded free trade and gained possession of Hong Kong.

Floods and famine caused great unrest in China, and in the 1850s and 1860s, the Taiping Rebellion called for reforms but was defeated after twenty million deaths. As the government got weaker, foreign countries carved out greater spheres of influence. China was torn over whether to adopt or reject modernization and foreign ways, and as the government weakened, a new group of Manchus led by the Dowager Empress Tz'u-hsi took power.

In the 1894–1895 Sino-Japanese War over Korea, a modernized Japan defeated China. A new emperor called for the Hundred Days' Reform, but was forced to flee. The Boxer Rebellion, in a riot of antiforeign feeling, killed many Chinese Christians and Europeans in 1899–1900. The Empress died in 1908, and Sun Yat-sen seized power in 1911 in a revolution based on reforms, equality and national pride.

Years of internal power struggles and civil wars followed: the opposing Chinese movements were the right wing Nationalist Chinese under Chiang Kai-shek and the Communists under Mao Tse-tung. The Communists gained glory from enduring The Long March in the face of Nationalist persecution and from their spirited fighting against the Japanese during World War II, and in 1949, China became a Communist country under the leadership of Mao Tse-tung.

China instituted strict economic controls, as well as a strict "one child" population policy throughout most of the country, and in the 1960s, after Mao's death, went through a ferocious "cultural revolution," in which many members of the educated classes were reassigned to agricultural labor to "re-educate" them to the problems of the laboring poor. This upheaval devastated China's economy, but gradually government strictures were loosened, toward more of a free market system, although the country remained communist. The economy grew rapidly, and China is now an economic powerhouse and a major trading partner of the United States and other countries. Throughout the twentieth century and up to the present day, there has been a conflict between China and the small country of Tibet, which China has claimed and Tibet has resisted. There are many historic and cultural ties, but Tibet continues to assert its cultural independence in the face of Chinese occupation and influence.

Japan

The Japanese migrated to their islands from mainland Asia, and by 300 A.D. had an emperor who claimed descent from the heavens. Within a few hundred years, Japan had adapted writing, art, medicine, a legal code, and other types of knowledge from the Chinese. The Japanese also adopted Buddhism, which coexisted with Shinto, the ancient Japanese polytheistic religion based on reverence for nature. The upper class wrote poetry, and Lady Murasaki Shikibu wrote *The Tale of Genji,* the world's first novel in about 1000 A.D. As the upper classes vied for power, Japan, although still nominally led by a shogun, fell into feudalism. Local areas were led by samurai and daimyo (warlords), who promoted both the ideas of honor and bravery and a warlike culture. Twice in the late 1200s, storms helped repel invasions by the Mongols. Various military leaders struggled for power, and the Ashikaga shoguns who prevailed in the 1300s supported Zen Buddhism, which led to the new art forms of the tea ceremony, landscape architecture, and Noh plays, dance dramas on religious subjects. The late 1400s was the Age of the Country at War as the old feudal system broke down, but the economy and arts flourished. By the early 1600s, severe internal fighting, notably by Oda Nobunaga and Hideyoshi, had led to the establishment of the Tokugawa shogunate, which remained in power until 1868.

Meanwhile, Portuguese traders and priests had arrived in Japan in the 1500s and quickly established trade and Christianity, but in spite of many converts, there developed ill-feeling against Christianity and foreigners. The shoguns banned most foreign contacts in the 1600s (including firearms), except for the Dutch, who were allowed to trade only in a restricted area. For the next 200 years, Japan developed in isolation, as the shoguns tried to weaken the daimyo's power. The country prospered as internal commerce and education spread, and kubuki theater, haiku poetry, and printmaking emerged, but the upper class, dependent only on their land, fell on hard times.

In 1853, Commodore Matthew Perry forced Japan to open trade with the United States, and trade with other nations followed. A movement to expel the foreigners failed, but instigators deposed the Tokugawa shogunate and put a Meiji emperor on the throne of Japan as a symbol of national unity. They kept actual power for themselves, recognizing the importance of Japan industrializing in order to defend itself and to compete in the modern world. They wrote the Charter Oath, ending feudalism and establishing an assembly, and bought out the daimyo's land, modernized the military, and abolished the samurai, who rebelled but were crushed.

The Japanese took enthusiastically to modernization, expanding education and voting rights and establishing a representative Diet (legislature), as well as producing a constitution guaranteeing many civil rights. Soon, Japan's modernized military defeated China, and then Russia, to become the leading Asian power in the early 1900s. Japan joined the Allies in World War I, picking up some German territories in Asia. Increasingly aggressive toward its neighbors in the 1930s, Japan allied itself with Germany in World War II, bombing the American navy base at Pearl Harbor, Hawaii, in the early morning of December 7, 1941, in retaliation for the American attempt to use an oil embargo to curb Japan's aggressive drive to acquire more land. After its defeat and occupation by the United States, Japan quickly reindustrialized and became one of the world's strongest economic powers, and a democratic constitutional monarchy.

AFRICA

It is thought that early forms of human life first appeared in Africa nearly 4 million years ago, and the civilization that later sprang up in Egypt along the Nile about 3000 B.C. was one of the earliest important ones. Just south of there, the ancient kingdom of Kush reached its height in the 200s B.C., with its farming, ironwork, temples, art, and trade. Kush was conquered by its rival, Axum, in the 300s A.D. Axum concentrated on trade, made Christianity its official religion (the first state in the world to do so), and eventually evolved into the modern state of Ethiopia.

Western Africa

In the western part of Africa, south of the Sahara, the Soninke people developed "silent barter" for their trade in salt and gold. Their state developed into Ghana, at its height about 1000 A.D. with a king, an army, many officials, and major trade. Unlike the population of Ghana, which was disrupted by rivalries as Mali was growing stronger, the Mandingo people of Mali converted to Islam, and their leaders Sundiata and Abubakari II greatly expanded the kingdom, promoting trade and exploration. Mali reached its height under Mansu Musa in the 1300s, developing much wealth and a great capital at Timbuktu with a palace, mosque, and university. But Mali, too, eventually grew weaker, and the Songhai people under Sunni Ali and Askia Mohammed captured much of the area, but were finally defeated by Moroccans, who were armed with guns, in 1590. With the burgeoning influence of the Europeans, much African trade shifted away from Sahara crossings and toward the Atlantic coast.

Western Africa was also the origin of the Bantu people, who began migrating from Nigeria south and east about 500 B.C., adapting new cultures, languages, crops, and metalworking techniques as they went. In the 700s A.D., the Luba formed a central African state that grew and spread as a series of loosely associated kingdoms by the 1600s. The Kongo empire developed near the mouth of the Congo River in the 1400s, trading with the Portuguese. The Bantu spread to southeast Africa as well, notably in a great but now-mysterious civilization that created the Great Zimbabwe, massive stonework ruins of a palace, fort, and temple.

Eastern Africa

The east coast of Africa from the time of Christ had been linked to Arabia by trade in gold, ivory, and slaves. Many Muslims settled in east Africa starting about 1000 A.D., spreading Islam and combining Arabic and Bantu to form the Swahili language.

Independent city-states flourished in this area, but most were captured by the Portuguese in the 1500s, then by the Arabs in the early 1800s.

Outside Influences

The coming of the Europeans and their settlement of the New World and creation of labor-intensive sugar, rice, tobacco, and cotton plantations there put a new emphasis on the practice of slavery, as did increasing contact with Arabia. In ancient civilizations all over the world, slaves were often war captives or people working off debt, but now slave raids became more common and more profitable, and the nature of slavery became more permanent. Most West African slaves went to the Americas and most East African ones to Arabia and India, where the slave trade went on long after it had been stopped in the West: it lasted at Zanzibar into the twentieth century.

Some African rulers such as those in Oyo, Benin, Dahomey, and Ashanti, all near the Niger River in West Africa, became heavily involved in supplying the slave trade, to gain advantage over their enemies and to buy European firearms. Others, such as King Affonso of Kongo, resisted and called eloquently for it to end. The slave trade imposed a terrible burden on Africa, causing the loss of millions of people, most of whom suffered terribly and many of whom died in transit.

There had always been opposition to slavery, and Britain led the way in outlawing the slave trade in its territories in 1807. Britain also used its warships throughout the 1800s to stop other countries, American, European, and African, from such trade. However, that trade went on illegally into the mid-1800s. In 1787, British abolitionists, including former slave Olaudah Equiano, established Sierra Leone as a haven for freed blacks. Free American blacks started settling nearby and in 1847 formed the country of Liberia, modeled after the United States. In the early 1900s, Marcus Garvey also promoted "repatriation" to Liberia, along with calling for black independence, but most non-African blacks, established for generations on other continents, stayed where they were.

Throughout the 1800s, European and American explorers such as Sir Richard Burton and Dr. David Livingston explored the interior of Africa, charting geographic features and making notes about plants and animals, and Henry Stanley explored and claimed the Congo for Belgium, whose king earned international outrage for the brutal conditions there. Christian missionaries offered education and medicine, while investors, spurred by the Industrial Revolution, looked for raw materials such as cotton, rubber, and gold, and diamonds, as well as more farmland.

European governments fought with the Africans over territory and usually prevailed because of superior arms. Some notable clashes were the Boers (Dutch), against the Khoisan and the Zulu; the French, against the Algerians and the Mandingo; the British, against the Sudanese, the Matabele, and the Ashanti; the Germans, against the Tanzanians; and the Italians, defeated by the Ethiopians. The Europeans also competed among themselves, with the French and British both making claims along the Nile. There was marked bitterness between the Boers and the British in South Africa from the 1600s onward, where the British won the bloody Boer War in 1902.

While the British succeeded in controlling most of the area from South Africa to Egypt, the French took much of north and west Africa and the Portuguese, Spanish, and Germans each took portions of the remainder. The Berlin Conference of 1885 set up free trade throughout much of Africa, dividing all of it, except for Liberia and Ethiopia, among the various European nations.

Most European countries preferred direct rule over their colonies, but the British followed indirect rule, in which local Africans ran the country under British guidelines, in preparation for eventual self-government. Since many Africans were subsistence farmers, there were clashes over taxes, always owed in cash. Although Europeans brought improvements in medicine and education, they saw the colonies as income producers, demanding labor from the indigenous people who were often treated harshly and whom the Europeans viewed as inferiors, and causing many disruptive changes in African traditional lifestyles.

An entire class of educated Africans did emerge, often encouraging independence movements. Soldiers from African colonies fought in both world wars, and after World War II most African countries won their independence.

THE AMERICAS

Native Americans

In recent years there has been increasing interest in and research about the pre-Columbian Americas and the people who lived here. Earlier erroneously called "Indians," they are currently erroneously called "Native Americans," since anthropologists traditionally thought that the first Americans came across the land bridge between Alaska and Siberia in the last Ice Age, about 12,000 years ago. Newer archaeological evidence suggests that there may have been multiple entry points from Asia as early as 40,000 years ago.

The many groups or tribes were culturally different from each other; some were hunters and gatherers while others farmed. In general, they had a great respect for the earth and for nature and did not conceive of individual land ownership. There are thought to have been almost 2,000 different languages, with very different sounds and grammars, spoken by the early inhabitants, including Quechua, still spoken by 5 million Peruvians, and Guarani, spoken by almost a million Paraguayans. Although there were no alphabets, the Mayans and, to a lesser extent, the Aztecs, had symbols with meaning, and various kinds of ornament, braiding, and belts were used as memory aids. Researchers have been translating Mayan symbols for over twenty years now, and with the spread of European alphabets, some American Indians began writing their groups' history, handed down through oral traditions, so there is an increasingly more complete written record being built of the past.

It is difficult to characterize Native Americans because the various groups or tribes were so culturally different from each other; some were hunters and gatherers while others farmed, growing crops native to the Americas such as potatoes, corn, squash, blueberries, tobacco, peanuts, peppers, tomatoes, pumpkins, avocados, and pineapples. Various civilizations in the Americas worked with metals such as gold and silver, but they did not have bronze or iron, nor did they have the wheel for transport, although they used the concept of the circle, and their only pack animals were the llama, the vicuna, and the alpaca, all in South America. They practiced many different religions, most polytheistic, and most had a concept of heaven. As in most places, warfare was common, although some groups, like the Hopi, were very peaceful. Although some groups practiced elements of democracy, particularly along the east coast of North America, others, like the Peruvian Incas, were totalitarian.

One of the significant groups, the Olmecs (1200 B.C.), whose artifacts were lost about the first century B.C. and not rediscovered until the twentieth century, are considered the original culture of Mexico. They had hieroglyphics and a number system based on three symbols, and they developed a calendar and recorded astronomical information. They also built temple pyramids with flat tops and probably had a very organized society, since they carved and moved enormous stone statuary heads. They also played a ceremonial ball game that ended in sacrifice of some players. About the time they disappeared, the city of Teotihuacán was built in Mexico by farmers and traders, many of whom were talented artists. The Maya built city-states with paved roads and strict social classes, but Mayan society collapsed by 1000 A.D. perhaps as a result of drought and/or over population, although that is not certain.

By 1325 A.D., the Aztecs, nomads from the north, had built Tenochtitlán, larger than any European city of the time, where Mexico City stands today. They eventually conquered most of Mexico, earning their neighbors' hatred by collecting tribute and vast numbers of prisoners for frequent sacrifice in religious rituals. The Aztecs were excellent farmers, engineers, and builders, who based much of their religion, calendar, and crafts on those of previous peoples, and who created co-ed schools for their children.

The Inca empire was even stronger, encompassing much of the west coast of South America and including about 6 million people. Like the Aztecs, the Incas, who terraced their mountainous land for crops and developed irrigation, were sophisticated farmers and builders. They conquered many of their neighbors, learning their neighbors' techniques for metalwork, weaving, and pottery, and imposing strict control over them socially and politically, including holding slaves and practicing human sacrifice. Both the Aztecs and the Incas were conquered relatively quickly by the small numbers of Spanish who behaved ferociously toward them, in both cases helped by the unhappy groups that formerly paid tribute and were subjected to harsh treatment.

There were great numbers of smaller Indian groups north of Mexico: the Anasazi (now known as cliff dwellers, or Pueblos, since Anasazi was considered a derogatory term) built huge apartment houses of adobe all over the southwest from about 700 A.D. until they dispersed as a result of drought in the 1100s, and the Navajo, the Hopi, and the Apache (meaning "enemy"), took their place. Others were the Hopewell, or Mound Builders (after the large ceremonial and burial mounds they built), who farmed the central part of North America from about 500 B.C. to about 500 A.D., and the Mississippi, many different tribes of whom built thriving farms and cities with earthen mounds and pyramids along the lower Mississippi from about 1200 A.D. until about 1600 A.D.

The Eskimo or Inuit, who adapted to life in the Arctic by depending upon seals, walrus, fish, and caribou for all their needs, were probably the last migrants from Asia. The northwest coast people, including the Nootka, the Tlingit, and the Chinook, were unusual for valuing their possessions and observing their strict social order, as well as for not farming, since they could live off berries, fish, and wild animals because their area was so fertile.

On the east coast, the Creek Confederacy, including Choctaw, Chickasaw, and Cherokee, was strong. In the northeast, the Iroquois League, including the Seneca, Cayuga, Onondaga, Oneida, Mohawk, and Tuscarora, was dominant. The Plains Indians included Arapaho, Sioux, Pawnee, and Comanche. Most of these groups had a strong communal life run by a governing council and shared values of pride, self-reliance, and independence.

European Exploration

Christopher Columbus, an Italian exploring for Spain, arrived in the Caribbean in 1492. His was a controversial expedition, made up of adventurers from around Europe. He had been rebuffed in his plans by the Portugese (who approved his round earth theory, as did many knowledgeable mariners in Europe at the time, (but rightly rejected his proposed distances as too short) and by some Italian states, so he was pleased when King Ferdinand, encouraged by Queen Isabella, of Spain agreed to fund him. Coincidentally, Columbus left Spain the day the Jews were expelled as part of the Spanish Inquisition, giving rise to modern speculation that he might have been partly Jewish. Three times Columbus visited the New World, at various islands in the Caribbean, convinced at times that he had found India, Japan, or China, but baffled that it did not resemble any known descriptions.

There are still grand Columbus Day celebrations and parades, especially in the Italian-American community, but Columbus in recent years has fallen into disfavor with some who judge him by modern standards. Undeniably, he was a product of his times: brave, fearless, adventuresome and cruel, but he was indeed the first to open the New World to Europe, boldly risking his life, and those of his men (including an African) to do so, and he took some Arawak Indians back to Spain to prove his feat.

Was he the first to "discover" America? Not according to those who were already there; additionally, many modern Portuguese think their explorers were the first in the years just before Columbus. The Irish make the case for St. Brendan crossing the North Atlantic in a skin boat about 800 A.D. Scandinavians tout the Vikings, who certainly made it from Iceland to Greenland by the year 1000 A.D. West Africans suggest the short trip across the Atlantic from West Africa to the east part of Brazil, based on pre-Columbian sculptures with Negroid features found in Central America. And the Norwegian explorer, Thor Heyerdahl, proved in the 1950s that it was possible to go by his raft *Kon-TiKi* across the South Pacific from the west coast of South America to the islands of southeastern Asia (or vice versa?). The first "discoverers," of course, were those who became known to the Europeans as "Indians," today's Native Americans.

But, whether or not he was the first external explorer to arrive, Columbus opened the door for those who followed him to the New World. Just as he had followed the example of Bartholomeu Dias, who sailed around Africa, so did Vasco da Gama follow both their examples to reach India in 1497. Some of the most famous adventurers in the New World were Juan Ponce de León, who explored Puerto Rico in 1508 and Florida in 1513 for Spain; Vasco Núñez de Balboa, who crossed Panama and discovered the Pacific in 1513 for Spain; and Ferdinand Magellan, a Portuguese sailing for Spain, whose expedition successfully went around the globe from 1519 to 1522, although he himself was killed by inhabitants of the Philippines.

Magellan's voyage was particularly important, as it showed that the oceans were connected and that the world was larger than originally thought, and it gave valuable information about trade winds, water streams, and methods of navigation. Spain and Portugal quarreled over their various claims to new parts of the world and finally settled their dispute with the Treaty of Tordesillas in 1494, partially negotiated by the Pope. It allowed Spain to claim all new land west of a point about 1,100 miles west of the Azores (off the coast of Spain) and Portugal to claim all new land east of there, which gave Brazil and ports around Africa and Asia to Portugal, and effectively gave Spain most of the Americas, which included the majority of Central and South America and the southern part of North America. England, the Netherlands, and France also got small parts of South America and the Caribbean.

Later, Hernando Cortés conquered the Aztecs of Mexico in 1521 with a small army that included some Africans traveling with the Spaniards, many indigenous Tlaxcalan Indians who feared and hated the Aztecs for their ferocity, and Malinche, an Aztec noblewoman who had been sold into slavery. The Emperor Montezuma was killed, many Aztecs died of smallpox, and Cortés and Spain gained great wealth and glory. Francisco Pizarro defeated the Incas in 1532: the Spanish captured the Inca leader Atahualpa, ransomed him for a huge sum, then killed him anyway and took over the empire. In the 1540s, Hernando de Soto explored what is today the southeastern United States and Francisco de Coronado the southwest, including the Grand Canyon, claiming the land for Spain.

The Spanish set up their colonies in what came to be known as Latin America under rule by viceroys, or king's governors, but weakened their power by establishing *audiencias* (councils to advise them), trying to enforce limits on foreign trade, as did all the powers to a lesser extent, and barring those born in the New World from reaching high office. Additionally, much gold and silver mined in their colonies was used to buy goods from other countries, so the great wealth of the Spanish New World in the 1500s and 1600s had flowed away by the 1700s. The *encomienda* was the privilege granted throughout the Spanish colonies to certain members of the upper class, allowing them to hold large tracts of land passed on by a system of primogeniture and forcing Indians to work for them, with strict limits on how much labor could be compelled and with the directive to protect the Indians and supervise their needs. But the limits were unenforceable, given the isolation of most areas, and their needs were often ignored. Forced labor soon gave way to a system of debt peonage, a kind of sharecroppping or serfdom.

There also arose a large class of *mestizos*, of mixed Indian and white descent, in part because in the beginning few women came from Spain. Additionally, the Spanish brought in the printing press, established universities (there were five in Spanish America by the time Harvard was begun), and converted the Indians wholesale to Catholicism. The Church played a major role in settlement, particularly in the area that is now California, where a series of deliberately spaced missions staffed by priests provided shelter for travelers as well as serving the local population. There is much controversy about the role of the Church in regard to its treatment of the Indians, but it was generally better toward them than were other institutions.

The Spanish were not the only ones exploring the New World. Giovanni Caboto (John Cabot), another Italian, sailing for England, claimed Newfoundland in 1497. In 1562, the English Captain John Hawkins traded goods and slaves to the Spanish settlements in the Caribbean. Sir Francis Drake made a fortune for England when he seized Spanish silver in the Atlantic and sailed homeward around the world across the Pacific (to avoid other Spanish ships) in 1577–1580.

Later, Henry Hudson, an Englishman sailing for the Dutch, named and claimed the Hudson River Valley in 1609. The Dutch later established New Amsterdam there, renamed New York by the British when they took it, along with the rest of the Dutch territory, in 1664. In 1614, the Dutch explorer Adriaen Block landed on Block Island, east of Long Island.

After being reprimanded by his government for exploring for the Dutch, Hudson sailed for the English. On his fourth and last trip to America, he explored and claimed the area around Hudson Bay in Canada for England before he was set adrift in a small boat with his son and a few faithful sailors, by the rest of his mutinous crew, never to be seen again. A few years later, a small colony of Swedes and Finns settled New Sweden in 1638 in Delaware, giving America the log cabin. The colony was taken over by the Dutch in 1655 and then by the English when they later defeated the Dutch.

The Dutch also gained major trading rights in Asia and controlled much of the trade in the Atlantic, including slaves. In 1619, the Dutch introduced Africans in North America as indentured servants, and by the 1640s they were being imported as slaves. The Spanish, Portuguese, and English had been trading slaves in South America and the Caribbean throughout the 1500s, particularly with the development of the sugar plantations. Black slavery was never widespread in Spanish America, except for the sugar plantations of Cuba and Puerto Rico, but was common throughout the rest of the Caribbean and on Brazil's sugar plantations.

Unlike the Catholic Spanish and Portuguese, the Protestant Dutch were not interested in converting the Indians, but were concerned solely with trade. As a result, the Netherlands was the most prosperous country in Europe and it was difficult to get people to move to New Amsterdam, even for large grants of land, so some Dutch landowners turned to using slave labor. One English settler, Lady Deborah Moody, got permission from the Dutch to establish a colony on Long Island, where she bought land from the Indians and promoted religious freedom, after she clashed with the Puritans.

The Dutch controlled the Hudson Valley and had good relations with the Iroquois Indians (known first as the Five, and then as the Six, Nations), with whom they traded for furs. In 1664, as part of a European conflict, the English so intimidated the Dutch with their seapower that Peter Stuyvesant, the Dutch governor of New Amsterdam, surrendered without a battle, giving the English control of all Dutch territory in North America.

The English and French explored the northern areas unclaimed by the Spanish and Portuguese and both of the former fished the Grand Banks off eastern Canada, as well as searching for the northwest passage. Sir Walter Raleigh who claimed Virginia for the "Virgin Queen," Elizabeth I of England, founded a settlement on Roanoke Island off the coast of North Carolina in 1587, where Virginia Dare, the first English child in the New World was born. But when Raleigh's ships returned with supplies three years later, all the settlers had disappeared and only the mysterious word "Croatoan" was carved on a post: their fate still remains a mystery.

English settlers founded Jamestown, Virginia, the first permanent English settlement in North America, in 1607, hoping to make their fortunes with gold or silver or to find a way to the Pacific, as the Spanish had. Instead, farming was difficult and over half the colonists died of starvation the first winter. The winter of 1609–1610 was called "the starving time," as it was even worse. The Powhatan Indians helped the colonists with food but were not always friendly: many settlers and Indians were killed, and the chief's daughter, Pocahontas, saved John Smith from being executed in 1608. But eventually the colony prospered, largely through tobacco farming. Pocahontas was later taken prisoner by the English and ransomed by her father, but she had fallen in love with and married John Rolfe, who took her to England where she was a great social success but died of smallpox in 1617. Although Virginia origi-nally had a House of Burgesses for representative government, in 1624 it became a royal colony run by the king's governor.

English Puritans (Separatists called "Pilgrims") led by William Bradford, including twenty-eight women, landed at Plymouth Rock in 1620 seeking religious freedom. The Protestant Reformation had left England officially Protestant in the 1500s, but the Puritans did not approve of the Church of England, which they wanted to "purify" since they considered it still too much like the Catholic Church. In one of the great ironies of history, they had had religious freedom after they left England for the Netherlands in 1607, but they did not like the Dutch policy of religious tolerance nor did they like their children absorbing Dutch culture and ways, and they did not promote religious freedom in the colonies they established.

Originally headed for Virginia, the Pilgrims landed in Massachusetts, first at Provincetown and then at Plymouth. They agreed among themselves to the Mayflower Compact in which they promised to obey the laws they would jointly create, setting the precedent for participatory government. Over half of them died during the first year, but the Indian Squanto and others taught them to grow native foods, so in November of 1621, the settlers and the Indians celebrated the first Thanksgiving together.

In 1630, another group of Puritans headed by John Winthrop founded the Massachusetts Bay Colony with nearly a thousand people who settled in several towns in eastern Massachusetts. By 1640, more than 20,000 English were living in the colony, and Anne Bradstreet's first famous volume of poems, *The Tenth Muse Lately Sprung Up in America,* was published in 1650. Puritan men who were loyal church members had the right to vote and each town was represented in the General Court, the governing body, but all citizens were forced to adhere to the Puritan church

Colonial Life

Eventually, Anne Hutchinson and Roger Williams, among others, were run out of Massachusetts for religious nonconformity, and they founded towns in Rhode Island. When Rhode Island was chartered in 1644, it included votes for all adult males (this was later changed to males owning property) in addition to religious tolerance. As well as various Christian churches, the first synagogue in North America was built at Touro in 1763, about one hundred years after the first congregation had been formed. Although Jewish men were allowed to vote in Rhode Island, most colonies banned them from doing so because they were not members of the established church, but by the time of the American Revolution, there were about 2,500 Jews in America, some of them religious refugees from Latin America, as well as from Europe.

Thomas Hooker's band of settlers founded Hartford in 1636, which joined with Windsor and Wethersfield in 1639 to form the Fundamental Orders of Connecticut. By 1662 Connecticut had secured a charter from England, which expanded the boundaries and gave the settlers self-government. New Hampshire broke away from Massachusetts to become a royal colony in 1679, but Maine remained part of Massachusetts until it became a state in 1820.

In one of the oddest series of historical events, after more than seventy years of English settlement in Massachusetts, accusations of witchcraft were made in the town of Salem during the summer of 1692 by a number of young girls who claimed that they were being tormented and "proved" it by fits and peculiar behavior. Two hundred people ultimately were accused, including a West Indian slave, a respected minister, seventeen other men, and a large number of older women, among them the governor's wife. Those who confessed and named others as witches were freed, but those who denied being witches were tried and convicted on specious evidence with single witnesses and no cross-examination. Whether the girls' behavior was caused by hysteria, delusion, a suggestive book on witchcraft, or ergot (a fungus that causes hallucinations and grows on rye, a dietary staple at the time), the result was nineteen people convicted and hanged during the aberration known as the Salem Witch Trials. The trials finally ended in the fall of 1692 as the accusations got wilder and people began to doubt the accusers. Those in prison were released and the courts later annulled the convictions and awarded reparations to the relatives of those who had been killed. The incident continues to capture the imagination of Americans. In 1953 Arthur Miller's play, *The Crucible,* dealt with the events of Salem as a metaphor for the anti-Communist hysteria.

There were English settlements along the Atlantic seaboard as far south as Georgia as well as throughout New England. Generally, south of New England, the colonies tended to have a less religious flavor, and religious men like Lord Baltimore and William Penn provided for freedom of worship. In the southern states, many settlers were Church of England rather than more earnest Protestant sects, and economic success (also valued in the north), rather than religion, was often their focus.

The former Dutch colony New Netherland was given by Charles II of England to his brother the Duke of York, and a portion of it, called New Jersey, became a royal colony. James treated the Dutch in New York fairly, allowing them their own language and religion, but he allowed no settlers a voice in the government, which became a major problem when he inherited the throne and moved to abolish representative government in New England as well. When James was driven from the English throne, his colonies reverted to their self-government.

William Penn, a member of the Society of Friends, or Quakers, was given Pennsylvania as a proprietary colony, with a strong owner or ruler, by the English king in 1681 in payment for a debt. Penn shortly afterward was granted Delaware in order to have a coastline, and he promoted his colony with pamphlets in various languages promising cheap land (for which he paid the Lenape Indians, whom he treated fairly), religious freedom, and representative government. People came in droves, all nationalities, including many Protestant Germans called "Deutsche" for German, who became known erroneously as "Pennsylvania Dutch," and all religions. By the 1750s, Philadelphia, "The City of Brotherly Love," carefully laid out as a planned city by Penn himself, was the largest, most prosperous port in the colonies.

Another proprietary colony was Maryland, which was established by Lord Baltimore in 1634 as a home for persecuted Catholics, with religious freedom for Protestants also: the Toleration Act was passed there in 1649, guaranteeing freedom of religion to all Christians. The governor's manager, Margaret Brent, as his representative temporarily received the right to vote but as a female was refused a seat in the assembly.

In 1663, Charles II of England gave a charter for Carolina (Latin for Charles), which provided a rigid system of social classes, to a group of British noblemen. The northern section was settled in large part by Virginians who were subsistence farmers as well as tobacco growers and lumbermen, while the southern part drew a mix of Europeans of many different religions, emigrants from the West Indies, and African slaves needed for the major crops of indigo and rice. After constant power struggles, North and South Carolina became separate royal colonies with representative assemblies.

The last North American English colony was Georgia, whose founder James Oglethorpe arrived in 1733 with the first group of debtors released from English prisons. Not only was Georgia to receive debtors and other criminals, who each received fifty acres free, but it was to buffer the more northern colonies from the Spanish in Florida. Slavery and rum sales were not allowed at first, but it was difficult getting others to settle there, in spite of much cheap land. By the 1750s slavery was permitted, and by 1752 Georgia had become a royal colony.

Throughout the English colonies, the Great Awakening of the 1730s and 1740s was led by the English clergymen John Wesley and George Whitefield. They were joined by local preachers such as Jonathan Edwards of Massachusetts and their movement stressed free will, freedom of religious choice, repentance, and salvation through reading the Bible, contributing to the trend toward schooling and democracy.

The French were not idle during this time. In 1524, they hired the Italian explorer Giovanni da Verrazano in a fruitless quest to find a water route to Asia through America, and Jacques Cartier claimed eastern Canada for France by exploring the St. Lawrence River in 1534. Samuel Champlain founded Quebec, the first permanent French colony in North America in 1608, and explored Maine, Nova Scotia, and many other areas of the Northeast. Champlain was a fur trader, as was Louis Joliet, who explored the Great Lakes and the Mississippi with the priest Jacques Marquette. Sieur de La Salle sailed the Mississippi River south to the Gulf of Mexico, claiming its valley for France. French settlements grew up in Louisiana (named after the French kings) and around the St. Lawrence River in Canada. The French owned much land in North America, but they found the slave-run sugar plantations of the West Indies much more valuable than the fur trade, although in general the French were known for getting along with the Indians better than other groups got along with the Indians. France was the major power in Europe throughout the 1600s and fought the British, in Europe and in the New World, for supremacy throughout much of the 1700s.

In 1759, the French General Montcalm lost the most important battle of the French and Indian War at the Plains of Abraham in Quebec City to the English General Wolfe. The war was named by the British because they fought against the French and most Indians. Some Indians fought on the British side, notably the Iroquois, whose alliance was brokered by Molly Brant, a Mohawk woman who was the partner of an Englishman. In the peace that ensued, the 1763 Treaty of Paris let the French keep their rich Caribbean sugar colonies, while giving Canada to the British. This turning point established that most of North America would be English-speaking, not French-speaking. For this reason, the French and Indian War, part of the seven years' War in Europe, was a very significant war for Americans, and the source of later Quebec separatism, though its significance is often ignored today.

Near Alaska, the Russian explorer Vitus Jonassen Bering crossed from Siberia through the Bering Sea to the Arctic Ocean in 1728 without getting to the American mainland, but later sighted Alaska. The Russians traded with the Aleuts, but no other Europeans showed up until 1775, when both Spanish and English ships arrived, the latter sailing through the Bering Sea and into the Arctic Ocean in search of the northwest passage. In this same period, Captain James Cook was exploring not only Newfoundland and then the northwestern coast of America, but also Hawaii, Tahiti, New Zealand, Australia, and other areas of the Pacific. In Alaska, the French appeared in 1786. Spain, alarmed, sent an expedition in 1788 and founded a settlement in 1789.

In 1788, the British explorer John Meares landed fifty Chinese laborers to build a settlement, and traders from the United States arrived. Captain George Vancouver explored the area for the British several times in the 1790s. By then the Russians had established a major presence, with trading posts, forts, churches, and settlements, although they were never to be very successful with the colony.

The competition among the various countries was fierce all over the Americas, fueled by both greed and patriotism, and privateering (a country approving its private captains' raiding other countries' ships and sharing the spoils between crew and crown) and outright piracy (individual ships robbing other ships and frequently killing their crew for purely personal gain) were the rule rather than the exception. Since the Spanish had great silver and gold mines in South America, their ships were frequently the victims of raids by the English, the French, and the Dutch. Sir Francis Drake was the most famous of the privateers, but Piet Heyn in 1628 captured an entire Spanish silver fleet for the Dutch, while Edward Teach, known as Blackbeard, was the most famous pirate of this period.

Most countries granted rights to private joint-stock trading companies for exploration and settlement, including England, France, the Netherlands, Sweden, and Russia. Exploration and settlement were risky and expensive, and sometimes ships went down or settlements failed. Few individuals could afford to gamble their all on success, but the hope was that success would bring riches to investors and it sometimes did. The Spanish at first were mainly conquistadors, who looked for wealth, and Catholic priests, who looked for converts. Few conquistadors brought their families or intended to stay permanently in the New World once they had made their fortunes, unlike the English, and, to some extent, the French, both of whom turned early to permanent settlements and agriculture.

Relationships with the Indians were uneasy. Early on, the ferocity of the Spanish treatment of them was referred to as the "Black Legend," but some Catholic priests, most notably Bartolemé de Las Casas, interceded for the Indians in a lifelong campaign. The Catholic Church disapproved of slavery since most Indians were not enslaved when the Europeans arrived, and when the Indians were converted, it was considered wrong to enslave fellow Christians. Most slavery in Europe had died out by about 1000 A.D., although serfdom, in which the peasants were tied by law to the land and/or its lord, remained until 1863 in Russia, about the same time the slaves were freed in the United States.

Conversely, the Church tolerated slavery of Africans, who were usually enslaved before the Europeans purchased them, often by other Africans specifically for sale to Europeans for firearms and other manufactured goods, and their conversion later was not considered a reason for freeing them. Both Indians and Africans were treated very harshly and provided much labor for new enterprises in mining and agriculture. Africans usually better withstood the climate, in many places much like Africa, and working conditions, and had more immunity to European diseases.

The Indians were much more vulnerable than were Africans to disease, and the great majority who died as a result of contact with the Europeans, including nearly all the Arawaks of the Caribbean, died of diseases such as smallpox, typhus, and measles, rather than in the ensuing battles, much as the Europeans died from the Asian plague in the 1300s. Interestingly, historians are divided about whether syphilis was brought by Europeans, as it was in the South Pacific where it decimated native populations, or whether it originated in the Americas, since there was no recorded instance of it in Europe until after contact with the New World.

From its inception in the New World, slavery was a thorny and disputed issue. Approximately 10 million Africans made the horrific journey in harsh conditions across the Middle Passage, the route across the Atlantic, so named because it was the middle part of the journey. It is estimated that as many as one-third may have died on the way, and approximately 500,000 ended up in what became the United States. Most of the rest went to the Caribbean or South America. Brazil was the last country in the Western Hemisphere to outlaw slavery, which it did in 1888. But from the earliest practice, there had been severe misgivings about slavery, particularly by the Quakers and other religious groups.

It is a truism that slavery survived so long in the South and in the Caribbean because the labor was needed for large-scale agricultural production of cotton, rice, sugar, and indigo, while in the North, small-scale dairy and truck farming, crafts, and eventually industry shaped the society. Northern society also included a higher level of education dictated by mandatory education in New England village settlements spurred by Puritan desire for literacy to enable reading of the Bible.

By the 1770s about 12,000 slaves lived in New England, where they generally worked as household servants, farm laborers, or craftsmen and could buy property and had the right to trial by jury. Similarly, in the middle colonies, about 35,000 slaves worked in farming or industry, and from the earliest days Quakers spoke out against slavery. In the same period, the vast majority of American slaves lived in the Southern colonies, where they worked on plantations and in various trades. But they were heavily restricted by slave codes that forbade their learning to read and write, to meet together, to leave the plantation, or to own weapons, and they were often treated harshly.

There were, of course, free black settlers, some of whom were quite economically successful, and some of whom owned slaves themselves, as did some Indians: most Cherokee later fought on the side of the South in the Civil War for that reasons. Thomas Fuller was a favorite of early antislavery activists to demonstrate black competence in mathematics and mental calculation, and Benjamin Banneker, son of a

North Carolina tobacco farmer, was a self-taught mathematician and astronomer who in the 1790s helped survey and lay out the new national capital of Washington, D.C. More often, free blacks were small craftsmen, farmers, or businessmen, such as the furnituremaker Thomas Day of Milton, North Carolina, whose father was descended from pre-Revolutionary free blacks and whose mother was the daughter of a wealthy land-owning doctor. Many free blacks had come to America as **indentured servants**, as had many whites. Usually the agreement was to work four to seven years for someone, often learning a trade in the process, to pay off the ship's passage, and then the indentured servant was free. Bacon's Rebellion in 1676 Virginia included both black and white indentured servants who felt they had been cheated by their masters. Over half of white colonial immigrants, even more in Virginia, Maryland, and Barbados, where Oliver Cromwell forcibly shipped thousands of his defeated enemies, were thought to have been indentured servants. But by the end of the 1600s, indentured servitude for many blacks had become indefinite in length and had morphed into slavery, legal by then in all the colonies. While today black Americans make up about 15 percent of the U.S. population, they made up about 20 percent of the population of the thirteen colonies at the time of the Revolutionary War.

In Indian-European relationships, unfortunately much of the tone was set by Cortés' treatment of the Aztecs and by Pizarro's treatment of the Incas, exacerbating relationships to this day between the descendants of both the Spanish and the Indians in Latin American countries. Farther north, Indians sometimes provided food and know-how to the early settlers of New England, but King Philip's War, in which over a period of eighteen months in 1675 and 1676, members of several tribes wiped out more than half of the colonists' settlements, with atrocities on both sides, caused lasting fear and bitterness between the two groups.

It is fashionable today to see the Indians as early, peaceful ecologists who could do no wrong, but that view, despite its many elements of truth, is also quite simplistic. The evidence that pre-Columbian Indians held slaves, practiced human sacrifice, and, in the case of the Aztecs, may have been cannibals, shows that no one group had a corner on morality: indeed, the autobiography, *The Soveraignty* [sic] *& Goodness of God: A Narrative of the Captivity, Sufferings, and Removes of Mrs. Mary Rowlandson, Who was taken Prisoner by the Indians with several others, and treated in the most barbarous and cruel Manner by those vile Savages: With many other remarkable Events during her Travels,* reflected the view of many fearful settlers during and after King Philip's War, as did the existence of "Indian-holes" built into early settlers' houses to allow for hiding during attack. It must be noted, however, that if the Indians had written their own story, they certainly would have stressed their internment and sale into slavery in the West Indies as a result of that war, along with other harsh treatment, so the settlers' exclusive ability to write presented a biased view of Indians for years. Additionally, much of the worst treatment of the Indians came not in the 1600s and 1700s, but in the 1800s, as the western land grab by more and more settlers resulted in increasing disregard for the rights of the Indians.

The newcomers were viewed by those already in the Americas with suspicion or friendliness and subsequently treated both well and badly, much like modern responses to current immigration. Concomitantly, many settlers often lived peacefully with their new neighbors, but many clashed fiercely with them. In 1637, after a series of raids on each other's villages, the Puritans set fire to a Pequot village, killing nearly 400 women, children, and old people. During King William's War of 1689–1697, the French under Count Frontenac incited the Abnaki to raid English settlements. On one particularly bloody day, March 15, 1697, they killed twenty-seven women and children, including a newborn, and marched the baby's mother, Hannah Duston, and nursemaid 100 miles. Then Hannah killed nine of her captors, scalped them all to prove her feat, and escaped in a stolen canoe. By contrast, in 1758, when French and Shawnee warriors captured Mary Jemison, she retained the customs she learned from them for the rest of her life.

Revolutionary War

Internal clashes were also common: the most significant was to be the strains between the English colonists and their mother country, which had always existed to some extent but were intensified by the results of the French and Indian War, which ended in 1763. Britain, triumphant in Canada and most of the rest of North America (except for Spanish holdings in the south and west), tried to raise taxes on the colonies to help pay for that war, arguing that the colonists got the major advantage of Britain's triumph.

The colonists' view was that they contributed simply by living with the hazards of the New World and that they objected to additional taxation because they had no representation in Parliament. Britain's response was that they had "virtual representation," meaning they were represented by Parliament in general, even if they had no specific representatives, as was the case with many parts of England and the rest of Great Britain. England had taken Wales and Ireland in the 1500s and joined with Scotland in 1607, forming Great Britain. At the time, British citizens had more rights and freedoms than most other groups in the world.

A more practical reason for the colonists' discontent was that they had for many years ignored unenforced British laws, often by smuggling, such as the Hat Act and the Iron Act, forbidding colonial export and production of those goods, respectively, to ensure a market for Britain, contributing to an independent spirit and a feeling of separation. The relatively sudden enforcement of those laws, such as the Navigation Acts, which limited much colonial trade only to Great Britain, plus the barring of settlement west of the Appalachians, came as something of a shock. In the 1760s, the Sugar Act, the Stamp Act, and the Townshend Acts, all imposing new taxes on goods, along with the Quartering Act, which required the colonists to house and feed British troops, caused enormous resentment.

Groups of American patriots such as the Sons and Daughters of Liberty and Committees of Correspondence sprang up throughout the colonies to resist the British. Anger was particularly great in Boston, where in March of 1770 a group of British soldiers fired on a mob that had been taunting them with snowballs, sticks, and rocks, killing five, including Crispus Attucks, a former slave. In a triumph of public relations, the Boston Massacre gained much support throughout the colonies for the people of Boston, as did the Boston Tea Party, in which colonists, dressed as Indians, dumped several hundred chests of British imported tea into Boston harbor.

In response, Britain passed the Coercive Acts, called in America the "Intolerable Acts," closing the port of Boston and ending self-government in Massachusetts.

It was in this unsettled period that Phillis Wheatley, a slave born in Senegal and living in Boston, had her book, *Poems on Various Subjects, Religious and Moral* published, the first book of poetry published by an African-American woman. A Continental Congress met to discuss action against the British and groups started stockpiling arms and gunpowder. In 1774, Parliament passed the seemingly unrelated and reasonable Quebec Act, expanding the province of Quebec and guaranteeing religious freedom to the French Catholics who lived there, but it fanned colonial anti-Catholicism and was viewed as an attempt to restrict Massachusetts', Connecticut's, and Virginia's claims to the west.

By April of 1775, British troops were marching on Concord and Lexington, Massachusetts to destroy the stockpiles of weapons there. The colonists were warned of the British intent by William Dawes and Paul Revere (about whose feat Henry Wadsworth Longfellow later wrote "The Midnight Ride of Paul Revere"), and open fighting broke out. The British destroyed the weapons, but the colonists attacked the troops all the way back to Boston.

A month later, Ethan Allen and his "Green Mountain Boys" took the British fort at Ticonderoga, New York, and the Second Continental Congress met and named George Washington the commander of a new American army. In June, at the Battle of Bunker Hill (really Breed's Hill), more than 1,000 British were killed and almost half as many Americans. By the early part of 1776, the British had been driven from Boston. About the same time, American troops won a decisive victory at the Battle of Moore's Creek Bridge in North Carolina.

A short while earlier, Thomas Paine published the very influential pamphlet "Common Sense," arguing for independence, and on July 4, 1776, the Second Continental Congress adopted the Declaration of Independence ("All men are created equal . . ."), written by Thomas Jefferson with input from the other delegates, arguing that the people had a right to abolish King George III's unfair government and declaring independence from that government. When Jefferson, who objected to slavery as an institution although he owned slaves himself, included the slave trade as an abuse of George III's power, the South objected and that portion was left out. It has been estimated often that roughly 25 percent of the colonists felt strongly inclined toward independence, an approximately equal number was loyal to the crown, and about half had no strong feeling either way. Benjamin Franklin, Samuel Adams, John Adams, John Hancock, Patrick Henry, and Richard Henry Lee were some of the other significant voices behind independence.

The biggest problem for the Americans was financing the war, as Congress had no power to raise money, many states refused to give, and militiamen were often willing to fight only in their local area. The British also had tremendous problems, chief among them having to supply troops 3,000 miles away, formal fighting deployment against American guerilla tactics, and mixed feelings in Britain about the war. Additionally, the British had contracted with the German state of Hesse to hire mercenary soldiers to fight the war, many of whom were unenthused about it and ended up deserting to live in the new country.

That summer of 1776, Washington's forces were unable to hold New York or New Jersey against superior British troops, and retreated first to Morristown, New Jersey, then to Valley Forge, Pennsylvania. They suffered tremendously that winter from the cold and from lack of supplies, but eventually triumphed at Trenton and

Princeton, New Jersey the following winter. When the Americans, led in part by Benedict Arnold who later defected to the British side, defeated a British force of 5,000 at Saratoga, New York a few months later, the French, who had been secretly providing weapons and supplies to the Americans, decided to openly provide help and recognize American independence. The Marquis de Lafayette, a young man who later played a part in the French Revolution, worked closely with General Washington.

Eventually Spain and the Netherlands, as well as high-ranking military men from Prussia (Baron von Steuben) and Poland (Kazimierz Pulaski and Tadeusz Kosciuszko) came to the Americans' aid. None of these countries was a democracy, but all were interested in weakening Britain. Two other young men whose deaths became legend, in part because of their youth, patriotism, and charming personalities, were Captain Nathan Hale, a school teacher who was quoted as saying "I only regret that I have but one life to give for my country," when he was hanged by the British for spying in 1776, and, on the other side, Major John André, a poet and humorist hung by the Americans for spying and arranging for Benedict Arnold to change sides.

In 1778, George Rogers Clark and a small band captured the British forts west of the Appalachians, and in the South, where the British were strong, Francis Marion "the Swamp Fox" and others effectively practiced guerilla warfare. Other important American generals were "Mad" Anthony Wayne, Israel Putnam, Henry "Light-Horse Harry" Lee, Philip Schuyler, Horatio Gates, Daniel Morgan, Benjamin Lincoln, and Nathanael Greene. The American victories at Kings Mountain, Cowpens, and Guilford Court House, all in the Carolinas, drove the British to a few coastal cities, with major strongholds at Yorktown, Virginia and New York City. With the help of the French, the Americans defeated the British forces under General Cornwallis, who surrendered at Yorktown in October 1781, and, although the peace treaty was two years away, the bulk of the fighting was over.

About 5,000 black Americans fought in the war, including Peter Salem and Salem Poor, honored for "outstanding heroism" at Bunker Hill, and some slaves were falsely promised their freedom when the war ended. Some states enlisted slaves in the army and then granted them their freedom, and other states provided for gradual abolition, while a Massachusetts court ruled in 1783 that its constitution outlawed slavery. Pennsylvania, Connecticut, and Rhode Island all began the gradual abolition of slavery in the early 1780s, and even Virginia and North Carolina started allowing owners who so desired to free their slaves.

Aside from the story of Betsy Ross helping to design the first flag and sewing it, women played other parts in the war, making uniforms and bullets, collecting supplies, providing nursing, cooking for the troops, and even acting as spies and messengers. Deborah Sampson of Massachusetts fought in several battles disguised as a man, and Margaret Corbin and Molly Pitcher took over in battle from their fallen husbands. In spite of Abigail Adams' famous letter urging fairness to women, written to her husband serving in the Continental Congress, women remained limited in voting, property, and custody rights.

The Treaty of Paris of 1783 gave the Americans not only independence but the land west to the Mississippi (frontierspeople such as Daniel Boone and his family had been settling there since before the revolution) except for Canada, which the

British retained, and Florida, which belonged to Spain, as well as fishing rights in the northern Atlantic. The thirteen states signed the Articles of Confederation in 1781, establishing a weak government that was generally unsuccessful because of its lack of military, financial, and internal power. The government successfully divided up the land immediately south of the Great Lakes, known as the Northwest Territory, which later became the states of Wisconsin, Michigan, Illinois, Indiana, and Ohio. It also banned slavery and encouraged public education there. Such events as states minting their own money (useless outside their borders), conducting their own foreign policy (unenforceable), and dealing with such incidents as Shays' Rebellion (farmers defying the government of Massachusetts over foreclosure laws, representation, and a weapons arsenal) caused widespread dissatisfaction and desire for a stronger government.

During the hot summer of 1787, delegates from most of the states convened in Philadelphia at the Constitutional Convention and drafted the U.S. Constitution. Although many famous names were present and George Washington headed the convention, James Madison, Alexander Hamilton, and John Jay had enormous influence defending the proposed constitution in *The Federalist Papers*. The Constitution ("We the people of the United States, in order to form a more perfect union . . .") was a series of compromises between large states and small, slave states and free, Federalists and anti-Federalists. The Connecticut Compromise provided for a House of Representatives and a Senate, to assuage the power struggle between large and small states. The three-fifths compromise counted a slave as three-fifths of a person for both representation and taxation purposes. Congress was given the power to tax imports but not exports (notably southern tobacco). Finally states could import slaves until 1808, at which time Congress would have the right to decide the future of the slave trade. It was officially ended then, but Eli Whitney's 1793 invention of the cotton gin meant demand for slaves kept expanding, and illegal trade was carried on.

Significant powers, many financial and military, were delegated to the federal government, along with separation of powers (separate branches for the executive, representative, and judiciary) and a series of checks and balances. Many powers were reserved for the states. Specified important individual rights (with the odd exception of the right to vote, which was left up to the states) such as freedom of religion, speech, press, assembly, and petition; freedom from unreasonable search, seizure, arbitrary arrest, self-incrimination, and cruel and unusual punishment; and the right to bear arms, were provided by the first ten amendments, known as the Bill of Rights.

The Constitution was approved by the states in 1788, and George Washington became the first president in 1789. John Jay helped shape the Supreme Court, and Alexander Hamilton established a federal banking system that also assumed the war debt and promoted a tax on liquor to get the country's finances in order. The liquor tax led to the Whiskey Rebellion in western Pennsylvania, but the federal government prevailed.

John Adams and Thomas Jefferson were elected the new president and vice president in 1797, when Washington's two terms were up. Both Washington and Adams were successful in maintaining neutrality during the French Revolution and staying out of war with Great Britain and Spain. The Alien and Sedition Acts passed by Congress in 1798, in response to the threat of war, imposed on freedom of speech and led to a strong interest in states' rights to oppose the federal government's power. However, under the leadership of Chief Justice John Marshall, the Supreme Court in the case of *Marbury v. Madison* asserted its right to rule on the constitutionality of federal and local laws, strengthening the federal government. In the War of 1812, the United States fought Britain successfully again, strengthening the federal government and crushing any hope of Britain regaining control.

The 1800's

A new American intellectualism took shape during the 1800s, with such writers as James Fenimore Cooper, Nathaniel Hawthorne, Herman Melville, Walt Whitman, Mark Twain, and Emily Dickinson writing from an American point of view, as did the Transcendentalists Ralph Waldo Emerson, Margaret Fuller, and Henry David Thoreau, who pioneered peaceful civil disobedience as protest and whose philosophy would later influence Mohandas Gandhi and Martin Luther King, Jr. Painters, too, emphasized American themes, such as the Hudson River School and Native American subjects. The uniqueness of the American landscape also was reflected in the growth of the conservation movement in the late 1800s, and in the early 1900s John Muir convinced President Theodore Roosevelt to set aside vast tracts of land for national parks.

Throughout the 1800s, the United States continued to grow and to expand, including buying the Louisiana Territory through the Louisiana Purchase from France and obtaining Florida from Spain. As the idea of Manifest Destiny (that the United States should own "from sea to shining sea") spread, Texas gained its independence from Mexico and joined the United States. In the 1840s, an open war with Mexico resulted in the United States taking much of the Southwest. Henry David Thoreau, a leader of the Transcendentalist movement, first practiced civil disobedience to protest this war. The United States also acquired the Oregon Territory from Britain, gained Hawaii, bought Alaska from Russia, a purchase known as Seward's Folly, and in 1898 picked up Puerto Rico, Guam, and the Philippines in the Spanish-American War.

Farther south, the ex-slave Toussaint L'Overture had led a successful rebellion, resulting in Haiti's independence from France in 1804, and many Latin American countries declared their independence, mostly from Spain. President James Monroe supported them with the Monroe Doctrine, barring further European interference in the New World. Simón Bolívar liberated much of northern South America and freed the slaves there, while José de San Martin led the fight in the southern part of the continent. Brazil achieved its independence from Portugal peacefully in 1822, and Mexico, after several efforts at rebellion, became independent in 1821, although there were terrible battles later between conservatives and liberals. In the early 1860s, Mexican conservatives, supported by France, installed the Austrian Archduke Maxmilian as emperor, but under U.S. pressure, and after defeat in the *Cinqo de Mayo* (May 5) battle at Puebla in 1862, the French withdrew their support. The archduke was shot and the liberals returned to power.

During the 1800s and early 1900s, immigration was tremendous. People came, many through Ellis Island, near New York City, seeking land, political freedom, religious freedom (especially European Jews), gold (in California in 1849), jobs, and food (the Irish fleeing famine). Life was hard and dangerous for many settlers, but difficult in the cities as well, where reformers like Jane Addams worked to improve slum life.

As the country and the population grew, Indians and slaves became increasingly major issues. The U.S. military (including "Buffalo soldiers," as black soldiers were called by the Indians, who were fascinated with their hair) fought the Indians for years, beginning with forced resettlement in the West, the "Trail of Tears" for Southeastern Indians under President Andrew Jackson. In 1849, the Bureau of Indian Affairs was formed, and after the Civil War followed the policy of trying to force the Indians onto reservations, usually poor and undesirable land. The government agents dealing with the Indians were often corrupt, and treaties were repeatedly broken as reservation land became desirable. The army tried to move the Indians off their reservations in the Black Hills of South Dakota in 1876 after gold was discovered there. In one battle of that attempt, "Custer's Last Stand," fought at the Little Bighorn River in Montana, General George Custer and his men were killed by Sioux and Cheyennes led by Sitting Bull and Crazy Horse. Conversely, in 1886 Geronimo and his southwestern Indians surrendered, and at Wounded Knee, South Dakota, in 1890, the army killed almost 300 disarmed Sioux, including women and children. By the end of the 1800s, most Indians had been pushed onto reservations, in spite of negotiations by such leaders as Tecumseh. Most of the buffalo that were a staple for many Native Americans had been killed. The poignant words of Chief Joseph of the Nez Perce summed up the Indian view in 1877: "I am tired of fighting. . . . My heart is sick and sad. From where the sun now stands I will fight no more, forever."

Reformers were dismayed at the treatment of the Indians, and many people did not understand their various cultures. The federal government tried, in the Dawes Act of 1887 that gave individual ownership of land to individual Indians and gave the vote to those who left the reservations, to include them in the larger society. However, land speculators and unscrupulous officials took advantage of the Indians in many ways, and they often lost their land.

On the slavery issue, neither the free nor the slave-holding states wanted to be outnumbered, so a series of compromises let in alternate free and slave states, while trying to restrict slavery in the new territories. The Missouri Compromise of 1819 let in Missouri as a slave state and Maine as a free state, and in the 1830s, Arkansas and Michigan came in as slave and free, respectively. In 1845, Florida and Texas came in as slave states, balanced by Iowa and Wisconsin as free ones.

By 1850, hostility was great between the North and the South, but a compromise crafted by Henry Clay and supported by Daniel Webster and John C. Calhoun, admitting California as a free state but giving the South more support on the capture of fugitive slaves and the new territories the right to vote on slavery, was accepted. Many people did not agree with the Compromise of 1850, especially the Fugitive Slave Act, requiring local governments to help in returning escaped slaves to the South. The Kansas-Nebraska Act of 1854, effectively wiping out the Missouri Compromise, and allowing new territories, even in the North, to make their own decisions about slavery, was even more unpopular. So was the Dred Scott Decision of 1857, in which the Supreme Court, sympathetic to the south, ruled that Scott was not a free man, although he had been taken into a free territory, and that he did not have the right to sue, since, as a slave, he wasn't really a citizen. The court further ruled that the Missouri Compromise, banning slavery from some states, was unconstitutional, further upsetting abolitionists.

Sojourner Truth, Frederick Douglass, Harriet Tubman (who later spied for the Union army), and other former slaves, along with abolitionists both black and white, worked for the end of slavery and helped slaves escape to the North or to Canada on a secret route of safe houses known as the Underground Railroad, which was not actually a railroad. However, runaway slaves were supposed to be returned to slavery, and shortly after the Dred Scott decision, John Brown was hanged for leading an armed rebellion against slavery at Harper's Ferry, Virginia. Many abolitionists, like Susan B. Anthony and Elizabeth Cady Stanton, also called for women's rights, starting at the Seneca Falls Convention of 1848, and Harriet Beecher Stowe published the widely read, antislavery novel *Uncle Tom's Cabin* in 1852.

Besides slavery, other major issues dividing North and South were tariffs and states' rights versus the power of the federal government. Finally, the Civil War broke out at Fort Sumter, South Carolina in 1861 under President Abraham Lincoln, when the Southern states, later under Confederate President Jefferson Davis, tried to leave the union. The North was shocked when the South quickly won the First Battle of Bull Run in Virginia, but west of the Appalachians, the Union army secured Missouri and captured Forts Donelson and Henry between Kentucky and Tennessee. The North barely prevailed at Shiloh, against General Albert Johnston, who was killed.

Union forces under General Ulysses Grant continued to move south along the Mississippi, splitting the South as they took Memphis and Vicksburg, a stronghold of Confederate troops. The Union army later took Port Hudson and New Orleans, gaining control of the entire Mississippi by the middle of 1863. In the east, however, the Confederates, led by Generals Robert E. Lee, "Stonewall" Jackson, and J.E.B. Stuart, won the battles of Richmond and Second Bull Run. They were stopped by Union forces under General George McClellan at the 1862 Battle of Antietam, the bloodiest battle of the war. After heroic effort under Generals Robert E. Lee and George E. Pickett, Confederate forces were beaten by Union troops led by General George G. Meade at Gettysburg in 1863, the northernmost battle of the war.

That same year, the Union army took Chattanooga, then won the battles of Lookout Mountain and Missionary Ridge, and moved further south to capture Atlanta. The following year, Union General William T. Sherman fought his way across Georgia from Atlanta on a "March to the Sea." Finally, Confederate General Lee surrendered his army to General Grant at Appomattox, Virginia in 1865 and the war was over.

In spite of draft riots in some Northern cities, the industrial North had defeated the rural South after four years, leaving it devastated economically, socially, and politically. Hundreds of thousands of Americans were dead on both sides, including black soldiers, who were mostly in the Union army, although the Confederacy had been first to take black volunteers. Black Americans, both male and female, went on to serve in the military throughout the twentieth century, and the Tuskegee Airmen of World War II were black pilots, led by Captain Benjamin O. Davis, Jr., whose father had been the first black general in the U.S. Army.

The Southern slaves were freed by the Emancipation Proclamation of 1863 and later amendments banned slavery, made blacks full citizens, and gave voting rights to black men. Many women contributed to the war effort through nursing and raising money for supplies, and Clara Barton, who had led the nursing effort in the North, formed the American Red Cross after the war. President Abraham Lincoln was assassinated by the actor John Wilkes Booth at Ford's Theatre in Washington, D.C. on April 14, 1865, near the end of the war, which made Reconstruction even more difficult.

Hostility was still so great that President Andrew Johnson became the first president to be impeached, although he was not convicted, when he was too conciliatory toward the South. With military governments in the former Confederate states, some black men were elected to office during Reconstruction, but soon the old guard was in control and blacks were again second-class citizens, often kept from voting by unfair requirements and regulations.

In the years after the Civil War, also known as the Gilded Age, the Industrial Revolution was in full swing: gigantic fortunes were made by "robber barons" such as John D. Rockefeller, Andrew Carnegie, and Cornelius Vanderbilt in railroads (many built before the war and many built by Chinese immigrant labor), oil, steamships, and steel. Samuel Morse had earlier invented the telegraph, and Alexander Graham Bell's patent of the telephone and Thomas Edison's invention of the lightbulb and other uses for electricity were the forerunners of the Wright brothers' invention of the airplane in 1903 and Henry Ford's use of the assembly line to build affordable cars in the 1920s.

Black Americans produced a series of inventions: Elijah McCoy's lubricating cup that allowed machinery to be oiled while running, Jan Matzeliger's shoemaking machine, Granville T. Woods' telephone transmitter, Lewis Latimer's electric devices, and Garrett Morgan's gas mask and automatic stop sign were among the many new innovations of the period by various inventors of all backgrounds.

The period of the 1890s through the 1920s was known as the "Progressive Era," in which reforms were made toward increased social justice, equality, education, and public health and safety, despite continuing racial and religious prejudice.

THE TWENTIETH AND EARLY TWENTY-FIRST CENTURIES AROUND THE WORLD

As the twentieth century opened, Europe dominated much of the world. Europeans had colonized most of Africa and many parts of Asia, including much of the Middle East, which was largely held by the Ottoman Empire. The "Sun never set on the British Empire," which included Australia and India as well as Canada and various smaller parcels, and France, too, had colonies in Africa, South America, and the Caribbean. Spain also still held colonies in many parts of the world including the Spanish Sahara, although the United States had taken much Spanish territory, notably Cuba, Puerto Rico, and the Philippines at the end of the Spanish-American War.

The unification of Germany in 1871 and the unification of Italy about the same time led to colonization, particularly in Africa and Asia, by those two new European powers. Germany, because of its investments, was a strong influence in the Ottoman Empire: indeed, some historians have suggested that German observers at the Turkish slaughter of the Armenians in 1894 and 1915 picked up techniques, to be used later in World War II, of mass slaughter of unwanted minorities.

The New World was strong and growing, and both North America and Latin America (so-called because the most common languages were Spanish and Portuguese, originally based on Latin) had many immigrants from all over the world: European immigration was especially strong in the United States and in Argentina. In 1910, Mexico had another revolution in reaction to peasant poverty and landlessness that lasted off and on until 1917 when a modern constitution established somewhat more stability. But, partly because of rapid population growth, land reform continues to be a major issue in Mexican political life, although since the 1970s much of the country's revenue comes from oil.

Two years before the death of Queen Victoria in 1901, the Boer War broke out in South Africa as the English colonists fought the Dutch colonists for much of the territory. After a brutal war of three years in which atrocities were practiced by both sides, the British won, although they alienated much of Europe in the process, and all of South Africa became a British colony.

Shortly afterward, in 1904, the Russo-Japanese War was fought, with the Japanese winning a year later, in part because of their early attack on Port Arthur before any declaration of war, used to such good effect that they many years later made a similar stealth attack on Pearl Harbor, drawing the United States into World War II. But most European and American world feeling in this early period supported the Japanese, in part since Russia was viewed as a threat because of its size. The American president Theodore Roosevelt won the Nobel Peace Prize for brokering the peace that called for Japan to gain in land and influence. In this period there was also much unrest in both China and the Ottoman (Turkish) Empire of the Middle East.

World War I

Starting in the 1890s, a terrific naval arms race was underway, as Germany sought to become, and Britain to remain, preeminent at sea. The major powers in Europe aside from Britain, France, and Germany were the tottering Austro-Hungarian Empire, which controlled much of central Europe, the problem-laden Russian Empire, and the declining Ottoman Empire, the "sick man of Europe." Against this background, the Germans, with France and Russia on their borders, formed an alliance with the Austrians and Italians (the Triple Alliance), while the French, Russians, and English formed a somewhat less committed alliance, the Triple Entente.

The Balkan area of southeastern Europe, coveted by the Austrians, the Russians, and the Turks, was commonly referred to as a "tinderbox waiting for a spark." The spark was provided by Gavrilo Principe, a Serbian schoolboy nationalist who assassinated the heir to the Austrian throne, the Grand Duke Franz Ferdinand, and his wife Sophie in the city of Sarajevo in the Austrian territory of Bosnia-Herzogovina on June 28, 1914.

The Austrian and Serbian governments negotiated and Serbia apologized and disclaimed responsibility for the act of a lone terrorist, while Austria demanded rights to additionally investigate. A leisurely month later, on July 28, the Austro-Hungarian Empire, confident of the "blank check" it had from its ally Germany to provide support no matter what, declared war on Serbia. The alliance system pulled more and more countries into war: Serbia was defended by Russia, which was allied with France, which was allied with England, which were both pledged to defend Belgium, which the Germans marched through on their way to France.

Eventually the Ottoman Empire and Bulgaria joined Germany and Austria to become the "Central Powers," and a number of other, less important countries, among them the United States, later joined the "Allies." World War I had begun. A slogan of war in England was "Home by Christmas!" but the British foreign secretary Sir Edward Grey was chillingly prescient when he said "The lights are going out all over Europe." One reason for the false confidence was that Europe had not seen a major war since the days of Napoleon a hundred years earlier (the Crimean War was fought in an isolated area of Russia and other wars had been very short). There was a general feeling that any war would last only a few weeks or months while strengthening patriotism in and bringing glory to the countries involved.

But no one had reckoned with the change that the Industrial Revolution would bring. The most important weapon of the early days of the war was the machine gun, invented by the American Richard J. Gatling during the Civil War, but now, in a variety of forms, in widespread use for the first time. Germany's Schlieffen Plan, which involved quickly attacking France so Germany would not have to fight a two-front war (against France and Russia simultaneously), was predicated on a quick defeat of the French, leaving the Germans free to settle in for a long battle against Russia.

But France was not defeated as planned: both sides had machine guns, and the French and British dug into trenches and stopped the Germans at the Battle of the Marne (the beginning of the "Western Front") while the Russians attacked from the east (the "Eastern Front"). The Italians, recoiling from the aggressiveness of the Germans and Austrians, left their alliance, and in 1915 joined the war on the side of the Allies, in a secret agreement that promised Austrian land to the Italians.

In the meantime, poison gas, first used by the Germans in 1915 at Yprés, blinding soldiers and causing them to drown in their own lung fluid, was being deployed as a weapon by both sides. In 1915, the Allies saw terrible defeats at Gallipoli while trying to resupply Russia and defeat Turkey, and at Tannenberg in Russia. In 1916, the long and grueling battles of Verdun and the Somme lasted for many months with a million and a half casualties combined and no real victors, to the bafflement of the generals, who had never seen a war of sustained fighting like this.

That same year, the Easter Rebellion broke out in Ireland, as the mostly Catholic Irish demanded independence from the mostly Protestant British, who harshly put down the rebellion. In 1921, Ireland was divided into two: the largely Catholic Irish Free State got Home Rule in 1922 and complete independence in 1948, and largely Protestant Northern Ireland remains as of this writing part of Great Britain, although the struggle between the nationalist guerilla Irish Republican Army and the Protestant establishment has continued since the late 1960s. Ireland remained neutral in World War II, much to the dismay of the embattled British.

In World War I, the "war to end all wars," poison gas and bombs were dropped from planes, which were also new to battle, and on the seas, the Battle of Jutland, off the north coast of Germany, was the only major sea battle and essentially a draw. German Undersea boats, or U-boats, however, waged submarine warfare across the Atlantic, sinking many Allied ships, most famously the *Lusitania*, in 1915.

Under the rules of war prevailing at the time, countries were not allowed to sink enemy civilian ships, but the Germans claimed that the British were carrying contraband war materials on their civilian ships, and Germany took out ads in all the New York papers warning Americans not to take passage on the *Lusitania*, as it would be sunk. Few people believed them, but when it was hit, it went up like a rocket, confirming the Germans' suspicions and killing all aboard, including 200 Americans.

When the Americans finally got into the war in 1917, their joining had more to do with German and Russian politics than anything else. Revolution broke out in Russia after years of terrible casualties and deaths: the Russians lost 2 million men in 1915 alone and were sometimes sent into battle armed with shovels against Germans armed with machine guns. When the Communist Party managed to seize control of Russia, Vladimir Lenin's slogan was "Peace, Land, and Bread," and he immediately moved to make peace with the Germans. The Russians gave up 2 million square miles of land to Germany with the Treaty of Brest-Litovsk and got out of the war early.

The other Allies were horrified, because the Russian defeat meant that from herein the war would be fought on the Western Front, and it looked as though the Allies would lose. But the U.S. entry into the war, partly as a result of the Zimmerman telegram, in which the German Foreign Secretary encouraged Mexico to take back the American Southwest, brought fresh supplies of materials and men under General Pershing. American victories at Chateau Thierry and elsewhere helped the Allies finally win the war. Because the Allies were mostly democratic countries and the Central Powers were not, World War I is sometimes known as the war fought "to make the world safe for democracy."

The victors were unhappy with Russia, their former ally, to the extent that they invaded Russia at Archangel and at Murmansk, both near the Arctic Circle, to retrieve supplies and to resist the Communist Revolution, causing ill feeling that would last for many years. More importantly, with Germany defeated, it would not be allowed to keep the land it had gained at Brest-Litovsk, but the other Allies were not inclined to return it to the Russians, and much of that territory became new countries. The end of the war, at the eleventh hour of the eleventh day of the eleventh month of 1918, originally called Armistice Day but celebrated now as Veterans' Day, brought about many changes in the map of Europe.

The new countries were Poland, Finland, Czechoslovakia, Estonia, Latvia, Lithuania, and Yugoslavia. Russia was shrunk, as were Germany and Austria. Hungary became a separate country. The Ottoman Empire was collapsing as Arab countries fought for independence simultaneously with the larger war, and Bulgaria lost its Mediterranean access for siding with Germany and Austria, while Rumania picked up land. France (Alsace-Lorraine) and Italy (parts of the Tyrol) each gained small areas, although not nearly enough to make up for the loss of an entire generation of young men. Some German colonies in Africa and the Pacific were parceled out, but the tremendous loss of life and feeling of civilization's ruin were overwhelming.

To make things worse, the flu epidemic of 1918–1919 killed at least 20 million people around the world. Over 10 million people died in World War I, most of them in battle (including colonial troops from Africa and Asia), and the battles were so long and so horrific that they changed the face of war. Technology had shaped this war, and technology helped to end it. By 1916, the English were building the tank, which could roll impervious over no man's land, the land between the Allied and the German trenches, and through machine-gun fire. This advance, combined with the American strength, finally brought the war to an end.

Five separate treaties were signed with the defeated nations (a newly independent Hungary was the fifth one), but the Treaty of Versailles, signed with the Germans, contained the seeds of World War II: the Germans had to admit guilt for starting the war (a reference to their "blank check," although the Austrians had declared war originally); give up much land including a corridor to the sea for the new country of Poland: pay heavy reparations; limit severely the size of the German army and navy (with no air force or submarines permitted); and demilitarize the German land west of the Rhine River (on France's border).

World Between the Wars

The American president Woodrow Wilson toured Europe to great acclaim, discussing his Fourteen Points of fairness and human rights and unsuccessfully urging fairer treatment for Germany. But Clemenceau in France as well as leaders of other countries felt the Germans should be punished more. Wilson also promoted a League of Nations to keep the peace, but the isolationist Congress, much to Wilson's dismay, refused to let the United States join, so the League was rather ineffectual. To this day there is a controversy over whether the conditions of Versailles (where the treaty with Germany was signed) were too harsh or too light, but they certainly were problematic.

The Russian Revolution was a tremendous upheaval. Not only did Vladimir Lenin, Joseph Stalin, and Leon Trotsky of the more radical wing of the communists (the Bolsheviks) prevail over Alexander Kerensky's democratic Provisional government (which took over after the Czar's abdication), but they also defeated the communist/socialist Mensheviks, a more moderate Marxist group. The Russian royal family, the Romanovs, were executed in secret without a trial, giving rise to ongoing rumors over the years that Alexander or Anastasia, Czar Nicholas' son and one of his daughters, had somehow escaped and were still alive. Alexander was a hemophiliac, which had given the opportunistic monk Rasputin, who said he could cure Alexander, an unhealthy and unpopular hold over the Czarina Alexandra.

These personal issues, together with the dismal performance of the unprepared and undersupplied Russian army in World War I, helped contribute to the Communist (Reds) takeover, which nevertheless took several years to consolidate because of such internal opposition as the Whites (anticommunists), the Greens (wanting Ukraine independence), and a military dictatorship (under General Kornilov). Trotsky managed to forge together a powerful Red Army, while Lenin worked on reformulating the structure of the government, including workers' groups as part of the government structure, seizing Russian Orthodox Church property, and distributing land to the peasants.

Lenin died in 1924, wanting Trotsky as his successor, but Stalin drove Trotsky out of the country and later had him assassinated in Mexico. Stalin took control, implementing many harsh measures and purges, including widespread executions and starvation that were devastating to his own citizens and to idealists around the world who believed in the Russian communist experiment. But Stalin greatly developed the military/industrial base that would help save the country and the world from Germany in World War II

The triumph of communism in Russia (whose name was now officially changed to the Union of Soviet Socialist Republics, of which Russia was the largest of sixteen republics) helped shape the interwar years for all of Europe, mostly by other countries' negative reactions to it. Major political movements in addition to communism (government owns every means of production, controls all needs, and disallows religion and monarchy), were socialism (government owns the major means of production, controls major needs, and often contains strong elements of democracy), fascism (strong anti-communist nationalistic government exists to be glorified and to glorify the state and controls many aspects of personal life) and, of course, democracy (personal freedom and the will of the people are foremost).

Countries can be more or less involved in the economic and/or personal freedom issues, and religious groups were often more inclined to support fascism because of its strong anticommunist component. Antifascists were often inclined to support communism for its resistance to fascism. Democracy frequently seemed weak or ineffectual in providing for its people in comparison to fascism, communism, or socialism, and economic issues were exacerbated by the worldwide Great Depression of the 1930s.

These issues were especially mixed in the Spanish Civil War of the mid-1930s, in which the democratic government, led by the King, oddly was supported by the Russian Communists, while the Catholic Church generally supported the Fascists, and most democratic nations remained neutral. Fascism triumphed in Spain under General Francisco Franco, and remained the form of government for many years, as it did in Portugal under General Antonio Salazar. This was possible partly because the Spanish and Portuguese stayed out of World War II. Portugal became a more democratic state in 1974, and King Juan Carlos took the throne as a constitutional monarch to lead Spain as a democracy in 1975.

In the interwar years, Great Britain was stunned by King Edward VIII abdicating his throne for an American divorcee; France had a series of unstable coalition governments, including Leon Blum's Socialists, which had the unfortunate effect of garnering more approval for the Fascists for their defense of private property and the Church; and Germany was in major upheaval. Germany's strong military government had resigned near the end of World War I and Kaiser Wilhelm II abdicated, so it was a liberal socialist democratic government that reluctantly signed the Versailles Treaty in 1919, providing much ammunition for later militaristic claims that Germany had been sold out by its democratic government. Many different political parties arose in Germany to challenge the weak and ineffectual Weimar Republic led by the old and frail World War I hero Paul von Hindenburg. In 1933 fascists under Adolf Hitler, calling themselves the National Socialist (Nazi) party, took control of the government, partly through being elected and partly through illegally banning the elected communists from the Reichstag, the representative body. The Fascists thereby gained a majority. Hitler promised to make Germany great again and to get rid of the provisions of the Versailles Treaty. Hungary, Romania, Austria, Bulgaria, and Greece became military dictatorships in the same period.

While this political situation was building in postwar Europe, the Middle East was very unstable because of the fall of the Ottoman Empire. At the end of World War I, England and France had been given mandates to administer several Middle Eastern countries, and much of the Arabian peninsula became independent, partly through the efforts of the British adventurer T. E. Lawrence ("Lawrence of Arabia") during World War I. In the Ottoman Empire, Young Turks had rebelled and established a parliament in 1908, and hundreds of thousands of Armenians were massacred in Turkey in 1915. In 1917, the "Balfour letter" lent British support to the idea of a separate Jewish state.

In Africa, independence movements against the colonial powers were under way, but most would not see results until after World War II. In Asia beyond the Middle East, India's independence movement from Britain was gaining strength under Mahatma Gandhi and it would succeed in 1947. Japan, which had fought in a minor way on the Allied side in World War I, gaining some former German colonies in the Pacific, was becoming increasingly militarized. Throughout the 1930s Japan preyed upon its neighbors, taking Manchuria and Korea. China resisted very little as it was involved in a series of major, internal civil wars for many years, which generally consisted of right-wing military fighting left-wing opponents after the fall of the emperor in 1911. Sun Yat-sen tried to put together a socialist democratic movement, but after being shunned by the Western democracies, he turned increasingly to the Russians.

By the late 1920s, the opposing Chinese movements were the nationalist Chinese under Chiang Kai-shek and the communists under Mao Tse-tung. In the 1930s and 1940s, the communists gained glory from their spirited fighting against the Japanese and from enduring The Long March in the face of nationalist persecution. The civil war raged right through World War II as a splintered China fought Japan, and in 1949 China became communist under Mao after a post–World War II civil war between communists and nationalists.

But the interwar years were not all political: much cultural and social history was being made. The Roaring Twenties was a decade of relieved reaction to the end of World War I and encompassed improved rights for women in many countries, particularly Great Britain and the United States, where suffrage, short hair, freedom from corsets, smoking, makeup, short skirts, and other social changes were widespread. Other notable movements were jazz and dances like the Charleston; the American expatriate movement in France, which consisted of artists and writers such as Josephine Baker, Ezra Pound, James Joyce, Ernest Hemingway, and F. Scott Fitzgerald, a group Gertrude Stein called the "lost generation;" the Harlem Renaissance, a flowering of black artists and writers; the international rise of abstract painting; Prohibition in the United States, giving rise to speakeasies and organized crime; and perhaps most of all, technology that influenced social and cultural life.

Although most had been invented before the war, some major innovations that became widespread in the 1920s were automobiles (particularly spurred by the American Henry Ford's retooling for assembly-line work in his factories), airplanes, radios, electricity, indoor plumbing, telephones, record players, and many household appliances. In 1927, Charles Lindbergh's flight across the Atlantic and in 1937 Amelia Earhart's disappearance during her attempt to fly around the world fired the public imagination for air travel, including zeppelins and blimps. Beryl Markham was an Englishwoman flying in Africa; and in the United States, Willa Brown, a black woman, made a reputation as an aviator and later trained pilots for World War II, notably the famed black Tuskegee Airmen. The first forty years of the twentieth century were also the years of glory for the great ocean liners (the *Titanic*, hit by an iceberg, went down in 1912).

Because the financial situation was overheated but precarious, many farmers first started suffering the effects of the coming Great Depression in the mid-1920s.

A crippling strike in England in 1926 hurt the economy, as did rampant inflation, especially in Germany and many other parts of Europe. The American stock market went higher and higher, reaching its apogee just before the crash of October 1929, which eventually extended into a worldwide economic depression that essentially lasted until the outbreak of World War II.

The Great Depression years were very hard on millions of people around the world, both in the industrialized countries where subsistence farming was no longer widely practiced and in undeveloped countries which no longer found a market for many of their raw materials and agricultural goods. The severe economic hardships contributed greatly to the unstable political situations in many places, and the United States was one of the places most changed by the Depression years. Interestingly, most socialist, fascist, and communist countries had many more social services in place than did the United States, which practiced a more hands-off, or laissez-faire, capitalism. The Republican president Herbert Hoover, who had done so much in helping the United States administer aid to a devastated Europe after World War I, could not seem to act in any meaningful way to help his own countrymen, many of whom were standing on bread lines and being fed by soup kitchens. He even called out federal troops who attacked the desperate veterans of World War I who gathered en masse in Washington, D.C. to demand their promised war bonuses early.

The Democrat Franklin Delano Roosevelt, a wealthy New Yorker, was elected president in 1932 and immediately set about creating a safety net of social agencies to create work and stabilize the economy. The Civilian Conservation Corps (CCC) planted needed trees and crops, especially in the "Dust Bowl" of the Midwest and built parks and recreation facilities. The Works Progress Administration (WPA) employed many in building roads and bridges, and even took hard-to-place people such as artists and writers, who produced public works such as murals and history/ guidebooks. The Public Works Administration (PWA) planned and carried out large, public projects such as highways and bridges. The Tennessee Valley Authority (TVA) brought electricity to rural areas and created flood control and conservation projects. Roosevelt also created a whole series of deficit spending and cooperative initiatives, including food distribution and Social Security. His wife Eleanor pressed for civil rights and help for the poor and, as a couple, they were beloved by much of the country and reviled by many wealthy Republicans, who called Roosevelt a "traitor to his class" and predicted ruination by socialist projects.

The late 1930s saw an increasingly dangerous situation in Europe, where strong nationalistic leaders in several countries passed laws against minorities, especially Jews. In Germany, at fascist dictator Adolf Hitler's behest, Jews eventually were forced to wear a yellow, identifying Star of David, and they were banned from owning guns, attending school, holding many jobs, and owning property (much of their property was destroyed during Kristallnacht, "the night of broken glass," in nationwide rampages against them.) Jews were also increasingly jailed, and eventually put into concentration camps (originally set up for political prisoners), along with political enemies, Slavs, homosexuals, the handicapped, Gypsies, and other "undesirable" groups who could be "scapegoated" or blamed for anything wrong with Germany and the countries Germany later took over. Many of these prisoners were deliberately killed (the "Final Solution"), many tortured and/or used for medical experiments, and many more died of starvation and overwork in slave labor, all in the series of events known as the Holocaust. Over 11 million people died in the Holocaust, about 6 million of whom were Jewish. The United Nations helped set up the state of Israel after the war as a Jewish homeland—a direct result of the Holocaust.

Hitler had made an alliance with Italy's fascist dictator Benito Mussolini, calling themselves the Axis powers, since Berlin and Rome were to be the new axis on which the world spun. Since the major purpose of fascism is to glorify nationalism and the state, those fascist leaders immediately looked to expand their countries. After Italy being defeated in an attempt to take Ethiopia in 1896, Mussolini took Ethiopia for Italy in 1935. In 1938, Hitler, after increasing the strength of the armed forces and remilitarizing the Rhineland, both against the provisions of the Versailles Treaty, annexed Austria in the action known as the "the Anschluss" and took part of Czechoslovakia.

Czechoslovakia was a contentious issue, as Neville Chamberlain representing England and Edouard Daladier representing France agreed at Munich in Germany without the presence of the Czechs or Russians to let Hitler take the western part (the Sudetenland) of Czechoslovakia, since it contained many ethnic Germans. This policy was hailed by many who remembered the horrors of the last war as promoting "peace in our time," but when Germany took the rest of Czechoslovakia in 1939, it was clear that "**appeasement**" would not stop Germany.

World War II

In August of 1939, the Germans and the Russians, both of whom viewed each other as major threats, signed a nonaggression treaty (much to the dismay of England and France), agreeing that if either took a portion of Poland, the other would remain neutral. On September 3, 1939, the Germans marched into Poland, ostensibly to take back the Polish Corridor, the German land that had been given to Poland after World War I so Poland could have access to a seaport, but in reality to grab the entire western portion of the country. England and France declared war on Germany. Shortly afterward, Russia, afraid of the German advance and also greedy for more land, took the eastern portion of Poland, executing several thousand Polish army officers at the Katyn Forest, as well as establishing military bases in the Baltic countries—Lithuania, Latvia, and Estonia—and, in the following year, Finland.

The Russians' main concern was that those countries would not be able to provide adequate defense and that the anticommunist fascist Germans would invade Russia again as the expansionist Germans did in World War I; conversely, those smaller countries, which had only gotten independence after World War I, were uncooperative with the Russians, as they viewed the Russian threat as equal to or greater than the German threat.

As autumn progressed, little else happened, and the winter became known as "the phony war." But in the spring of 1940, the Germans made quick, fierce "**blitzkrieg**" attacks on their neighbors, quickly overrunning Denmark, Norway, Belgium, the Netherlands, Luxembourg, and, in June of 1940 after only a few weeks of fighting, France. The French quickly declared Paris an "open city" to keep it from being destroyed. When the Germans took Belgium, they were able to move north around the French defenses known as the Maginot Line, and they trapped much of the French and British armies at Dunkirk on the English Channel. The "miracle of Dunkirk" was the British rescue of most of those soldiers, although their equipment and arms were lost, and many French soldiers returned home to live under the German occupation.

In the summer of 1940, Germany began extended bombings known as the "**the blitz**" on England, causing great hardship and much loss of life. The Royal Air Force with great losses defended England and attacked Germany, and it is of those pilots that Prime Minister Winston Churchill said "Never before has so much been owed by so many to so few." England did not surrender, but by the following spring the Germans were in control of Bulgaria, Greece, and Yugoslavia, preparing for their attack on Russia on June 22, 1941, known as "Operation Barbarossa."

Nearly a million people died of starvation and disease in the German siege of Leningrad, and the Russians resisted tenaciously, helped tremendously by an unusually fierce and early winter. But the Germans rallied, and in the summer of 1942, the great Battle of Stalingrad began, with bombardments and fires by the Germans, and ferocious house-to-house fighting. The Russians, military and civilian, fought heroically under Soviet General Georgi Zhukov, and in February 1943, the German army surrendered, turning the tide of the entire war in Europe and putting the Germans on the defensive for the first time.

Meanwhile, the war raged on elsewhere. North Africa was particularly contested, partly because of the many colonies there and partly because of the Suez Canal. The British were determined to retain control of the canal, and the Germans to gain control of it because of the access it provided across the Red Sea to India and the rest of Asia, especially to the oil deposits in the Middle East. In the early 1940s, the Italians and British battled in Libya and Egypt. The Germans sent troops under General Erwin Rommel ("the Desert Fox") against whom the British sent troops under General Bernard Montgomery, who managed to defeat the Germans by the end of 1942 and save the Suez Canal. By that time, the American General Dwight Eisenhower was directing much of the Allied fighting in North Africa, and by the summer of 1943, the Allies had prevailed there in "Operation Torch," giving them a foothold from which to invade Europe.

Except for Britain and Russia, which were still fighting the Germans, and the five neutral countries (Switzerland, Portugal, Spain, Ireland, and Sweden), Germany had the rest of Europe, although there were resistance movements in many areas and several governments in exile in London, including Charles de Gaulle's Free French.

Although the Americans had been helping Britain and Russia with the lend-lease plan (promoted by President Franklin Roosevelt), allowing them to obtain ships and supplies, the Americans did not enter World War II until December 7, 1941, two and a half years after it had begun, when the Japanese, who had not declared war, attacked the American naval base at Pearl Harbor, Hawaii at dawn without warning. The Americans were stunned by the devastating loss of men, ships, and planes, just as they were a short time later when the Japanese attacked the American base at Manila in the Philippines, destroying many of the planes massed there. The Japanese attack was a deliberate policy, provoked by the American embargo of oil to Japan in the face of continued Japanese aggression throughout the 1930s toward its neighbors. As the European countries ignored their Asian colonies because of the war in Europe, Japan aggressively took them over, along with Korea, Manchuria, and parts of China, added to the German colonies and parts of Russia Japan had gained before and after World War I. When the Americans declared war on Japan after the Pearl Harbor attack, Japan's allies, Germany and Italy, declared war on the United States.

As the war raged through the Pacific, the Japanese took the Philippines, Burma, Singapore, Thailand, Malaya, Borneo, Java, Sumatra, French Indochina, and many small islands. In addition to jungle fighting, much of the Pacific war was fought at sea and in the air. As the Japanese planned to attack Australia, the Americans and the other Allies rebuffed them at the battle of the Coral Sea, and then won the Battle of Midway, turning the tide of the war in the Pacific, much to the relief of the Australians whose armies were mostly fighting elsewhere. The Allies used an "island-hopping" strategy to work their way toward Japan, gaining Allied footholds by ferocious fighting on alternating islands.

The Japanese idea of honor provided for no surrender and for harsh treatment of those who did surrender. The Japanese were notorious for treating both prisoners of war such as in the Bataan death march and civilians in captured areas such as at the "Rape of Nanking" very badly.

The great loss of life at the Battle of Okinawa, one island south of the main Japanese homeland, convinced the Americans that the casualties in an invasion of Japan itself would be so great that they should be avoided by the dropping of atomic bombs (the first and only time they have been used in war) on Nagasaki and Hiroshima. Many of those killed were Japanese civilians, but President Harry Truman defended his decision on the grounds that it was his duty to save American soldiers' lives if he had the means to do so, and he was generally supported by the American public. The United States, through fear of spies, also put many American Japanese (and some Germans and Italians) in internment camps (as had been done with some Germans in World War I) when the war began, most of the adults legal aliens who did not recover their property when the war was over. The U.S. government years later apologized and paid minor restitution for its action.

Meanwhile, back in Europe, in 1942 the Allies attempted a small invasion on the French coast at Dieppe, but they were rebuffed. Stalin kept pointing out that the Russians were carrying the brunt of the war in Europe on the Eastern Front, and there were stories beginning to circulate about the atrocities and killings in the concentration camps. By 1943, the Allies had invaded Italy successfully, and the Italians deposed their government, killed Mussolini, and changed sides in the war.

The Allies' preparations for an invasion of Occupied France (held by the Nazis, including the cooperating Vichy government in the south) came to fruition on June 6, 1944. After much careful planning under General Eisenhower, they invaded Normandy in the operation known as D-Day (for "deployment day"). After much loss of life and heavy fighting, the Allies got their foothold and headed east, driving the German army before them.

In the winter of 1944–1945, the Germans made one last desperate push to the west at the Battle of the Bulge, but failed to defeat the Allies. As the other Allies drove east into Germany, the Russians headed west into Poland and Germany, both armies meeting in Germany and liberating concentration camps in Poland and Germany along the way. One of the oddities of the Holocaust was that many more concentration camps were set up in Poland than in Germany and many more Polish Jews were killed than German Jews because there had been many more Jews living in Poland when the war broke out. Some Poles were complicit with the Germans in persecuting the Jews, although the Germans killed many Poles as well.

By the end of April 1945, Hitler had committed suicide, and Germany surrendered. The war in the Pacific theater continued until Japan surrendered in August, after the dropping of the atomic bombs. World War II was finally over, after the deaths of 45–70 million people. The Allies set up an international court and tried leaders in both Germany and Japan for "crimes against humanity," and established the United Nations, headquartered in New York City, to try to keep the future peace.

Cold War

Generally speaking, in Europe countries were to influence the areas they had liberated: that meant that the democracies were to influence western Europe, and Russia was to influence eastern Europe. Russia, which had borne the worst brunt of the war, losing 20 million people, was obsessed with security and insisted on a buffer of communist countries (Poland, Hungary, Czechoslovakia, Yugoslavia, Romania, Bulgaria, Latvia, Lithuania, Estonia) between itself and Germany.

The Americans, having fought for democracy, were disappointed that it would not extend throughout Europe, but did institute it under the Allies in the three western parts of Germany (Russia administered East Germany as a communist country). General George Marshall led the effort known as the Marshall Plan to rebuild the defeated countries of Europe in order to avoid the bitterness and instability of the post–World War I years, so, in an odd irony, Germany's and other countries' economies rebounded with American help, while Great Britain, under a Labour government, was the last country to recover from the war, with war debts, shortages, and rationing lasting into the 1950s. The GI Bill helped U.S. veterans attend college and buy homes.

The hostility between eastern (aligned with the Soviet Union) and western Europe (aligned with the United States) was so great that it became known as the Cold War (as opposed to a shooting, or "hot," war) and lasted until the early 1990s. In 1948, the Soviets shut off access to the Allied part of Berlin, but the British and Americans responded with an airlift that lasted for over a year until the crisis was resolved. In 1961, the Berlin Wall was built by East Germany to keep its citizens from escaping into free West Berlin, and the tearing down of the wall by cheering citizens from both sides in 1989 during the fall of communism was seen as very symbolic. In the post-war years the United States and Russia were the two super powers: the United States had the bomb first, but that advantage was lost in the early 1950s. Then in 1957, Russia sent up Sputnik, the first satellite in space, which the United States quickly emulated, putting men on the moon in 1969 as part of the Space Race.

In Japan, the Americans under General Douglas MacArthur occupied and ran the country as a democracy for a few years until the economy was rebuilt and the political situation stabilized, and Japan quickly became a democratic, industrialized nation. In the rest of Asia and Africa, the situation was somewhat different. When Japan was defeated, some countries regained their independence and many that had been colonies of European powers now wanted independence. The communists, many of whom had gained their citizens' loyalty by fighting against the Japanese, led the independence movements in some areas. In 1949, China became a communist country, causing great concern in the Western democracies, who recognized Chiang Kai-shek's exiled government in Taiwan as the "real" China. "Red" China would not be allowed to join the United Nations until 1971, followed by U.S. president Richard Nixon's historic 1972 visit, which reopened relations with communist China.

In the United States, the anticommunist feeling grew into hysteria in the early 1950s, fed by Joseph McCarthy, a Republican senator from Wisconsin who accused many people in the State Department (most notably Alger Hiss, who was convicted of perjury) and other fields of having communist leanings. In Hollywood, the accusations degenerated into a "blacklist" of writers who were "blackballed" from working in their profession. Most of McCarthy's accusations had no basis (although American freedoms make it legal to be a communist and many idealists in the 1930s and 1940s had supported communism against fascism), and he was eventually discredited, but his crusade deepened the divide between generally hawkish Republicans and dovish Democrats.

Korea became involved in a civil war, and the United Nations intervened, defending the south from the communists, who were aided by the Chinese. The subsequent Korean War, called a "police action," lasted from 1950 to 1953 and resulted in a division of Korea, enforced by U.N. troops who are still there as of this writing, into the communist North Korea and the nominally democratic South Korea (often run as a military dictatorship).

The French tried to return to Indochina, where the Vietnamese, led by the Communist Ho Chi Minh, resisted them and called for independence. When it became apparent in the mid 1950s that the French were withdrawing, the United States began aiding the South Vietnamese against the communist North. As the fighting and the American help escalated in the middle 1960s under President Lyndon Johnson, the Vietnam War (America's longest war but never actually declared a war) became a hotly contested issue in the United States and abroad, with antiwar protestors in the streets. Their actions were partly because South Vietnam had a series of corrupt leaders; there was much disapproval of chemical warfare using napalm and Agent Orange; and American draft laws excused college students until 1969, so the war was disproportionately fought by the sons of the working class.

The war spread into surrounding countries, devastating Laos and Cambodia as well, and leading to the communist victory in Cambodia and the subsequent slaughter of several million people by Pol Pot's Khmer Rouge. At the height of the Vietnam War, over 500,000 American troops were fighting in Vietnam and over 58,000 were killed there. Feelings were and still are very bitter between "hawks" (those in favor of the war) and "doves" (those against it). Because of the controversy, President Lyndon Johnson declined to run for a second term in 1968. Finally, in 1973, President Richard Nixon withdrew American troops, and in 1975, the communists took over all of Vietnam.

Independence Movements

The aforementioned major theme worldwide after World War II was that the colonies of France, Britain, Spain, the Netherlands and even the United States were demanding and getting independence, in a nationalist movement that had begun even after

World War I, so that gradually colonial empires were falling apart. During the Cold War, the world increasingly divided into democratic and communist camps (free world and communist world), but these newly independent countries became known as the "Third World" (not allied with either, and aided by both sides to keep the other in check). Third World countries (with some exceptions) generally tended to be located in Asia, Africa, or South America, and tended to be agricultural, undeveloped, poor, and heavily populated, which meant that the competition and aid to gain their allegiance was intense for political reasons but also often was motivated by humanitarian and medical reasons.

In Africa, most colonies gained their independence in the years after World War II. Some colonies had peaceful transitions from Britain: Ghana, Nigeria, Cameroon, Sierra Leone, Tanganyika, Uganda, and Gambia. Other British colonies became the independent countries of Kenya, Zambia, Malawi, and Zimbabwe after a mix of negotiation and fighting. In the 1950s, France fought to keep Algeria, which got its independence in 1962. Colonies across Africa followed suit in the next two decades: by 1960, most other French colonies were free by negotiation and referendum. Both Angola and Mozambique fought Portugal and won after its dictator was overthrown at home in 1974.

The transition to independence in some places was difficult, as in the struggles in the Congo (which became Zaire and then the Congo again). Since the countries had been largely divided by Europeans ignoring tribal groups and migration patterns, many bitter civil wars as in Nigeria and between Rwanda and Burundi took place throughout the latter half of the twentieth century. The tensions were further heightened by fighting between blacks and whites. Whites were in the minority everywhere and often feared black majority government as in Kenya and Rhodesia. Many newly independent countries gave up their colonial names and took African names. In independent South Africa, legal segregation of the races (apartheid, instituted in 1948) was finally ended in the 1990s, universal suffrage was instituted, and a black president, Nelson Mandela, was elected.

In Asia, India got its independence from Great Britain in 1947, followed by a civil war in which over 2 million people were killed and Pakistan claimed independence from India. Japan had claimed before World War II that it was taking Asia for the Asians. Most countries there objected to being taken over by the Japanese, but did not want to revert to their former colonial status. In addition to Indochina getting free of the French, many other countries achieved their independence from European colonizers.

The British solution was to form a "commonwealth," which meant independence but voluntary association and recognition of the monarchy. Canada, a wealthy industrialized country that had become an independent Dominion in 1867, remained part of the commonwealth, as did Australia (which voted in late 1999 to remain with it), but some colonies still wanted, and achieved, complete severance, so the independence movements continued, through the Bahamas gaining their independence in 1974. Canada was a model of democratic socialist government throughout the century, but stumbled on the ethnic issue, as French Canadian activists in the largely French province of Quebec starting in the 1960s increasingly demanded recognition of French culture, including the imposition of strict French-only language laws. In a Quebec referendum in 1994, Quebecers voted by a tiny margin to stay with the nation, but activists vowed a different result next time. Interestingly, Native

Americans, who have a large chunk of northern Quebec as tribal lands, warned that if Quebec broke with Canada, they would break with Quebec.

Many Latin American countries had unstable histories of government by various dictators in the twentieth century, but by the 1990s, most were democracies. Their relationship with the United States was often strained: President James Monroe's 1823 establishment of the Monroe Doctrine (that no European countries were to interfere in the events of the Western Hemisphere, even to reestablish their hold in their colonies) helped the independence movements in nineteenth-century Latin America, but the "Roosevelt Corollary" of 1904, providing that the United States would mediate problems for the Europeans, was looked upon with hostility by most Latin American countries and often made the U.S. relationship with its neighbors very awkward.

In 1954, Puerto Rican rebels seeking independence bombed the U.S. Capitol building. By the late 1990s, extensive discussions were taking place, in Puerto Rico and on the mainland, about whether Puerto Rico wanted to continue its commonwealth status as a U.S. possession whose people already have U.S. citizenship; wanted to become independent as the Philippines did after World War II; or wanted to become a state.

The situation was exacerbated by the flirtation with communism in some Latin American countries and the concomitant horrified reaction in the United States, which illegally helped depose the socialist President of Chile and aided the fight against the Sandinista government of Nicaragua, much to the dismay of many. The United States also sponsored the failed Bay of Pigs invasion of Cuba by exiles in the United States a few years after Fidel Castro had announced he was a communist after defeating the dictator Fulgencio Batista and taking over Cuba in 1959. When Russia was discovered putting missiles in Cuba, the United States successfully demanded their removal ("the Cuban missile crisis" of 1962). The United States also placed an embargo on trade with Cuba after the government nationalized most property, including that owned by Americans, which, together with various communist economic policies in Cuba, crippled the economy and is still in place at the time of this writing. Many other countries continued to trade with Cuba, most notably Canada, which placed a strain on U.S.-Canadian relations.

Cultural Change

The 1950s was the period of the *Brown* decision, in which the Supreme Court of the United States in 1954 outlawed the concept of "separate but equal," established by the Court in *Plessy v. Ferguson* in 1896. The *Brown* decision did away with de jure (legal) segregation and President Harry Truman already had integrated the military in 1948, although de facto (in fact) segregation remained in many places. The lawyer for the NAACP (National Association for the Advancement of Colored People, which had been founded early in the century by a coalition of blacks and whites), who argued the case before the Supreme Court, Thurgood Marshall, later became the first black (the preferred designation by the 1960s) Supreme Court Justice. Marshall was appointed by President Lyndon Johnson, who was also active in the passage of the Voting Rights Act of 1965, which eliminated unreasonable state requirements for citizens registering to vote, used in some Southern states to keep blacks disenfranchised.

Much public feeling in favor of civil rights was aroused by the television coverage of peaceful protestors being attacked in Arkansas, Louisiana, Alabama, and Mississippi. Efforts at black voter registration and integrating schools and store lunch counters resulted in church bombings and violence against black citizens in many areas, but ultimately succeeded.

The civil rights movement gained momentum throughout the 1960s, in part from the efforts of Rosa Parks, an Alabama woman who refused to move to the back part of the bus she was on so a white man could have her seat. Her action sparked the Birmingham bus strike in which the young minister Dr. Martin Luther King, Jr. came to the forefront as a leader with his philosophy of peaceful civil disobedience to effect social change, based on the writings and actions of Thoreau and Gandhi. Ralph Abernathy and Jesse Jackson were also very active in the civil rights movement. The more radical Black Panthers (under Bobby Seale, Huey Newton, and Eldridge Cleaver), the Black Muslims (under Elijah Muhammad and Malcolm X), and the intellectual Angela Davis promoted black pride (often symbolized among the young of the time by an "Afro" hairstyle and the slogan "Black is beautiful"). King became the best-known black leader in the United States, giving his "I Have a Dream" speech in Washington, D.C. at the 1963 Freedom March.

President Richard Nixon instituted the still-controversial policy of "affirmative action," admissions and hiring preferences intended to make up for past discrimination against black citizens. As the black middle and upper classes grew successfully, taking advantage of newly opened educational and business opportunities, a crime-ridden underclass, partly a result of the general explosion of drug use in society and partly of the movement of prosperity to the suburbs, also emerged.

President Lyndon Johnson's "war on poverty" (originally conceived by President John Kennedy to help the rural poor), part of the "Great Society" concept, expanded the welfare state, especially in rural areas and in inner cities, with Aid to Families with Dependent Children, food stamps, and Medicaid. By the early 1990s, an increasing percentage of American children lived in poverty, partly as a result of single-parent families because of the high divorce rate and birth rates to unmarried teenage mothers, who, with some exceptions, generally earn low wages due to their youth and lack of skills. As the century began, births to single mothers dropped, the divorce rate was slightly down, and welfare had been strictly reformed.

The 1960s was a time of great tumult, both politically and socially. In tragic events that shocked the nation, President John F. Kennedy was assassinated in Dallas, Texas on November 22, 1963, and his brother Senator Robert Kennedy was assassinated in 1968, as was Dr. Martin Luther King, Jr. In unrelated killings, Malcolm X, the leader of the Black Muslims, was assassinated by one of his followers, as was George Lincoln Rockwell, the leader of the American Nazi party by one of his. In 1972, Governor George Wallace of Alabama was paralyzed in an attempted assassination during his presidential bid, and the spate of killings led many to despair about the future of politics in America.

In addition to the Vietnam War (see earlier) and civil rights, the women's movement was an issue. It got under way with the publication of Betty Friedan's *Feminine Mystique* and other books in the 1960s examining the state of women, followed by the founding of the National Organization for Women. The gay rights movement also began in this period, with the Stonewall riots in which gay bar patrons defended against ongoing police brutality in New York City, and elderly activists formed the Gray Panthers. The year 1968 saw a rash of strikes by students everywhere, most notably in France, where they almost brought down the government, and in China, in the midst of the Cultural Revolution. "Sex, drugs, and rock and roll" changed traditional standards for many people.

There was a new interest in ethnic roots and individual rights, partly exemplified by defiance of the drug laws by many people, particularly in the case of marijuana, and the sexual revolution, based in part on the development of the birth control pill, gained much momentum. AIDS would not appear until the late 1970s and would not become common for ten years after that. "The silent majority" was overshadowed by the active minority, as more and more citizens all over the world took to the streets and the airwaves to promote their views and causes. Rock music, begun in the United States as an amalgam of black and white Southern music, and often a voice for social change, made its way around the world with such artists as Chuck Berry, Elvis Presley, Bob Dylan, and the English groups the Beatles and the Rolling Stones.

In the 1970s, many industrialized countries suffered recessions and then inflation. The oil shortage of the early 1970s, a result of the banding together of many oil-producing countries into OPEC (Organization of Petroleum Exporting Countries) to affect the international market, gave impetus to the growing environmental movement and its demand for more ecologically friendly products, such as more efficient, less polluting cars, and Earth Day was celebrated for the first time. Rachel Carson's *Silent Spring,* about environmental problems caused by pesticides, and Marjorie Stoneman Douglas's *River of Grass,* about saving the Florida Everglades, although published earlier, became very influential in the movement.

A main political event of the time in the United States was Watergate, named after the building complex where four burglars working for the Republican party were found breaking into the Democratic party's headquarters. The ensuing investigation, initiated by *Washington Post* reporters Carl Bernstein and Bob Woodward, and attempted cover-up caused the resignations of many highly placed officials in Republican President Richard Nixon's administration, and eventually brought down the president himself. In August 1974, facing impeachment, he became the first American president to resign his office, which was taken over by Vice President Gerald Ford, who immediately pardoned Nixon.

Another significant event was the 1978 seizure of fifty-two hostages (and their release 444 days later) at the American Embassy in Iran by militant revolutionaries supported by the religious leader Ayatollah Khomeini in retaliation for U.S. support of the ousted Shah. This action heralded the growth of Islamic fundamentalism (also linked to nationalism and issues of control of oil) in the Middle East. In country after country, response to the seemingly unstoppable spread of "decadent" Western, mostly American, culture (often in the form of movies, pop music, clothing, and women's rights) was a hardening of traditional religious rules by conservative clerics. As of this writing, the latest country to go this route is Afghanistan, where the fundamentalist religious Muslims (the Taliban) controlling much of the country have banned women from working outside the home, receiving medical care, or attending school, along with imposing the mandatory wearing of the face- and body-covering chador, despite the efforts of the Karzai government.

On September 11, 2001, four passenger planes were hijacked by Islamic fundamentalist terrorists unhappy with U.S. influence. The planes were used as weapons to bomb significant U.S. locations. The two World Trade Center towers in New York City were each hit by a plane a few minutes apart and the Pentagon in a Virginia suburb of Washington, D.C. was hit by a third plane. The fourth plane, United Flight 93, was heroically thwarted when some of its passengers, alerted by cell phone to those previous crashes, diverted the plane from its presumed White House or Capitol target, overpowering the hijackers but not able to stop its subsequent crash in a Pennsylvania field. Over 3,000 people on the ground and in the air were killed in those events. Despite the fact that most of the hijackers were Saudi nationals, attention turned to the Taliban in Afghanistan, which supported Al Qaeda, a Sunni Islamic fundamentalist terrorist group, one of whose leaders, Osama Bin Laden, located in Afghanistan, was the Saudi architect behind "9/11." Later in 2001, the Taliban was removed as Afghanistan's government by Afghans allied with the United States and other countries. When U.S. attention later turned to Iraq with the invasion and subsequent occupation there, the Taliban regrouped and continues to be an aggressive presence in Afghanistan at this writing.

One of the less fundamental countries was Iraq, which, after a long war with Iran, attacked Kuwait in the 1990s and was in turn attacked by United Nations forces led by the United States. The Gulf War pushed Iraq out of Kuwait and only lasted a few weeks, but Iraq continued to create problems with its threats of biological warfare and was bombed several times in 1998 by the United States for refusing to cooperate with U.N. weapons inspectors.

In 2003, the United States, aided by Great Britain and a few other countries, invaded Iraq in a first strike unprecedented in U.S. history, because President Bush and his administration argued that Iraq, under its provocative, militaristic leader Saddam Hussein was developing biological and nuclear "weapons of mass destruction." This invasion was contrary to the wishes of most other countries and of the United Nations, whose inspectors did not find such evidence. By the time it became apparent that no such evidence existed, the United States was bogged down there, and Iraq had devolved into civil war between the Sunnis and the Shiites, which further destabilized the country. Saddam Hussein was deposed, tried, and executed, and Iraq became a hotbed of both internal religious strife and of Middle Eastern resistance to the United States, with a flow of fighters coming from other countries.

In an effort to win the "war on terror," the United States took "enemy combatants" to its naval base at Guantanamo Bay, Cuba, as the administration argued that they could be held indefinitely without being charged. When the Supreme Court struck down that argument, military tribunals were set up. Almost 4,000 U.S. soldiers have been killed in Iraq, as have very small numbers of soldiers of other participants. The estimates are that the war in all its incarnations has killed several hundred thousand Iraqis.

The 1980s saw a conservative resurgence in the West with the election of President Ronald Reagan in the United States and Prime Minister Margaret Thatcher in Great Britain. Taxes in both countries were cut and, in Britain, many social programs were privatized. In 1982, Argentina attacked and claimed the Falkland Islands, which it called the Malvinas, and which had been a source of contention between Britain and Argentina since the first half of the 1800s. But Britain defended vigorously and won, solidifying Thatcher's popularity for the next decade. In the United States, Reagan was also very popular, although his two terms were marked by the "Irangate" and "contra" scandals, investigations of clandestine foreign affairs operations, and by the burgeoning savings and loan scandal, brought about when Congress relaxed rules for the banking industry while guaranteeing losses, costing the country several billion dollars as a result of bad or criminal management. By the end of the century, the United States had a popular two-term Democratic president, William Jefferson Clinton, embroiled in a messy year-long sex scandal that led to his impeachment by a bitterly partisan House and subsequent acquittal by a more moderate Senate, both controlled by Republicans.

The election of 2000 was even more contentious. The Democratic candidate Al Gore won the popular vote, but Republican George W. Bush took the electoral vote. The deciding factor was the popular vote count in Florida: a confusing ballot, extensive absentee voting, and incorrect voter lists led to a narrow victory for George W. Bush after a month of each side contesting court decisions, when the U.S. Supreme Court stopped the count, thereby giving victory to George W. Bush, who was re-elected in 2004.

The election of 2008 was particularly historic because of its wide field of candidates, representing diversity of gender, religion, race, ethnic background, and iconoclastic views. Barack Obama became the first black Democratic nominee, beating out his closest competition, former first lady Hillary Clinton, who came very close to being the first female nominee. John McCain, Republican nominee, chose a female as his vice presidential running mate. In an Electoral college landslide in November 2008, Barack Obama was elected president, resulting in much approbation from the rest of the world.

The year 1989 brought the fall of the Berlin Wall, one of the most stunning events of the century, as it led not only to the reunification of Germany, but more importantly to the defeat of communism mostly because of widespread economic failure in most European countries: this was in sharp contrast to the communists prevailing during rebellions in Hungary in 1956 and in Czechoslovakia in 1968. Again, nationalism became a major force, especially in the former Yugoslavia, where the independence movements of Croatia, Slovenia, Bosnia, Kosovo, and Macedonia led to atrocity-laden civil wars throughout the 1990s. In 1999, NATO bombed Serbian Yugoslavia due to its harsh treatment and "ethnic cleansing" (driving out or killing) of ethnic Albanians (themselves Yugoslav citizens) supporting the Kosovar Liberation Army agitating for independence in the Yugoslavian province of Kosovo. The Soviet Union apart, with many of its sixteen republics gaining independence sometimes through military clashes. Despite having tremendous financial and social difficulties in making the change from communism, Russia, the largest of them stabilized its economy, partly thorough reliance on oil exports.

Many European countries, however, came together to form the European Union based on the Common Market, agreeing to free movement of goods and people, including a common passport and went on a common monetary system based on the "euro." It was also in the 1990s that the "Chunnel," the tunnel under the English Channel that linked England to France, was finished and opened to use. Refugee movement was tremendous as well, with major immigrations, often from third world countries to the industrialized West, for political reasons, as in the cases of Cubans, Nicaraguans, and Vietnamese, or for economic reasons, as in the cases of Algerians, Haitians, and Russians.

The twentieth century ended and the twenty-first began with computers changing the way people gather information and do business, much as science shaped life around the world throughout the century, with the development of communications (radio, movies, television, and telephones), transportation (the automobile, air travel, space exploration), electricity (appliances, heating, air-conditioning), nuclear power (the bomb and power plants), and modern medicine (antibiotics, contraception, transplants). At the start of the twenty-first century, over 6 billion humans were living out their stories and making collective human history on the planet Earth.

History Resources

Getting Started Educationally

Adamson, L. G. *A Reference Guide to Historical Fiction for Children and Young Adults.* Westport, Conn.: Greenwood Press, 1987 (plot summaries of well-written children's historical fiction).

Adamson, L. G. *Recreating the Post: A Guide to American and World Historical Fiction for Children and Young Adults.* Westport, Conn.: Greenwood Press, 1994.

Bennett, Clifford T., Joe Richelle, and Ken Watson. Review of "SVE Series on World and U.S. History." *Social Education.* April 1999: 164–166 (analyzes four CDs: African-American History, Columbus and the Age of Discovery, Cradles of Civilization, and The Greek and Roman World).

Bigelow, William. "Once Upon a Genocide: Christopher Columbus in Children's literature." *Language Arts.* 69, February 1992: 112–120 (revisionist view).

Crabtree, Charlotte. "Returning History to the Elementary Schools." In *Historical Literacy*, eds. Paul Gagnon and the Bradley Commission on History in the Schools. New York: Macmillan, 1989.

Fairey, Chad C., Clifford T. Bennett, and John Lee. "History Uninspired? A Critical Look at Tom Snyder's *American History Inspirer: The Civil War.*" *Social Education.* April 1999: 162–164 (grade 5–12 software lacks content and people but is strong in geography and causes of the war).

Hartman, D. K. and G. Sapp. *Historical Figures in Fiction.* Phoenix: Oryx Press, 1994.

Johnson, Nancy M. and M. Jane Ebert "Time Travel Is Possible: Historical Fiction and Biography—Passport to the Past." *The Reading Teacher.* March 1992: 488–495 (includes an extensive bibliography).

Kornfeld, John. "Using Fiction to Teach History: Multicultural and Global Perspectives of World War II." *Social Education.* September 1994: 281–286.

Lamme, Linda. "Stories from Our Past: Making History Come Alive for Children." *Social Education.* September 1994: 159–164.

Leeman, William P. "American History Websites for Use in Secondary Schools." *Social Education.* April 1999: 144–151.

National Standards for History (Basic Edition K–12). Los Angeles: National Center for History in the Schools, University of California, 1996.

National Standards for History (Grades 1–4) Expanding Children's World in Time and Space. Los Angeles: National Center for History in the Schools. University of California, 1994.

National Standards for History (Grades 5–12) Exploring the American Experience. Los Angeles: National Center for History in the Schools, University of California (no date).

National Standards for World History (Grades 5–12) Exploring Paths to the Present. Los Angeles: National Center for History in the Schools, University of California (no date).

Ravitch, Diane. "Tot Sociology: What Happened to History in the Grade Schools." *The American Scholar.* Summer 1987: 112–132.

Rudman, M. K. and S. P. Rosenberg. "Confronting History: Holocaust Books for Children." *The New Advocate.* 4, 1991: 163–177.

Sims, R. *Shadow and Substance: Afro-American Experience in Contemporary Children's Fiction.* Urbana, IL: NCTE, 1982 (analyzes historical context of books 1965–1979).

Stafford, Jan. "How to Teach about Religions in the Social Studies Classroom." *The Social Studies.* November/December 1993: 245–248 (includes suggested children's trade books).

Totten, Samuel. "Telling the Holocaust Story to Children." *Social Studies and the Young Learner.* November/December 1994: 5–8 (includes suggested children's trade books).

Tunnell, M. O. and R. Ammon, eds. *The Story of Ourselves: Teaching History through Children's Literature.* Portsmouth, N.H.: Heinemann, 1993 (contains annotated bibliography of historical literature).

History Content for Teachers

Ailslee, Thomas and Carol Gluck, eds. *Asia in Western and World History: A Guide for Teaching* (Columbia Project on Asia in the Core Curriculum). M. E. Sharpe, 1997.

Bailey, Jim. *Sailing to Paradise.* New York: Simon & Schuster, 1994.

Boatner III, Mark M. *Encyclopedia of the American Revolution.* Mechanicsburg, Penn: Stackpole, 1994.

Bobrick, Benson. *Angel in the Whirlwind: The Triumph of the American Revolution.* New York: Simon & Schuster, 1997.

Boorstin, Daniel J. *The Americans: The Colonial Experience.* New York: Random House, 1964.

Boorstin, Daniel J. *The Discoverers.* New York: Random House, 1983.

Boorstin, Daniel J. and Brooks Mather Kelley. *A History of the United States.* Englewood Cliffs, NJ.: Prentice-Hall, 1992.

Bose, Sugata and Ayesha Jalal. *Modern South Asia: History, Culture and Political Economy.* New York: Routledge, 1998.

Branch, Taylor. *Parting the Waters: America in the King Years 1954–63.* Touchstone, 1989.

Branch, Taylor. *Pillar of Fire: America in the King Years 1963–1965.* New York: Simon & Schuster, 1998.

Branham, Charles R. *Profiles of Great African Americans.* Lincolnwood, Ill.: Publications International, 1998.

Brinkley, Douglas. *American Heritage History of the United States.* New York: Viking, 1998.

Burkholder, Mark A. et al. *Colonial Latin America.* 3rd ed. Oxford: Oxford University Press, 1997.

Burns, Edward McNall, Philip Lee Ralph, Robert E. Lerner, and Standish Meacham. *World Civilizations: Their History and their Culture.* 7th ed. New York: W. W. Norton, 1986.

Campbell, I. C. *A History of the Pacific Islands.* Berkeley: University of California Press, 1990.

Canning, John, ed. *One Hundred Great Kings. Queens and Rulers of the World.* New York: Bonanza, 1967.

Cantor, Norman F. *The Civilization of the Middle Ages.* New York: Harperperennial, 1994.

Catton, Bruce et al. *The American Heritage New History of the Civil War.* New York: Viking, 1996.

Champagne, Duane. *Native America: Portrait of the Peoples.* Detroit, Mich.: Visible Ink Press, 1994.

Christian, David. *A History of Russia, Central Asia and Mongolia: Inner Eurasia from Prehistory to the Mongol Empire.* Blackwell, 1999.

Countryman, Edward. *The American Revolution.* New York: Hill & Wang, 1985.

Crow, John A. *The Epic of Latin America.* Berkeley: University of California Press, 1992.

Davies, Norman. *Europe: A History.* New York: Oxford University Press, 1996.

Davis, Kenneth C. *Don't Know Much the Civil War: Everything You Need to Know About America's Greatest Conflict But Never Learned.* New York: Avon, 1997.

Donghi, Tulio Halperin and John Charles Chastien. *The Contemporary History of Latin America.* Durham. N.C.: Duke University Press, 1993.

Evans, Harold. *The American Century (20th).* New York: Knopf, 1998.

Fleming, Thomas. *Liberty: The American Revolution.* New York: Viking, 1997.

Foote, Shelby. *The Civil War: A Narrative* (3 vols.). New York: Random House, 1974.

Gibbon. Edward. *The History of the Decline and Fall of the Roman Empire* (6 vols). London, 1776–1787.

Grun, Bernard. *The Timetables of History.* New York: Simon & Schuster, 1982.

Hale, J. R. *Renaissance Europe,* Berkeley: University of California Press, 1971.

Haley, Alex. *The Saga of an American Family.* New York: Doubleday, 1976.

Hart, Liddell. *History of the First World War.* London: Pan Books, 1970.

Hart, Liddell. *History of the Second World War.* London: Pan Books, 1973.

Hart, Michael. *The One Hundred: A Ranking of the Most Influential Persons in History.* Secaucus, NJ.: Citadel Press, 1987, 1995.

Hobsbaum, Eric J. *The Age of Extremes: A History of the World 1914–1991.* New York: Vintage, 1996.

Hughes, Robert. *The Fatal Shore: The Epic of Australia's Founding.* New York: Vintage, 1988.

Iliffe, John. *Africans: The History of a Continent.* New York: Cambridge University Press, 1996.

Johnson, Charles et al. *Africans in America: America's Journey Through Slavery.* San Diego: Harcourt Brace, 1998.

Johnson, Paul. *A History of the American People.* New York: HarperCollins 1999.

Jones, Constance. *1001 Things Everyone Should Know about Women's History.* New York: Doubleday, 1998.

Josephy, Alvin M. *The Indian Heritage of America* Boston: Houghton Mifflin, 1991.

Kanellos, Nicolas. *The Hispanic Almanac: From Columbus to Corporate America.* Detroit, Mich.: Visible Ink Press, 1994.

Karnow, Stanley. *Vietnam.* New York: Penguin, 1983, 1991.

Maier, Karl. *Into the House of the Ancestors: Inside the New Africa.* New York: Wiley, 1997.

Manchester, William. *The Glory and the Dream: A Narrative History of America 1932–1972.* Boston: Little Brown, 1973.

Manchester, William. *A World Lit Only by Fire: Life in the Middle Ages.* New York: Little Brown, 1992.

McElvaine. Robert S. *The Great Depression: America, 1929–1941.* New York: Times Books, 1994.

McNeill, William. *Plagues and Peoples.* New York: Doubleday, 1976, 1989.

Metaxas. Eric. *Amazing Grace: William Wilberforce and the Heroic Campaign to End Slavery.* New York: HarperOne, 2007.

Nies, Judith. *Native American History.* New York: Ballentine, 1996.

Norton, Mary Beth et al. *A People and a Nation: A History of the United States.* 3rd ed. Boston: Houghton Mifflin, 1990.

Noss, John B. *Man's Religions.* 4th ed. London: Collier-Macmillan Limited, 1968.

Palmer, R. R. and Joel Colton. *A History of the Modern World.* 8th ed. New York: McGraw-Hill, 1998.

Reader, John. *Africa: A Biography of the Continent.* New York: Knopf, 1999.

Richard, John. *Australia: A Cultural History (The Present and the Past).* Reading, Mass.: Addison Wesley, 1997.

Roberts, J. M. *A History of Europe.* Alan Lane, 1997.

Rogozinsky, Jon. *A Brief History of the Caribbean.* New York: Meridian, 1992.

Schlesinger, Jr. Arthur M. *The Cycles of American History.* Boston: Houghton Mifflin, 1986.

Skidmore, Thomas and Peter H. Smith. *Modern Latin America.* 4th ed. New York: Oxford University Press, 1996.

Stewart, Jeffrey C. *One Thousand One Things Everyone Should Know About African American History.* New York: Doubleday, 1996.

Takaki, Ronald. *A Different Mirror: A History of Multicultural America.* Boston: Little Brown, 1994.

Taylor, A. J. P. *The Origins of the Second World War.* London: Penguin Books, 1961, 1984.

Tessler, Mark. *A History of the Israeli-Palestinian Conflict.* Bloomington: University of Indiana Press, 1994.

Thomas, Hugh. *The Slave Trade: The Story of the Atlantic Slave Trade 1440–1870.* New York: Simon & Schuster, 1997.

Tuchman, Barbara. [World War One Trilogy] *The Zimmerman Telegram* (1958), *The Guns of August* (1962), *The Proud Tower* (1966). New York: Knopf.

Tuchman, Barbara. *A Distant Mirror: The Calamitous 14th Century.* New York: Knopf, 1978.

Vandiver, Frank Everson. *1001 Things Everyone Should Know About the Civil War.* New York: Doubleday, 1999.

Viault, Birdsell S. *Modern European History.* New York: McGraw-Hill, 1991.

Winchester, Simon. *The River at the Center of the World.* New York: Picador, 2004.

Winn, Peter. *The Changing Face of Latin America and the Caribbean.* Berkeley: University of California Press, 1995.

Zinn, Howard. *A People's History of the United States 1492–Present.* New York: Harperperennial, 1995.

History Content for Students

Armstrong, William. *Sounder.* New York: Harper, 1969 (early twentieth-century African Americans).

Borden, Louise. *The Little Ships: The Heroic Rescue at Dunkirk in World War II.* New York: Simon & Schuster, 1997.

Brink, Carol Ryrie. *Caddie Woodlawn.* New York: Macmillan, 1936 (pioneer life).

Burleigh, Robert and Bruce Strachan. *American Moments.* New York: Henry Holt and Co., 2004.

Burleigh, Robert and Wendell Minor. *Abraham Lincoln Comes Home.* New York: Henry Holt and Co., 2008.

Caselli, Giovanni. *The First Civilizations.* New York: Peter Bedrick, 1983.

Community Construction Kit (software). Watertown, Mass.: Tom Snyder Productions, 2008.

Corbishley, Mike. *The Roman World.* New York: Warwick, 1986.

Dalgliesh, Alice. *The Courage of Sarah Noble.* New York: Scribner's, 1954 (pioneer life).

Davis, Burke. *Black Heroes of the American Revolution.* New York: Harcourt Brace, Jovanovich, 1976.

Dorris, Michael. *Morning Girl.* New York: Hyperion, 1992 (Taino Indian girl).

Dower, Laura. *For Girls Only.* New York: Feiwel & Friends, 2008.

Fisher, Leonard Everett. *Great Wall of China.* New York: Macmillan, 1986.

Fisher, Leonard Everett. *The Tower of London.* New York: Macmillan, 1987.

Fisher, Leonard Everett. *Pyramid of the Sun, Pyramid of the Moon.* New York: Macmillan, 1988 (Toltecs and Aztecs).

Fleischman, Paul. *Bull Run.* New York: HarperCollins, 1993 (Civil War).

Forbes, Esther. *Johnny Tremain.* Boston: Houghton Mifflin, 1943 (American Revolution).

Fritz, Jean. *George Washington's Breakfast* and the rest of her series of books on the Revolutionary War (and a few on other subjects), from various publishers.

Giff, Patricia Reilly. *Lily's Crossing.* New York: Dell, 1997 (World War II).

Greene, Bette. *Summer of My German Soldier.* New York: Dial, 1973 (World War II).

Hakim, Joy. *A History of Us* (ten-book series on American history). New York: Oxford University Press, 1993.

Hamilton, Virginia. *The Bells of Christmas.* New York: Harcourt Brace, Jovanovich, 1989 (prosperous nineteenth-century African Americans).

Hamilton, Virginia. *Many Thousand Gone: African Americans from Slavery to Freedom.* New York: Random House, 1992.

Handler, Andrew and Susan Michaels. *Young People Speak: Surviving the Holocaust in Hungary.* Danbury, CT: Watts, 1993.

Haugaard, Erik Christian. *The Boy and the Samurai.* Boston: Houghton Mifflin, 1991.

Henry, Marguerite. *King of the Wind.* Rand McNally, 1948, 1976 (Arabian boy in Europe with horse in 1600s).

Hershfelder, Arlene. *Happily May I Walk American Indians and Alaska Natives Today.* New York: Scribner's, 1986.

Hesse, Karen. *Out of the Dust.* New York: Scholastic, 1997 (Great Depression).

Holman, Felice. *The Wild Children.* New York: Scribner's, 1983 (Bolshevik revolution).

How Would You Survive? (software). Watertown, Mass.: Tom Snyder Productions, 2008.

Hudson, Jan. *Sweetgrass.* New York: Philomel, 1989 (Blackfoot girl).

I Wonder Why Greeks Built Temples and Other Questions about Ancient Greece. New York: Kingfisher, 1999.

Interviews with History (software). Educational Publishing Concepts.

Kudlinski, Kathleen. *Night Bird: A Story of the Seminole Indians.* New York: Viking, 1993.

Kerby, Mona and Lynne Barasch. *Owney, The Mail-Pouch Pooch.* New York: Farrar, Straus and Giroux, 2008.

Lawson, Robert. *Ben and Me.* Boston: Little, Brown, 1939, 1988 (Ben Franklin).

Lawson, Robert. *Mr. Revere and I.* Boston: Little, Brown, 1951, 1988 (Paul Revere).

Lenski, Lois. *Indian Captive: The Story of Mary Jemison.* Stokes, 1941 (colonial white girl stays with Senecas).

Loverance, Rowena. *Ancient Greece.* New York: Viking, 1993 (and others in the series: Ancient Egypt, the Middle Ages, and the Renaissance).

Lowry, Lois. *Number the Stars.* Boston: Houghton Mifflin, 1989 (Holocaust and World War II in Denmark).

Lyons, Mary. *Letters from a Slave Girl: The Story of Harriet Jacobs.* New York: Scribner's, 1992.

MacLachlan, Patricia. *Sarah, Plain and Tall.* Trumpet, 1985 (pioneer life).

MayaQuest (software). Minneapolis: MECC, 1995.

McClintock, Barbara. *Adele & Simon in America.* New York: Farrar, Straus and Givoux, 2008.

McGaw, Jessie Brewer. *Chief Red Horse Tells about Custer: The Battle of the Little Bighorn.* New York: Elsevier, Nelson, 1981.

Meltzer, Milton. *The American Revolutionaries: A History in Their Own Words 1750–1880.* New York: Crowell, 1988.

Meltzer, Milton. *Rescue: The Story of How Gentiles Saved Jews in the Holocaust.* New York: Harper, 1988.

Miles, Miska. *Annie and the Old One.* Boston: Little Brown, 1971 (Navajo girl and grandmother).

Monjo, F. N. *The Drinking Gourd.* New York: Harper, 1970 (Underground Railroad).

Murphy, Jim. *The long Road to Gettysburg.* New York: Clarion, 1992.

Namioka, Lensey. *The Coming of the Bear.* New York: HarperCollins, 1992 (1600s Japan).

O'Dell, Scott. *Carlota.* Boston: Houghton Mifflin, 1977 (Mexican War).

O'Dell, Scott. *Island of the Blue Dolphins.* Boston: Houghton Mifflin, 1960, 1990 (Native-American girl lives in isolation).

Oregon Trail (software). Minneapolis: MECC, 1985 (and many subsequent updates).

Orlev, Uri. *The Island on Bird Street.* Boston: Houghton Mifflin, 1983 (Warsaw ghetto in WW II).

Platt, Richard and Manuela Cappon. *Through Time: Beijing.* London: Kingfisher, 2008.

Sensel, Joni. *The Humming of Numbers.* New York: Henry Holt and Co., 2008.

Sewall, Marcia. *The Pilgrims of Plimoth.* New York: Atheneum, 1986.

Sheinkin, Steve and Tim Robinson. *King George: What Was His Problem?* New York: Roaring Brook Press, 2008.

Sheinkin, Steve and Tim Robinson. *Two Miserable Presidents.* New York: Roaring Brook Press, 2008.

Sightseers. *Ancient Egypt, A Guide to Egypt in the Time of the Pharaohs.* New York: Kingfisher, 1999.

Sightseers. *Paris, 1789.* New York: Kingfisher, 1999.

Speare, Elizabeth George. *Calico Captive.* Boston: Houghton Mifflin, 1957 (white captives in colonial America).

Speare, Elizabeth. *The Witch of Blackbird Pond.* Boston: Houghton Mifflin, 1961 (Puritan America).

Speare, Elizabeth. *The Sign of the Beaver.* Boston: Houghton Mifflin, 1983 (colonial America with Native American).

Stanley, Jerry. *Children of the Dust Bowl: The True Story of the School at Weedpatch.* New York: Crown, 1992.

Steele, Philip. *Knights and Castles.* London: Kingfisher, 2008.

Steptoe, John. *Mufaro's Beautiful Daughters: An African Folk Tale.* New York: Scholastic, 1987.

Strachan, Bruce. *Ancient Egypt: A First Look at People of the Nile.* New York: Henry Holt and Co., 2008.

Sutcliff, Rosemary. *Blood Feud.* New York: Dutton, 1976 (English boy enslaved by Vikings) and others in the series about ancient Britain.

Talbert, Marc. *The Purple Heart.* New York: HarperCollins, 1992 (Vietnam-era United States).

Taylor, Mildred. *Roll of Thunder, Hear My Cry.* New York: Dial, 1976 and *Let the Circle Be Unbroken.* New York: Dial, 1981 (discrimination in rural Mississippi).

The Jean Fritz History Series (software). Watertown, Mass.: Tom Snyder Productions, 2008.

Timeliner (software timelines). Watertown, Mass.: Tom Snyder Productions, 1996.

Timeliner XE (software). Watertown, Mass.: Tom Snyder Productions, 2008.

Uchida, Yoshiko. *Journey to Topaz.* New York: Scribner's, 1971 (Japanese internment).

Uchida, Yoshiko. *Journey Home.* New York: Atheneum, 1978 (return to California).

Warren, Andrea. *Orphan Train Rider: One Boy's True Story.* Boston: Houghton Mifflin, 1996 (late pioneer life).

Wilder, Laura Ingalls. The *Little House* series. New York: Harper & Row, 1935–1953 (pioneer life).

Wisniewski, David. *Sundiata: Lion King of Mali.* New York: Clarion, 1999.

Yenne, Bill. *100 Events that Shaped World History.* Bluewood, 1993.

History Websites

www.erols.com/mwhite28/20centry.htm (Historical maps)

www.loc.gov (45,000 photos of Depression from Library of Congress)

www.mountvernon.org (Mount Vernon)

www.nytimes.com/learning (*New York Times* for grades 6 through 12)

www.metmuseum.org (Metropolitan Museum of Art)

www.si.edu (Smithsonian Museum)

www.vatican.va (The Vatican)

www.bl.uk (British Museum)

www.americaslibrary.gov/cgi-bin/page.cgi (American History)

www.americanhistory.si.edu (National Museum of American History)

www.fordham.edu/halsall/africa/africasbook.html (African History)

www.si.edu/anacostia (Museum of African American History and Culture)

www.pbs.org/wonders (Wonders of the African world)

www.latino.si.edu (Smithsonian Center for Latino Initiatives)

www.clpgh.org/cmnh/exhibits/north-south-east-west (Native American)

http://americanindiansinchildrensliterature.blogspot.com/ (American Indians in Children's Literature)

http://www.greece.kl2.ny.us/instruction/ELA/6-12/Tools/lndex.htm (Tools for Reading, Writing, Thinking)

http://rims.kl2.ca.us/foot_prints/index.html (Footprints Portal)

www.si.edu/nmai (National Museum of the American Indian)

www.omnibusol.com/medieval.html (Byzantine to French Revolution)

www.hudmark.com/schoolnet/history.html (Links to World History)

www.kamat.com/kalranga/timeline/timeline.htm (history of India)

www.pbs.org/greatwar (World War I)

http://www.npg.si.edu/ (The National Portrait Gallery)

library.thinkquest.org/15511 (Home front in World War II)

http://www.civiced.org/ (Center for Civic Education)

http://www.socialstudies.org/ (National Council for Social Studies) *http://www.nche.net/* (National Council for History Education)

http://teachinghistory.org/ (Center for History and New Media)

http://www.educationworld.com/history/ (Education World, Inc.)

http://www.americaninstituteforhistory.org/ (American Institute for History Education)

http://www.nationalhistoryday.org/ (National History Day, Inc.)

http://www.archives.gov/ (National Archives and Records Administrations)

http://dohistory.org/ (Do History Home)

http://www.history.com/classroom/ (Teaching American History)

http://www.h-net.org/ (H-Net: Humanities and Social Sciences Online)

http://www.ed.gov/programs/teachinghistory/index.html (U.S. Department of Education)

http://www.plimoth.org/ (Plymouth Plantation, Plymouth, MA)

http://www.archives.gov/index.html (National Archives and records Administration)

http://www.archives.gov/education/lessons/ (Teaching with Documents)

http://www.ala.org/ala/rusa/rusaourassoc/rusasections/historysection/histsect/histcomm/instructionres/usingprimarysources.cfm (Using Primary Resources)

CHAPTER 3

Geography

BASIC IDEAS

Geography, which comes from a Greek word for writing about the Earth, is the study of the Earth's surface and of how it is affected by the movements of land, sea, and air and by the interaction, deliberate and inadvertent, of the humans and animals who live on it. Geography is about where things are physically, as well as about the way people and nature affect each other and their environment (as of 2010 there were nearly 7 billion people on the Earth). One might think of these divisions as physical geography and cultural geography (the previous chapter on history addresses much of the latter). Geography vitally affects plant and animal life as well as such aspects of human life as diet, prosperity, accessibility, inventions, religion, clothing, and housing, since these are all shaped by climate, terrain, location, and resources. In pre-historic times, before history, economics, or government played large roles in human life, geography was the most important element in the lives (and deaths) of early humans, and it is still an extremely important influence.

Given its obvious importance, it is remarkable that Americans are relatively uninterested in geography. One suggestion has been advanced that because of the size and importance of our country, we have not had to learn much about the rest of the world; rather, the rest of the world has learned about us. But even within the United States, many people have a weak grasp of states and regions and of the geography that shaped and continues to shape them.

The earliest recorded geographers were the Greeks who mapped the coasts of the Mediterranean Sea. The Romans who followed them were famous roadbuilders who created an enormous empire, consequently becoming excellent mapmakers. North Africans and Arabs took the mapmaking lead during the Middle Ages, and Europeans made maps during the Crusades and the later Age of Exploration, but it was not until the twentieth century, partly a result of the wide-ranging wars and improved technology, including airplanes and advanced cameras, that most of the world, including the very remote parts of Asia, Africa, and Antarctica, were mapped. Some recent technological innovations in geography include the global positioning system **(GPS)**, which can be installed or used portably; that and other such advances allow the individual user to find absolute and relative location to anywhere on the globe. Additionally, the proliferation of geography and mapping websites bring easy geographic knowledge to the public.

Any study of geography should include maps, and every home and classroom should be well-equipped with a globe and with reliable and comprehensive maps. Referring to maps or globes will be very helpful to the reader of this chapter (as with the history chapter) and will make the information contained much more meaningful, less abstract, and more likely to be retained. An atlas will prove invaluable as well, in answering both general and specific questions about fluid information such as population, boundary changes, new countries, and recent events.

WATER AND LAND

It is thought that the Earth with its circumference of almost 25,000 miles and its diameter of about 8,000 miles (both fairly accurately estimated by the ancient Greek scientist Eratosthenes), is over 4.5 billion years old. Over two-thirds of the Earth's surface is water (almost 140 million square miles), most of it interconnected oceans. The major oceans are the Atlantic, which separates North and South America from Europe and Africa; the Pacific, which separates North and South America from Asia; and the Indian, which lies south of Asia. Lesser oceans are the Arctic in the north and the Antarctic (in recent years more often called the South Atlantic) in the south. Additionally, there are many smaller subdivisions of oceans, such as the Mediterranean Sea (part of the Atlantic), the South China Sea (part of the Pacific), and the Arabian Sea (part of the Indian).

Oceans can be the sites of *tsunamis*, series of enormous waves, which are created when an earthquake, volcanic eruption, underwater explosion or other disturbing event causes great amounts of ocean water to move quickly in reaction. On December 26, 2004, a giant earthquake in Indonesia caused tsunamis around the Indian Ocean basin, killing over 230,000 people (mostly in Thailand, Sri Lanka, Indonesia, and India) in one of the world's most devastating natural disasters. As a result there has been a new push for early warning equipment and communications in many Third World Countries.

The term sea also is used for large lakes sometimes, and there are other subdivisions of seas and oceans, such as **bays** and **gulfs** (similar partial enclosures of water by land). Freshwater bodies are usually called **lakes**, but also can be **ponds**, natural or man-made **reservoirs**, **swamps**, and, of course, **rivers**. Some of the world's most important rivers are the Mississippi, which drains the central United States; the Amazon, which drains the northern part of South America and contains more volume of water than any other; the Volga, the Danube, and the Rhine of central Europe; the Congo, which drains west central Africa; the Nile, which drains the northern part of Africa and is the only major river to run north, as well as the world's longest river; the Yellow and the Yangtze, which drain the central part of China; the Indus and the Ganges, which drain the northern parts of India; and the Tigris and Euphrates, which drain Iraq. These African, Indian, Chinese, and Iraqi rivers are also considered the cradles of human civilization, from which the first settlements grew.

Most of the Earth's land area (over 57 million square miles) is made up of the seven continents (although in some Latin American countries the Americas are viewed as one continent): by size they are Asia, Africa, North America, South America, Antarctica, Europe, and Australia. A look at the way the coastline of North and South America complements that of Africa makes clear the origin of **Alfred Wegener's** theory that the Earth's land mass was originally one large continent (**Pangea**) that broke apart through a process known as continental drift. A lava eruption about 200 million years ago that split North and South America, Africa, and Asia shows geologic likenesses on the various continents and probably released gases that were a factor in the extinction of much animal life of the time.

Islands (completely surrounded by water) are smaller than continents and usually considered part of the nearest one, such as Greenland and North America or Madagascar and Africa. Other important land designations are **peninsulas** and **capes** (similar lands mostly surrounded by or jutting into water), such as the Arabian Peninsula, the state of Florida, and Cape Horn (at the bottom of South America).

Water and land sometimes come together to connect or separate two great masses of either, such as **straits** (narrow waterways joining two larger ones, such as the Dardanelles, which join the Black Sea to the east side of the Mediterranean; the Strait of Hormus, which joins the Persian Gulf to the Gulf of Oman; and the Strait of Gibralter, which joins the Atlantic Ocean to the west side of the Mediterranean) or **isthmuses** (narrow strips of land joining two larger ones, such as Panama, which joins North and South America). Sometimes canals are dug in isthmuses to make quicker sea routes, as was done in Panama (the Panama Canal) and in Egypt (the Suez Canal), so both straits and isthmuses become strategic places to seize in time of war.

The part of the Earth that people see is called the **crust**, and it is the top portion of the **lithosphere** (the highest point on Earth is in the Himalayas, **Mount Everest** at just over 29,000 feet, and the lowest is in the **Marianas Trench** below the Pacific Ocean at over 36,000 feet, although the shore of the Dead Sea of Israel at 1,312 feet below sea level is the lowest land point). The bottom portion of the lithosphere contains great pieces of flat rock known as **plates**, which move and shift in response to heat and pressure in the hot core of the Earth below them. The plates' movement is called **plate tectonics**, and the movements can cause **earthquakes** and **volcanoes**, and shape **mountains** and other land forms, particularly noticeable by the Pacific Ocean plate's movement, known as the Ring of Fire. The other major plates are the North American plate, the South American plate, the Indo-Australian plate, the African plate, the Eurasian plate, and the Antarctic plate. In the United States, the most famous plate movement is at the San Andreas Fault in California, caused by the friction of the North American plate and the Pacific Ocean plate.

READING MAPS

A **globe** is a small model of the Earth showing the land and oceans on it, and it is generally proportionally accurate since it is the same overall shape as the Earth. A **map** is simply a flattened out globe or portion of a globe and has consequent advantages and disadvantages: the major disadvantage is that since the Earth is three-dimensionally round while a map is only two dimensional, there is unavoidably some distortion of proportion on a map. Hence, continents or countries may not appear accurately as to size: a common **distortion**, for example, is that on the widely used Mercator projection (a kind of map that shows all lines of longitude parallel and all lines of latitude the same length, even at the North and South Poles): Greenland appears about the size of South America, even though on a globe it is clearly only a small fraction of the same size. There are many projections, or attempts to accurately represent the Earth in two dimensions, and every projection will have some distortion, but as long as the reader knows this and allows for it, the map can still be very useful.

In spite of the distortion problem, maps have many advantages over globes: they are more compact, portable, accessible, and personalized (especially for travelers or students). Because they can focus on one small part of the world, they can give much more detailed information, and the smaller the area the map represents, the more accurate the picture and the less the distortion.

The most common function of maps is to show physical landmarks, both natural and manmade (such as mountains, highways, and political divisions), in relation to one another. However, many maps serve other functions, giving information on human culture (including population, religion, farming, dietary preferences, employment, and economics), natural resources (including plant, animal, and mineral distributions), past history, weather, **elevation** (height from sea level), and/or any other information a mapmaker chooses to include. Because information changes (particularly with new highways being built or with boundary changes as countries gain their independence), it is a good idea to check the date of any map being used.

One of the most important elements of a map is the **scale**, which shows how much real-life distance is symbolized on the map, usually in set bar lengths (one mile, ten mile, or even 500 mile), depending upon the size of the area reflected. It is most often grouped with other information, all of it together known as the "**legend**,"

or "**key**." The legend identifies what the various markings and colors indicate (such as capitals, elevations, kinds of roads, boundary markers, etc.), making it an important part of any map.

Any map is useless without an indication of direction. Most maps are oriented toward the north at the top, with the east on the right, the west on the left, and the south on the bottom, but it is important to be aware that occasionally a map will have a different orientation. The four main points of the compass (N, S, E, W), combined with the intervening main points (NE, SE, SW, NW), form a "**compass rose**," an indicator of direction that is often part of the legend.

For purposes of mapping and conveying information, the Earth is divided into northern and southern halves ("**hemispheres**" from "half globes") horizontally by the **Equator**, which is the imaginary line that encircles the world. Further, it is divided into eastern and western halves (also hemispheres) vertically by the **Prime Meridian**, a line that runs through Greenwich, England (the site of the Royal Observatory, which at the time of the dividing in 1884 had the most advanced geographic equipment). As the Prime Meridian circles the globe through the Pacific Ocean, it is known on the opposite side of the globe as the **International Date line**, since that is where the date, officially begun in Greenwich, officially changes as the 180 degree marker notes the passage of one day and the beginning of the next.

Reference has been made to lines of **latitude and longitude**. Lines of longitude are counted from the Prime Meridian, starting at zero, and are "long," ie., vertical, while lines of latitude are counted from the Equator, starting at zero, and are horizontal. The distance between each line of latitude is constant, but longitude lines come closer together the further they get from the equator, to meet at the **Poles**. Additionally, because the Earth is round and mathematicians have agreed upon 360 degrees in a circle, from the **Equator** to one of the Poles is 90 degrees (from Pole to Pole is 180 degrees), and from the Prime Meridian to the International Date Line is 180 degrees (with a little variation to allow for the zigzags).

Therefore, latitude can be either north or south, but it cannot be above 90 degrees. Halfway between the Equator and either Pole, then, is 45 degrees (either north or south). Similarly, longitude can be any number up to 180 degrees, either east or west, but above 180 degrees it moves into the opposite vertical hemisphere.

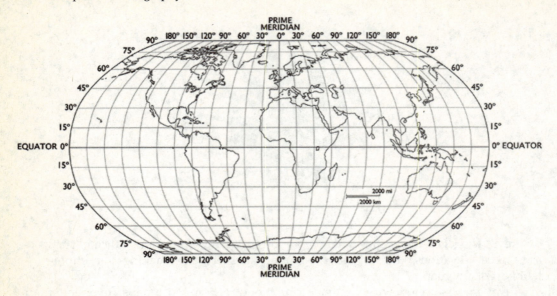

Combining any two measurements, such as 30 degrees north and 90 degrees west, would indicate a specific place on the Earth (in this case, the city of New Orleans).

But most places on Earth are not at exact coordinates, since each line of latitude, or **degree**, is about 69 miles, as are the lines of longitude at the Equator. The degrees, then, are further divided into **minutes** and **seconds** (distance, not time), such that every spot on Earth can be accurately described. A minute equals a little over one mile in length, and a second equals about 100 feet in length. This exactitude is especially important for ships at sea or planes flying in clouds, because of the dearth of landmarks.

In ancient times, many different cultures navigated using astronomy, but such navigation was not as accurate as with latitude and longitude because as the navigator's position on the Earth changed in relation to the sky (particularly between large areas such as between the islands of the South Pacific), it became more difficult to judge the proper placement of the stars and planets. Hence, as exploration grew, the need for accurate navigation grew.

THE PHYSICAL MOVEMENT OF THE EARTH AND ITS EFFECTS

The Earth, as the ancient Greek mathematician and scientist Aristarchus suspected, and the Renaissance Europeans Copernicus and Galileo confirmed, orbits around the sun. It takes a year for the Earth to make a complete orbit (moving through space at almost 67,000 miles per hour), but it also spins once every twenty-four hours on its axis, the measurement of a day (it has to spin at over 1,000 miles an hour to complete one turn in a day). During that spin, or rotation, the portion facing the sun has daylight and then darkness as that portion rotates away from the sun.

The lines of longitude on a map line up with the twenty-four hours in a day: it takes about one hour for the sun to move 15 degrees of longitude, and time on Earth is set by the Greenwich Prime Meridian (see above). There are twenty-four different time zones on the Earth, and as the sun passes directly overhead, it is noon in each one of them in succession (some of the time zones zigzag away from strict lines of longitude to accommodate putting various land areas such as states or small countries in the same time zone).

As the Earth circles the sun, it is at a permanent **tilt** of 23.5 degrees (which is why globes are usually made on a tilt). If the Earth were not tilted, every place in it would have unchanging seasons, since they would be the same distance from the sun at any given time. Because of the tilt, as the Earth circles the sun, either the Northern or the Southern Hemisphere gets more warmth and light because it is closer (moving a tilted globe around a lightbulb will show this concept clearly). When the Northern Hemisphere is closer, it is summer there and winter in the Southern Hemisphere, and when the Southern Hemisphere is closer to the sun, it is winter in the north.

The effects of the tilt and the orbit are exaggerated or lessened, depending on the location of a particular spot on Earth. For example, the regions around the Equator generally have warm weather all year because even with the tilt, they are always close to the sun. About March 23 and September 22 each year, known as the start of Spring and Fall, or the **equinoxes**, the sun, shines directly overhead on the equator. Its northernmost direct point (the **solstice**, June 22) is when it reaches the **Tropic of Cancer** (23.5 degrees north latitude) and its southernmost (the solstice December 22) is when it reaches the **Tropic of Capricorn** (23.5 degrees south latitude).

Conversely, the North and South Poles are usually cold because, being farthest from the Equator, they never get the full warmth of the sun. Beyond 66.5 degrees north or south latitude are the Polar regions, known as the **Arctic Circle** in the north and the **Antarctic Circle** in the south, where there is permanent frost (permafrost) although the tilt in the Earth dramatically lengthens and shortens the amount of daylight in summer and winter, respectively. The **temperate zones** lie between the Tropic and the Pole of either hemisphere and show the most seasonal change.

Seasons and climate can also be affected by other geographic factors, such as distance from large bodies of water (these tend to moderate climate), elevation (the higher the point, the colder, even though it is closer to the sun, because thinner air tends to lose warmth), and weather patterns (such as El Niño or La Niña, which can bring winds and rain or drought).

In October 2005, Hurricane Katrina hit the Gulf Coast portions of Mississippi and Louisiana, doing extensive damage. New Orleans sustained additional damage from flooding, and thousands of people fled, some out of area and some to the Superdome, while more thousands were stranded. Neighborhoods were destroyed and largely abandoned, and the local, state, and federal governments were all very slow to respond to the people's need for water, food, and shelter. Because New Orleans was so devastated and so many homes were destroyed, many people left and the population dropped by approximately half. The rebuilding process has been slow and is not yet completed.

In recent years, there has been an increased awareness about the warming of the Earth, referred to as **Global Warming**. Although the Earth's climate has changed through the ages naturally, most reputable scientists feel that increased consumption of fossil fuel, with the ensuing increased amount of carbon dioxide in the atmosphere, is hastening change. In 2007, former Vice President Al Gore shared the Nobel Peace Prize with the Intergovernmental Panel on Climate Change for sounding the alarm on this very important issue.

CONTINENTS

Asia

Asia is the largest continent, and in modern times it is sometimes referred to as Eurasia, since it is actually joined to Europe. Traditionally, the Ural Mountains in Russia have been the divider of Europe from Asia (Russia is usually studied with Europe, as it will be here, although more than 40 percent of its population is Asian), and at the Mediterranean Sea in the south, Asia, Europe, and Africa come together. In addition to the main land mass, Asia includes the subcontinent of India, the Indonesian and Japanese **archipelagos** (chains of islands), and many isolated islands in the South Pacific Ocean. Asia contains the largest country in the world (Russia, after the breakup of the Soviet Union) and the two countries with the largest populations (China, at almost 1.5 billion and India at approximately 1 billion).

Asia ranges from the Arctic Circle in the north to islands south of the Equator, with most of the continent lying in the more temperate zone of the Northern Hemisphere. It is bounded on the east by the Pacific Ocean and on the south by the Indian Ocean. Asia has many major rivers, including the Ganges River of India,

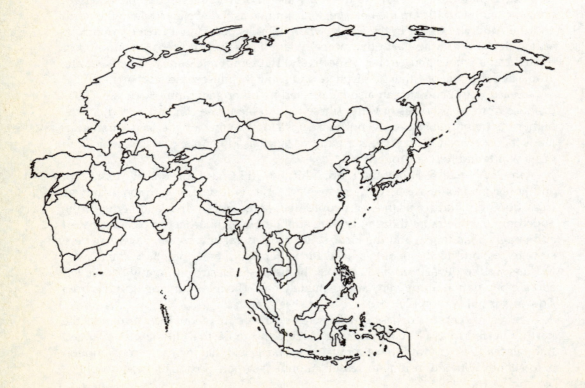

the Yellow and Yangtze Rivers of China, the Indus River of Pakistan and China, and the Mekong River of southeast Asia. It also has three international inland seas: the Aral, the Caspian, and the Black, all of which are on the western side of the continent. The highest mountains in the world are the Himalayas (including Mount Everest) along the border of northern India, Tibet, and China, and China's Gobi Desert is one of the largest in the world, as is the great desert of the Arabian Peninsula. By contrast, southeast Asia has some of the densest jungle and wettest rainforests in the world. In between lie a variety of land types and climates that have shaped a wide range of people and animals.

Because of the size of Asia, there is also an extremely wide range of culture and language, with concomitant clashes over land and over cultural hegemony. There are over 1,200 different language groups in India alone, and vast differences between Asian culture from different peoples in the same area to similar people in different areas (certain religions, for example, are found in most Asian countries, and many Asian countries contain a variety of ethnic groups). The major countries of Asia are China, Japan, Korea (North and South), India, Sri Lanka (Ceylon), Pakistan, Bangladesh, Indonesia, Malaysia, Singapore, Myanmar (Burma), Laos, Vietnam, Cambodia (Kampuchea), Thailand, the Philippines, Taiwan, Mongolia, Nepal, and Bhutan. The Middle East is also part of Asia, and includes Afghanistan, Iran (Persia), Iraq, Turkey (a tiny portion of which crosses the Mediterranean into Europe), Syria, and Lebanon, as well as the countries of the Arabian Peninsula: Israel, Jordan, Saudi Arabia, Kuwait, Qatar, the United Arab Emirates, Oman, and Yemen. Additionally, when the Soviet Union broke apart, most of its republics gained their independence, forming several new countries in both Europe and Asia, including Kazakhstan, Uzbekistan, Turkmenistan, Tajikistan, Kyrgyzstan, Azerbeijan, Armenia, and Georgia.

Many of the world's religions arose in Asia, beginning with the monotheistic religions of Judaism, then Christianity, and finally, Islam (Muslim). Traditionally, much of the Middle East has been Muslims, with smaller populations of Jews (now concentrated mostly in Israel), and Christians (including many Orthodox Christians, converted from Constantinople rather than, from Rome). Most of the rest of Asia has not traditionally been monotheistic with Buddhism, Hinduism, and Taoism making up the majority. China, North Korea, and Vietnam, as communist countries, are officially nonreligious. Islam (and Christianity to a lesser extent) has also spread throughout the rest of Asia, and some countries, like India, are a mix of religions. Religion has been a major political issue for some Asian countries such as Pakistan, India, Indonesia, and the Philippines, as well as for the Middle East.

There has traditionally been much cultural diffusion in Asia, such as Japan's early adoption of China's writing system, or the widespread practice of the Indian religions of Hinduism and Buddhism. The early Chinese invented pasta, gunpowder, paper, silk, porcelain, merit-based civil service, printing, and superior strains of rice. Many Asian foods, particularly in China and India, are made with small, chopped morsels that cook quickly and thus save fuel, which is important where the press of population uses up the forests. Asia also has tremendous natural resources, including many in isolated parts of Mongolia and in Siberia in Russia. While much of Asia is still poor and agricultural, many countries such as China, Japan, Korea, and India have become major industrial powers and hence world political forces.

Africa

Africa is the second-largest continent and stretches from the Mediterranean in the north to South Africa far below the Tropic of Capricorn. It is bounded on the east by the Indian Ocean and on the west by the Atlantic Ocean. Because it lies directly south of Europe and just west of the Arabian Peninsula, it has traditionally influenced and been influenced by both areas. North Africa, in particular, has been part of the whole Mediterranean civilization since ancient times, with some of the great Hellenistic thinkers in Alexandria, Egypt and some of Rome's greatest allies and adversaries in Carthage (currently Tunisia). North Africa has often been studied as part of the Middle East because when Arabs swept across the area spreading Islam in the 700s A.D., they brought not only their religion but the Arab language and culture as well, so North Africa has much in common with the Arab countries of the Middle East. In recent years, however, scholars have recognized that North Africa should be studied as part of Africa, since it has long been part of other African cultures as well.

Most of Africa lies north of the Equator, with a substantial portion lying south. Much of the northern portion of Africa is on the same approximate latitude as the southern United States, the central portion of Africa lies on either side of the Equator, and the southern portion of Africa is roughly on the same latitude as Brazil; so, although much of Africa is tropical, it also has parts with a temperate climate. Snow

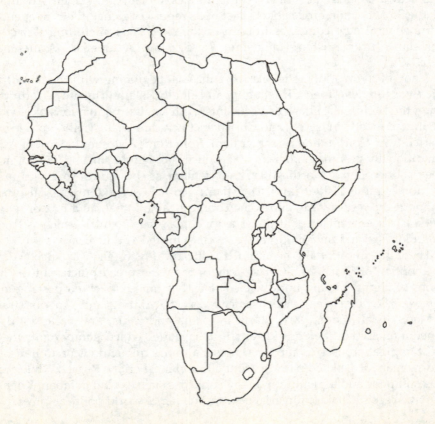

skiing, for example, is popular in mountainous parts of South Africa. Besides temperature and elevation, rainfall affects climate, and much of Africa is unique as **desert**: the Sahara Desert makes up much of North Africa and the Kalahari Desert is important in South Africa. By contrast, central Africa has some of the densest jungle and wide open **savannahs** (prairies) in the world.

Elsewhere on the continent, as in Asia, lie a variety of land types and climates that have shaped a wide range of people and animals. Africa has many unusual animals that have fascinated explorers and visitors over the centuries, including giraffes, lions, hippopotami, rhinoceroses, zebras, and lemurs.

Because of the size of Africa, there is an extremely wide range of culture and language, with the usual resulting clashes over land and authority. As in India, there are hundreds of different languages and vast differences among African culture. The ethnic rivalries in Africa have been exacerbated by the land divisions made by the former colonial powers of Europe in the nineteenth and twentieth centuries, by which similar cultural groups often were separated inadvertently into different countries, and which did not take into account seasonal movements of various nomadic tribes or groups. There are over fifty countries in Africa and some of the most prominent are: Ethiopia, Somalia, Sudan, Egypt, Libya, Algeria, Morocco, Mauritania, Mali, Niger, Nigeria, Chad, Congo (formerly Zaire), Uganda, Kenya, Tanzania, Mozambique, Zimbabwe, Zambia, Angola, Namibia, Botswana, and South Africa. Many African countries changed their names from European ones to African ones when they gained their independence in the half-century following World War II. Rwanda and Burundi, two small countries near Tanzania and Uganda, have been much in the news in recent years because of an ongoing civil war. The large island country of Madagascar (off the southeast coast) is also considered part of Africa.

Africa contains followers of all of the world's great religions, particularly Islam and Christianity: traditionally, the Muslim Middle East influenced East Africa, and European Christian missionaries influenced the rest of the continent south of the Sahara. Additionally, much of the population follows animist religions based on different local traditions. Many countries are a mix of religions, and religion has been a major political issue for some African countries such as Rwanda and Burundi. Race has often played a significant role in African politics, from slavery to the right to vote and/or hold property, and, often because of clashes over race (as well as over other religious or ethnic issues), many African countries have had a difficult time in the twentieth century making the transition to stable independence from the colonial powers who took over most of Africa in the nineteenth century. A civil war in Sudan since the 1990s has raised the specter of slavery again, as captives are bartered and sold. Between drought civil war, and the specter of genocide, the Darfur region, in particular, has suffered humanitarian crises since the 1980s.

South Africa, the last country to do away with apartheid (legal separation of the races), has become the major industrial power, and Africa has a number of big cities. Much of the continent is still agricultural and poor, and health care has become an increasing issue because of diseases, including AIDS, tuberculosis, and malaria. However, most countries have industries such as lumbering, mining, and manufacturing, and the continent has tremendous natural resources.

North America

North America is the third largest continent and ranges from the Arctic northern parts of Canada and Alaska to the tropical zones of Mexico and Central America. It is bounded on the east by the Atlantic Ocean, on the west by the Pacific Ocean, on the north by the Arctic Ocean, and on the south by the Caribbean Sea, the Gulf of Mexico, and South America. From north to south, it consists of Canada, the United States, Mexico, and the countries of Central America: Belize, Guatemala, Honduras, El Salvador, Nicaragua, Costa Rica, and Panama. Mexico and Central America are often studied with South America because they are culturally similar: together they are called **Latin America**, based on the largely Spanish and Portuguese (whose languages originated from Latin) settlement there after the coming of the Europeans.

Although there were thriving Native American groups living in North America at the time of the coming of the Europeans, they are in the distinct minority today (with varying rights of autonomy), and the United States and Canada share a common heritage of British settlement and language. Canada also has a significant minority of French background, and French influence in certain areas is very strong (there is a powerful independence movement in Quebec, a province whose population is 80 percent French in origin). There is also a large Hispanic influence and population in the United States, and there are substantial numbers of citizens of African (about 12–15 percent of the U.S. population), European, and Asian descent

(with large numbers of the latter particularly on the west coast). Both countries are home to many immigrants, so have a strong multicultural makeup. The cultures of Central and South America are largely Spanish and Indian based, although there are immigrants of other back-ground, with Spanish the main language, even for the many citizens of Native American descent.

Freedom of religion is widespread in North America, and the main religion is Christianity. Most people of Canada (heavily Catholic in French Quebec) and the United States (which also has a large Catholic population) practice various forms of Protestantism. Catholicism is the largest religion in Mexico and Central America, with significant other religious minorities all over the continent, including Jews and Muslims.

Canada is the second largest country in the world in land size, but has a population of about only 30 million: much of the country is classified subarctic or arctic and is very sparsely settled, although the coastal portions and southern border are temperate, and the British Columbia/Washington State area contains one of the great temperate rainforests of the world. Canada is made up of ten provinces (each headed by an elected premier), led by an appointed governor-general, who is advised by an elected prime minister and cabinet. The capital of Canada is Ottawa, although its largest cities are Toronto, Montreal, and Vancouver.

Canada and the United States share the longest unmilitarized border in the world. Both are stable democracies and are each other's major trading partner. They have been allies in both world wars, although there has been some diplomatic friction over the American Revolution, slavery, Vietnam, Cuba, pollution, and fishing rights. Canada, an industrial and agricultural country, has one of the highest standards of living in the world. Like most western European countries, Canada provides many social services for its citizens, including national health insurance, although it suffered economic stagnation in the 1990s, while the U.S. economy boomed.

The United States, the fourth-largest country in the world in land size, is made up of fifty states and over 300 million people. Each state is headed by an elected governor, and the country is led by an elected president. The capital of the United States is Washington, D.C. (District of Columbia), established on land given to the federal government by Virginia and Maryland. The largest cities, however, are New York, Los Angeles, and Chicago, and there are many others larger than Washington, D.C.

With its varied temperate climates and great prairies, forests, mountains, and waterways, the United States has enormous natural resources and is a major agricultural and industrial producer. The Appalachians are the great mountain range of eastern North America, as the Rockies are of western North America, and both of them include many other mountain range designations, such as the White, the Green, the Great Smokies, and the Catskills in the east and the Sierra Madre, the Cascades, Sierra Nevada, and the Grand Tetons in the west. The north central part of the United States contains the Great Lakes (Superior, Michigan, Huron, Ontario, and Erie), and some important rivers in the United States are the Mississippi, the Ohio, the Missouri, the Colorado (which carved the Grand Canyon), and the Rio Grande between the United States and Mexico. The highest mountain in the United States is Mount McKinley in Alaska. Alaska (separated from the rest of the continental United States by part of Canada) and the island chain of Hawaii are the only two states that are not contiguous to (joined to) the rest of the states.

U.S. influence has been strong around the world, especially in the areas of popular culture (particularly movies and television), science, inventions, consumer goods, and individual freedom. The United States reveres the concept of individual effort and opportunity, and provides fewer social services to its citizens than do other countries with comparable standards of living, a point of some contention among advocates for the poor. However, the populace in general has a very high standard of living, and the country is a magnet for immigrants hoping to share in the freedom and prosperity.

Mexico is a large and varied country made up of thirty-one states containing about 100 million people. It is a democracy in transition with an elected president and Congres, and its capital is Mexico City, the largest city in the world. Mexico is quite dry, with no major rivers, which has made it difficult for the populace to successfully farm and has contributed to the lower standard of living than in the more northern parts of the continent.

Mexico, Canada, and the United States formed **NAFTA** (the North American Free Trade Agreement) in the 1990s, which has made trade between them more open and less subject to tariffs, but has been somewhat controversial because of economic inequities caused by Mexico's lower standard of living and wage scale. There are substantial numbers of Mexican Americans living in the southwestern United States, which the United States took from Mexico in the 1840s. The residents have much cultural influence and contribute to substantial trade across the border. For these reasons and because of the higher standard of living in the United States, there are also ongoing issues of both legal and illegal immigration from Mexico.

Central America is much wetter and more humid than most of Mexico and produces rich harvests of coffee, bananas, and other crops. Political instability, however, has plagued many Central American countries, with the notable exception of Costa Rica, a stable democracy with a high literacy rate. Throughout the 1980s, El Salvador, Nicaragua, Honduras, and Guatemala were all involved in civil war. The Panama Canal is located in Panama, near where it joins South America, and was controlled by the United States throughout most of the twentieth century, although the United States agreed in 1979 that the canal would revert to Panama in 2000 and the canal subsequently was handed over.

North America is also generally considered to include the island of Greenland (owned by Denmark) and many islands of the Caribbean. The Caribbean islands are rich in ethnic flavor as a result of early settlement by various European countries, and by Africans, many of whom were brought as slaves, in addition to later arrivals of Asians. Because of the warm climate and beautiful scenery, tourism is big business throughout the Caribbean, even in Cuba, a communist country boycotted by the United States, but with the exception of Haiti, a poor country whose political instability has had severe economic consequences. The island chains of the Bahamas, the Greater Antilles (including Cuba, Jamaica, Santo Domingo [shared by Haiti and the Dominican Republic], and Puerto Rico), and the Lesser Antilles (including the Virgin Islands, Anguilla, St. Kitts and Nevis, Monserrat, Antigua, and Barbuda, Domenica, Guadeloupe, Martinique, St. Lucia, St. Vincent, and the Grenadines, Barbados, and Granada) link North America and South America.

South America

South America is the middle of the seven continents in size and ranges from well north of the Equator (Venezuela and Colombia) almost to the Antarctic Circle (the southern tips of Chile and Argentina). It lies directly south of North America and is bounded on the east by the Atlantic Ocean and on the west by the Pacific Ocean. It includes the islands of Aruba, the Netherlands Antilles, and Trinidad and Tobago on the northeast coast, and the Malvinas/Falkland Islands (owned by Great Britain) on the extreme southeast coast. The spine of South America is the Andes Mountain range, which runs up the west side of the continent, so most of the land area drains to the east, forming the river with the largest volume of water in the world, the Amazon of Brazil.

The **Amazon rainforest** is one of the natural wonders of the world and provides much of the needed oxygen for life on Earth, so it is natural that its clearing for agriculture concerns many people. Additionally, it has thousands of species of plants (including rare ones used in medical research) and animals. Another famous natural area is the **Galapagos Islands** (off the Pacific coast of Ecuador), where Charles Darwin's observations of tortoise and bird life led to his theory of evolving species.

Because the mountains are so high, their altitude affects climate in many instances: the city of Quito, Ecuador is on the Equator but cold most of the year, as are many parts of Peru, Bolivia, Chile, and Argentina. Their climate is in contrast to the many low-lying coastal areas known for their steamy tropical heat. Because much of South America lies south of the Equator, the seasons, like those in Australia and in the southern part of Africa, are the opposite to those in North America and Europe.

There were thriving Native American cultures, most notably the Inca when Europeans arrived in South America, and there are still many indigenous people throughout the continent. Although much of South America was settled by Spain (with Spanish becoming the most common language), the largest country, Brazil, went to Portugal as a result of the **Treaty of Tordesillas** (1494) in which the Pope divided up newly discovered regions (so the language of Brazil is Portuguese). The Netherlands (Dutch Guiana, now Suriname), Great Britain (British Guiana, now Guyana), and France (French Guiana, still an overseas department of France) also got small portions, including the Falkland Islands, a wool-producing area still owned by the British, near the tip of South America. Other countries in South America are Argentina, Bolivia, Chile, Colombia, Ecuador, Paraguay, Peru, Uruguay, and Venezuela.

The people of South America are a mix of American Indian; those descended from Spanish and other European settlers (particularly in Argentina and Uruguay, where many Italians and Germans settled); and African, most originally brought as slaves. **Mestizo** refers to those of mixed European and Native American ancestry. South America and the Caribbean islands received the vast majority of slaves brought to the New World, and in 1888, Brazil was the last country in the Western Hemisphere to do away with slavery. Catholicism is the major religion, although evangelical Protestantism is growing stronger. The continent has many natural resources, and some parts of South America are sophisticated and industrialized, but much of the populace tends to be poor and to work in some form of agriculture.

Argentina is a major producer of beef and is very industrialized, as is Venezuela, which also is an important oil supplier. Brazil and Colombia are famous for growing coffee, while Chile is known for mining and industry. Peru, a difficult land to travel across because of the high mountains, has a major tourism site at Machu Picchu, the famous Inca ruins. Because the gap between rich and poor is great, the illegal drug trade, which can be very profitable, has flourished, causing major political and social problems in some countries such as Colombia and Bolivia. Most of the countries of South America are democracies, although traditionally many have been politically unstable and governments often turn over due to scandal or power struggles.

Antarctica

There is an old joke that asks "What continent's people have the highest I.Q.?" and the answer is "Antarctica—no one lives there but research scientists!" Antarctica (opposite of the Arctic, which is frozen water and so not a continent) is one of the world's last great frontiers, shared and administered by many nations doing research there. It is the third-smallest continent, and it has been studied and mapped

by various kinds of scientists eager to learn about the land, the ice, and the living creatures there, including much about the geologic makeup of the Earth and of past ice ages through core samples of earth and ice. Antarctica has no permanent human inhabitants, but has much animal life on both the continent and in the water around it, including seals, walruses, whales, and penguins, in spite of its harsh climate. Winter temperatures go below −120 degrees Fahrenheit in Antarctica, since it and the opposing Arctic region are the farthest distances from the Equator (and so from the direct rays of the sun) as it is possible to be on the Earth.

The winter was particularly harsh on the group of explorers with Captain Robert Scott of Great Britain, who reached the South Pole in 1912, only to find that the Norwegian explorer Roald Amundsen had arrived a month earlier. On the way back to their base, Scott and his men all died, but their diaries survived to tell their story.

Because Antarctica is a circle located at the "bottom" (although there is really no top or bottom in space) of the Earth, it faces the continents of Australia, Africa, and South America, as well as the country of New Zealand, and the South Atlantic, South Pacific, and Indian oceans: the water around Antarctica is sometimes known as the Southern Ocean. Antarctica is larger than either Australia or Europe, and is almost entirely covered by ice, which is over two miles thick in some places, and which constantly breaks off into the surrounding sea. Antarctica remains relatively unpolluted, although the air and oceans around it are affected by pollution elsewhere, and increased tourism there is bringing pollution problems. Because of its location and isolation, Antarctica is a prime site for monitoring ozone holes and global warming.

Europe

Europe is the second smallest continent (after Australia). It is bounded on the east by the Ural Mountains of Asia and by the Black Sea, on the south by the Mediterranean Sea, on the west by the Atlantic Ocean, and on the north by the North Sea and Arctic Ocean. Many of the countries of Europe (where the Industrial Revolution began) are heavily industrialized and have some of the highest standards of living in the world, including more social services than are provided in the United States.

Europe's climate is varied, since the continent ranges from the Scandinavian countries and Russia within the Arctic Circle to the palm-lined shores of the Mediterranean Sea. It also has many valleys and mountain ranges, so elevation affects the climate in many places. Additionally, the British Isles and the Atlantic coast of Europe are surprisingly moderate in climate in spite of their latitude because of the warming effects of the **Gulf Stream**, which crosses the Atlantic and runs north

along the European coast. Some of the major mountains of Europe are the Alps of central Europe, the Urals of eastern Europe, the Pyrenees between France and Spain, and the Appennines of Italy. Europe has many important rivers, including the Danube, the Volga, the Rhine, the Seine, and the Tiber.

Europe has varied cultural and national groups, speaking a polyglot of languages. Switzerland has four official languages and even such a small country as Belgium has cultural disagreements between the speakers of French and Walloon (Flemish). French has traditionally been the second language for many Europeans, particularly of the middle and upper class, but English is replacing it as a necessary language. Most of Europe is Christian, divided between a Catholic majority in the southern portions and a variety of Protestant sects in the north, although there is much intermingling. There is a small but significant Jewish population, even after the genocidal effects of the Holocaust, and there are increasing numbers of Muslims, many coming from Algiers (to France) and Turkey (to Germany).

England was the home of the **Industrial Revolution** in the 1700s and 1800s, and the technological and scientific advances throughout most of Europe in those periods and in the twentieth century led to European ascendancy in the 1800s and consequent colonizing and empire-building, such that Europe had a tremendous influence on the rest of the world, disproportionate with its size. In the twentieth century, it continued to become heavily industrialized, leading to its generally high standard of living, but it was also a central site of World War I and World War II, two debilitating wars that together killed almost 70 million people and left many people, particularly in Germany and Austria, questioning their cultural heritage. Europe since has been a leader in promoting human rights and providing charitable relief in less fortunate parts of the world.

The worldwide, century-long trend toward nationalism affected Europe as much or more than other parts of the world, as colonies gained their freedom and European empires disappeared in the twentieth century. Even within Europe, many new countries appeared after World War I, when the Austro-Hungarian, Russian, and Ottoman Empires fell apart, and again after the fall of communism, when many of Russia's former republics gained their independence and countries such as Czechoslovakia and Yugoslavia each broke apart into separate nations.

In an opposite movement, East and West Germany became one, and most western European nations came together to form the European Union (there is additional information on these phenomena in Chapter 2).

Most Western European countries are representative democracies, some with a strong socialist flavor. Eastern Europe was mostly under the dominance of the Soviet Union for much of the twentieth century, particularly after World War II, and some of those countries have had a difficult transition to democracy (and some have not made the transition) since the breakup of the Soviet Union. Russia, in particular, has suffered enormous economic problems, which have affected its political stability, in the change to a free market economy. The rest of Eastern Europe in general is poorer, less educated, and less industrialized, with much more subsistence forming and far less world influence, than Western Europe, but after many years "behind the **Iron Curtain**" (isolated by the Soviet Union) many countries there are changing their economic and political systems to more closely reflect those of the rest of Europe, hoping to share in the general prosperity and freedom.

Australia

Australia is the smallest continent and is also a country. Reference to it often includes New Guinea and the Solomon Islands to the north (site of much fighting during World War II), the double islands of New Zealand to the southeast, the island of Tasmania just off the south coast, and an array of microscopic islands and island chains to the north and east, including Micronesia, Melanesia, Polynesia, and others, all under the umbrella name of Oceania. Australia is bounded on the east by the Pacific Ocean, on the south and west by the Indian Ocean, and on the north by Indonesia. Australia is largely flat and largely dry (most of western Australia is desert), unsuited for many types of agriculture since only 6 percent of the land is arable (able to grow crops), although it does have valuable minerals and a major sheep-farming industry. Because it is so isolated, it is unique in its animal life, with species found nowhere else, including kangaroos, wallabies, koala bears, flying possums, platy-puses, and wombats. Most of the human population lives near the ocean in wetter, more fertile areas than the great dry interior known as the outback.

The original settlers of Australia, Aborigines, are far outnumbered today by those of British descent: Britain in the 1700s began using Australia as a penal colony, a use that continued until 1839. Australia, made up of six states, became an independent country in 1901, although it remains part of the British Commonwealth. In late 1999, voters decided by referendum, perhaps surprisingly, not to replace the Britain-appointed governor with an Australian president, breaking all official ties with Great Britain. The population today is largely white and of British descent, although the Aborigines (who invented the boomerang) have gained ground in recent years in obtaining tribal lands with some autonomous government. Oddly, although the largest cities are Sydney (with its famous Opera House) on the southern east coast and Melbourne on the eastern south coast, the capital of the country is Canberra in the southeast interior between them.

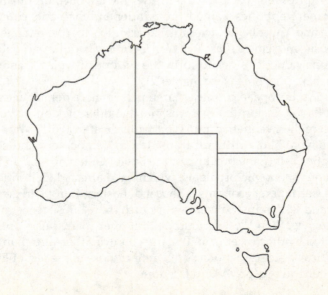

Geography Resources

Getting Started Educationally

Andrews, J. L. "Putting America on the Map: The Voyage of Columbus." *Learning.* 88, 17, 1988: 64–65.

Atkins, Cammie. "Introducing Map and Globe Skills to Young Children." *Journal of Geography.* March 1984: 228–233.

David, D. W. "Big Maps—Little People." *Journal of Geography.* March/April 1990: 58–62.

Forsyth, A. S. "How We Learn Place Location: Bringing Theory and Practice Together." *The Social Studies.* November/December 1988: 500–503.

Geography for Life: National Geography Standards. Washington, D.C.: Geography Education Standards Project, 1994.

Hatcher, Barbara. "Putting Young Cartographers 'on the Map.'" *Childhood Education.* May/June 1983: 311–315.

Hertzberg. Lanny. "World Exploration." *Electronic Learning.* November/December 1990: 42–43.

Kirman, Joseph M. "Radarsat Satellite Images: A New Geography Tool for Upper Elementary Classrooms." *Social Education.* April 1999: 167–169 (includes a site for images: www. radarsatinaction.com).

Melahn, D. "Putting Itin Perspective: Geography Activities for Primary Children." *Journal of Geography.* July/August 1989: 137–139.

National Geographic Society, 1145 Seventeenth Street, N.W., Washington, D.C. (800–638–4077).

Pattison, W. D. "Territory, Learner, and Map." *The Elementary School Journal.* 67, 1966: 146–153.

Rand McNally Notebook World Atlas. No bibliographic information contained (widely available inexpensive, clear, up-to-date map booklet).

Reissman, Rose. "Exploring Geography with Newspaper Maps." *Learning.* October/November 1994: 65.

Rice, Gwenda, H. "Teaching Students to Become Discriminating Map Users." *Social Education.* October 1990: 393–397.

Van Cleaf, D. W. Strengthening Map Skills through Orienteering. *Social Education.* 45, 1981: 462–463.

Geography Content for Teachers

Barnes, Ian et al. *The History Atlas of Asia.* New York: Macmillan, 1998.

Brock, Jan O. M. *The Study and Teaching of Geography.* Columbus, Ohio: Merrill, 1980.

Castro. F. A. *A Quick Way to Learn Geography: The World.* New York: Merriam Webster, 1991.

Davis, Kenneth C. *Don't Know Much about Geography.* New York: Avon, 1995.

De Blij. H. J. and Peter O. Muller. *Geography: Regions and Concepts.* 6th ed. New York: John Wiley & Sons.

Harper, Robert A. and Theodore H. Schmudde. *Between Two Worlds: A New Introduction to Geography.* 2nd ed. Boston: Houghton Mifflin, 1978.

Kasule, Samuel. *The History Atlas of Africa.* New York: Macmillan, 1998.

McEvedy, Colin. *The Penguin Historical Atlas of the Pacific.* New York: Penguin, 1998.

Oxford Atlas of the World. 3rd ed. New York: Oxford University Press. 1995.

Time Almanac 1999: The Ultimate Worldwide Fact and Information Source. Boston: Information Please, 1999.

Content for Students

Adams, Simon. *The Kingfisher Atlas of Exploration and Empires.* London: Kingfisher, 2007.

Adams, Simon. *The Kingfisher Atlas of the Modern World.* London: Kingfisher, 2007.

Africa Trail (software). Minneapolis: MECC, 1995.

Allen, Thomas. *Where Children Live.* Englewood Cliffs, N.J.: Prentice Hall, 1980.

Amazon Trail (software). Minneapolis: MECC, 1996.

Balsley, Irol W. *Where on Earth?* Good Apple, 1986.

Buettner, Dan. *Soviet Trek: A Journey by Bicycle Across Russia*. Minneapolis: Lerner, 1994.

Burnie, David and Juniper, Tony. *Endangered Planet*. London: Kingfisher, 2007.

Burnie, David and Lewis, Anthony. *The Kingfisher First Dinosaur Picture Atlas*. London: Kingfisher, 2008.

Chancellor, Deborah. *Maps and Mapping*. London: Kingfisher, 2007.

Chiasson, John. *African Journey*. New York: Bardbury, 1987.

Crosby, Nina E. and Elizabeth H. Marten. *Know Your State*. DOK Publications, 1984.

Cross Country USA (truck travel software). Didatech Software.

Destination: Rain Forest. Edmark, 1995.

Ehrlich, Amy and Minor, Wendell. *Rachel: The Story of Rachel Carson*. New York: Voyager Books, Harcourt Inc., 2008.

Frank, John and Sylvada, Peter. *How to Catch a Fish*. New York: Roaring Brook Press, 2007.

Geosafari (electronic globe that asks geography questions).

Harrison, Ted. *O Canada*. Ticknor & Fields, 1993.

Hynes, Margaret. *Polar Lands*. London: Kingfisher, 2007.

Inspirer Geography Series (software). Watertown, Mass.: Tom Snyder Productions, 2008.

Irizarry, Carmen. *Passport to Mexico*. New York: Watts, 1987 (and other countries in the series).

Kandoian, Ellen. *Under the Sun*. New York: Dodd, Mead, 1987.

Kingfisher Young People's Atlas of the World. New York: Kingfisher, 1997.

Knowlton, Jack. *Maps and Globes*. New York: Crowell, 1985.

Lewin, Ted. *The Reindeer People*. New York: Macmillian, 1994.

Mapmaker's Toolkit (software). Watertown, Mass.: Tom Snyder Productions, 2008.

Mapping the World by Heart (software). Watertown, Mass.: Tom Snyder Productions, 2008.

My First Amazing World Explorer: CD Rom Activity Pack. Multimedia, 1996.

National Geographic World Atlas for Young Explorers. Washington, D.C.: National Geographic Society, 1998.

National Inspirer: U.S. Geography Scavenger Hunt (software). Watertown, Mass.: Tom Snyder Productions, 1997.

Neighborhood MapMachine 2.0 (software). Watertown, Mass.: Tom Snyder Productions, 2008.

Nicholaus, Bret and Lowrie, Paul. *KidChat Oh, The Places To Go!* New York: Roaring Brook Press, 2007.

Onyefulu, Ifeoma. *A Is for Africa*. New York: Cobblehill, 1993.

Priddy, Roger. *Wipe Clean United States Activity Atlas*. New York: Priddy Books, 2007.

Quest for the Pole. New York: Scholastic, 1988.

Revkin, Andrew. *The North Pole Was Here*. London: Kingfisher, 2007.

SimCity 3000 (and the rest of the series that allows students to deal with geography in creating a town or city). GameSpot, 1999.

Swan, Robert. *Destination: Antarctica*. New York: Scholastic, 1988.

The Golden Spike: Building America's First Transcontinental Railroad (software simulation). Washington, D.C: National Geographic Society.

The Great Maine to California Race (software). Hayden Software, 1983.

Weiss, Harvey. *Shelters: From Teepee to Igloo*. New York: Kingfisher, 1997.

Where Are We? (software). Watertown, Mass.: Tom Snyder Productions, 2008.

Where in the World Is Carmen Sandiego? (and other titles in the Carmen Sandiego series that focus on different areas of the world and different eras). Broderbund Software, 1986.

Young People's Atlas of the United States. New York: Kingfisher, 1997.

Geography Websites

www.50states.com (U.S. by State)

www.maps.yahoo.com (Maps Anywhere in the U.S.)

www.mapquest.com (U.S. maps)

www.mapsonus.com (U.S. maps)

www.atlas.usgs.gpy (U.S. Topographic Maps)

www.atlapedia.com (Physical and Political World Maps)

www.nationalgeographic.com (National Geographic Society)

www.edhelper.com (Thousands of Lesson Plans with Geography)

www.pbs.org/neighborhoods/history/#us (Neighborhoods)

www.census.gov (U.S. Census Bureau Demographic Profiles of States, Cities, and Towns)

http://www.nationalgeographic.com/resources/ngo/education/ideas.html (National Geographic Society)

http://www.nps.gov/ (National Park Service)

http://www.ncge.org/ (National Council for Geographic Education)

http://www.mapping.com. (David Smith's Mapping.com)

http://www.onlineclass.com/ (Online Classes)

http://www.aag.org/Education/center (Association of American Geographers)

http://www.education-world.com/soc_sci/geography/index.shtml (Education World, Inc.)

http://geosim.cs.vt.edu/ (Departments of Geography and Computer Science, Virginia Tech)

http://www.oxfam.org.uk/education/resources/mapping_our_world/ (Mapping our World)

http://www.usgs.gov/ (U.S. Geological Survey)

http://education.usgs.gov/common/lessons/index.html (U.S. Geological Survey)

http://ncge.net/geography/education (National Council for Geographic Education)

http://www.geog.psu.edu/gouldcenter/ (Peter R. Gould Center for Geography Education and Outreach)

http://www.educationatlas.com/geography-education.html (Education Atlas.com)

http://www.earthforce.org/section/resources/ (Earth Force: Tools for Teachers and Example Atlantic Hurricane Map)

http://weather.unisys.com/hurricane/index.html (Unisys Weather: Hurricane/Tropical Data)

http://nationalatlas.gov/ (National Atlas Home Page)

http://www.greatbuildings.com/ (Architecture Design Images)

http://www.eduplace.com/ss/maps/ (Outline Maps)

http://ngm.nationalgeographic.com/mapmachine#theme=Street&c=0|0&sf=187648892.534865. (Map Machine)

http://www.colorado.edu/geography/gcraft/notes/mapproj/mapproj_f.html (Map Projections)

CHAPTER 4

Economics*

THE BASIC PREMISES

Economics is the study of human solutions to the problem of scarcity. It investigates how humans deal with unlimited wants and needs in the face of limited natural, human, and capital resources. All societies must decide what goods and services will be produced, distributed, and consumed.

Economics, then, is the study and management of financial resources, and it is generally divided into two parts, macroeconomics and microeconomics. **Macroeconomics** studies the performance of the economy as a whole, including government policies such as the actions of the Treasury, the Federal Reserve, and even Congress. **Microeconomics** looks at the behavior of individuals in the market and the factors that affect their choices and behavior (which restaurant will you eat at, which movie will you buy a ticket for, which apartment will you rent, which job will you take?). In private life, individuals make economic choices for themselves, but personal economic choices may have positive or negative consequences on society as a whole, such as when someone chooses to donate money to a cause, to have a child, to declare bankruptcy, or to engage in risky or dangerous behavior (which can leave society having to choose whether or not to pay the ensuing medical bills and/or disability benefits).

Money spent on one thing is gone and cannot then be spent on another, a concept known as "**opportunity cost**." Decision making, by society or by individuals, requires analysis of consequences in the form of benefits and/or possible losses, since there is often an economic reason for the decisions people make. Is it better to spend money on a bigger house or a newer car, on food or medicine, on tennis lessons or a new piano, and what will be the consequences of each choice? In making such decisions, people and societies often use past decisions or experience, for good or for bad, to guide them.

---

*Substantial portions of this chapter were adapted from *Voluntary National Content Standards in Economics.* Copyright © 1997, National Council on Economic Education, New York, NY 10036. Used with permission.

In the free-enterprise system, markets exist when buyers exchange money for goods and services from sellers, determining **market prices** (seen operating in purest form at flea markets, for example). By the natural laws of **supply and demand**, prices go up when there is a shortage of a product available and they go down (on sale) when there is a surplus, affecting both buyers and sellers: hence, Christmas trimmings are more valuable in November than in January. **Equilibrium price** is the price at which the quantity supplied of something equals the quantity of that thing demanded, so both the quantity and price do not change (i.e., the number of people wanting hot dogs at a ball game equals the number of hot dogs available, so they are not put on sale nor is the price raised). **Relative price** is the price of one good or service compared to the prices of others. Changes in the price of one good or service can lead to change in prices of many others, since markets may affect each other. In other words, if gas prices rise, the market for big cars may drop.

Competition among sellers lowers costs and prices, and encourages producers to produce more of what consumers are willing and able to buy (the price of many goods, such as video players, drops after they come on the market, as a result of competition). Competition among buyers increases prices and gives goods and services to those who are willing and able to pay the most for them (such as tickets for the Superbowl). Changes in the level of competition can affect price (if there are three movie theaters in your town, prices of tickets should drop, but if two shut down, the remaining one may raise the price due to lack of competition). Competition usually results in lower prices, higher quality, and better customer service, as sellers compete to get buyers' business. Conversely, competition among buyers results in higher prices and more profit for sellers, such as the huge increase in real estate prices in the late 1970s and early 1980s as millions of baby boomers tried to buy houses. There was a similar increase in real estate prices after 2000, as lending rules were relaxed and so more buyers rushed into the marketplace. Because of the demand, real estate prices rose to unsustainable heights, then dropped because many people could not keep up with their increased payments on their large, adjustable rate mortgages. The resulting wave of foreclosures, particularly in fast-growing areas where prices had risen highest, hurt the real estate market and banks that held overvalued mortgages, produced economic uncertainty, and helped severely weaken the economy by 2008. The weak economy was a pressing problem both in the United States and around the world, to the extent that governments intervened financially to prop up their economies in order to avoid a replay of the Depression of the 1930s.

THE HISTORY OF ECONOMICS

Economics has been a factor of life throughout recorded history, and, by extension, trade—from the silent barter of early Africa to the sophisticated maneuverings of the U.S. Federal Reserve—has been an integral part of human experience. But trade is often awkward: if the two people don't need what each other has, more and more parties are drawn in, to satisfy each trader's needs, so eventually money was invented. The early Lydians originated the use of money, and Marco Polo in the 1200s reported on Chinese money and banking. Most other civilizations followed suit, although even today there are cultures that use jewelry, cattle, or other goods for trade purposes. **Money**, whether in the form of cash or credit, makes it easier to trade, borrow, save, invest, and compare the value of goods and services. The real value of money (which is issued by governments and usually backed by gold or silver) is the goods and services it can buy (money on a desert island is valueless because there is nothing that can be done with it), so that doubling the amount of money available would only increase inflation (prices rise) but not allow the consumer to buy more.

Money permits specialization, rather than barter, increasing overall levels of both production and consumption. Plato and Aristotle wrote about division of labor (including slavery) and the use of money in ancient Greece, and by the Middle Ages, the concepts of banks (for safekeeping money) and checking accounts (from bankers' letters of credit stating that people had money on deposit for safekeeping) were born, as people found it difficult and unsafe to carry large amounts of gold to buy and sell ever-larger amounts of goods as trade grew. The early Chinese also established the use of money, banking, and checks. The idea of selling both land and labor as marketable goods rather than simply viewing them as fixed inheritances or serfdom also grew. Over the centuries, various businesses offered credit to their reliable customers in the form of charge accounts that could be paid monthly, and by the 1960s, the **credit card**, which could be used at any number of businesses, local or international, was firmly established as part of modern life.

Although economics has such a long history, it has only been studied and analyzed as a specific discipline in the last few hundred years. Jean Baptiste Colbert and the physiocrats of 1600s France are known for their theories of **mercantilism** (how the economic system should work to the state's advantage), and Adam Smith, a Scotsman, wrote the first economics book, *An Inquiry into the Nature and Causes of the Wealth of Nations*, published in 1776. He suggested that society would be best served if people just looked out for their own interests, without much government interference (**laissez-faire** economics, French for "leave it alone") since that would lead them to act in ways that are good for society (lowering prices and increasing consumer choice through competition in the market).

Smith thought that labor was the main source of wealth, so that wealth could be increased by making labor more effective, especially through the use of **capital** (accumulated resources available for investment, which in turn would contribute to the economy). Smith's ideas form the basis of **capitalism**, or the free enterprise/free market system, as they call for the least government regulation and the most initiative or freedom by the individual. But many people now feel Smith's ideas do not provide for enough protection for those who are not able, for one reason or another, to compete effectively in the marketplace. Thomas Malthus in 1798 expanded the laissez-faire idea to argue that it was little use to help feed the poor, as they would reproduce and there would be more mouths to feed and more unemployment because the population always increases faster than the food supply (perhaps understandably, economics in this period was known as the "dismal science"). Rather, he suggested that lowering the birth rate would help lessen poverty.

Economics began to be studied in earnest in the 1800s, and a variety of economic theories, often mixed with government, came into being. David Ricardo in 1817 applied the idea of laissez-faire to wages, stating that when labor is scarce, wages are high but that wages drop when the labor supply increases. He believed investment was better spent on infrastructure, rather than on wages and salary.

An important political and economic theory of the 1800s was **communism**, an idealistic system laid out by Karl Marx and Friedrich Engels, who together co-authored *The Communist Manifesto*. They suggested that workers should own the means of production and share in the labor and profits, an idea summed up in the phrase, "From each according to his ability, to each according to his need." Communism in practice, however, has turned out to be a system in which the government owns all the means of production and regulates the economy (and incidentally many other aspects of life, including religious belief). That degree of central planning and lack of freedom, combined with the natural human response toward lethargy if there is no reward for hard work, has proven to be so cumbersome and unwieldy that it could not provide for the needs of the people. Marx argued that economic forces shape history, and, ironically, formerly communist countries, such as Russia and the former East Germany, have gone to a free enterprise system (as have even currently communist countries such as China and Vietnam to some extent unofficially), and those communist countries that have not, such as North Korea, are suffering economically.

Socialism, based on the government owning only the major means of production (as a safety net for the population) and attempting to equalize distribution of income, while encouraging free enterprise in other areas, a concept known as a "**mixed economy**," also sprang up at this time and currently is widely practiced in Europe, usually under democratic governments. "**Utopian socialists**" such as Charles Fourier in France and Robert Owen in Scotland set up model communities with idealistic principles of sharing for workers, but lack of cooperation within caused them to fail. The United States is a **capitalist**, or free enterprise, country that has some socialist elements, such as Social Security, food stamps, and free public education, Medicare, unemployment insurance, and industrial and agricultural subsidies.

Other important economic theories include first Jeremy Bentham's and then John Stuart Mill's ideas on **utilitarianism**, the greatest good for the greatest number of people. Mill also valued individual freedom and the greatest good, but argued that government intervention was necessary to accomplish social justice and reforms. Thorsten Veblen's theory of **conspicuous consumption** postulated that people buy useless goods to establish high social status. Most significant to the twentieth century, John Maynard Keynes' theory on **deficit spending** was that the government should spend money it does not yet have to stimulate the economy and pull the country out of a recession or depression. Keynes' ideas were used by many governments in the 1930s to help end the Great Depression, influencing aspects of Franklin Roosevelt's New Deal and, after World War II, the Marshall Plan in which the United States helped to rebuild Europe economically. Similarly, John Kenneth Galbraith promoted a strong economic role for government, but another influential economist, Milton Friedman, advocated for free markets and a reduced economic role for government.

In nondemocratic societies, a dictator may decide how to regulate resources; or the army, the religious establishment, influential branches of government, or private people may have more input than others. Under **fascism** (a kind of dictatorship practiced in Germany and Italy before World War II and continuing in Spain and Portugal into the 1970s), the government regulates the economy by force in order to make the nation stronger than its rivals. Other dictatorships may structure the economy simply so the dictator and his or her associates can make money off the people (such as with Ferdinand Marcos and with the Duvaliers in the Philippines and Haiti, respectively).

GOVERNMENT INVOLVEMENT IN ECONOMICS

It is clear that governments frequently get involved in their economies, ostensibly for the good of the citizens. If there were no regulation at all, for example, there would be no protection for consumers from a producer who either buys up or drives out of business all the other producers of a good or service, thus creating a **monopoly** in which one person or company owns all of one good or service, or an **oligopoly** in which a small number of sellers or providers dominate a market or an industry. The opposite situation is "**pure competition**," which means an open market of products and information, with easy entry and exit. However, without regulation, neither would there be protection for ethical producers from unethical ones who pollute the environment, use child labor, or underpay their workers, all in order to produce a cheaper product (in fact, this was largely the situation in England and, to some extent, in the United States, France, and Germany at the beginning of the Industrial Revolution).

So twentieth-century governments, in part as a result of the Great Depression of the 1930s, often participate in some kinds of economic activity (usually public utilities, roads and transportation, and public schools and hospitals), and regulate most other kinds through licensing various service providers and requiring the safety of products, in addition to providing general requirements for the good of society in relation to such things as fraud, the minimum wage, rent control or subsidies, safety regulations (with both consumers and workers in mind), labor laws, and environmental protection. There are many areas of life in which the government intervenes (often to protect the economic or social rights of the poor, the weak, or the handicapped), and there is much disagreement about the extent to which it should do so.

Different societies have valued different economic priorities, although public policies often try to improve future standards of living. Most of the Western world, for example, believes free, public education is something that government should provide for its people for the good of society, but Western Europe often provides free college tuition and preschool, while the United States generally provides only K–12. Similarly, most European countries provide national health insurance, but the United States provides it only for the elderly (Medicare) and the very poor (Medicaid). By contrast, the United States spends much more on defense than do most European countries, making it a major superpower and giving it an enormous amount of influence and responsibility in the world.

In poorer countries, public health may be a greater priority than education, although they are often linked. Which choice is better is something the individual societies must work out, and in democratic countries, the citizens vote for representatives who reflect their concerns and beliefs about how to allocate resources. Fairness is a concept that is very important to most people, and power struggles about who gets what reflect status and influence in society. Often the poor have little influence, while wealthy corporations may have excessive influence. People who get little help from their government, whether or not they are rich or poor, may resent the help that others get, feeling that that help unfairly affects competition. Conversely, programs that benefit many people, such as Social Security or public schooling, are generally popular.

The cost of government policies sometimes exceeds the benefits of those particular policies, perhaps because of demands by special interest groups or because social good, rather than an economic goal, is being pursued (public transport, for example, rarely pays for itself outside of big cities, but society generally feels obliged to provide some form of it for those who cannot drive). Some public policies cost more than the benefits they generate (a park operating at a loss because few people use it), or one group enjoys the benefits while another one pays the costs (as in money taken from young workers to pay Social Security to older workers or property taxes for schools paid by people with no children). Most governments also redistribute income, often through income tax, to attempt to compensate for market failures. Generally, such policies exist in the name of the greater good for society, but it is often hard to measure the success of government programs (supporters of welfare reform consider it a success to get people off welfare, but opponents worry about those who have used up their benefits but are still unemployed). Many farmers receive large subsidies because the government wishes to keep farmers in business to guarantee stable food supplies, and some businesses (such as defense industries) are protected by tariffs or quotas because their products are considered important.

Often political influence plays a part in protecting special interest groups (such as Angora goat farmers in Texas), creating unfairness to taxpayers and to the larger society. Another problem arises when different government policies conflict: for example, subsidizing tobacco while trying to persuade people not to smoke.

Governments usually provide for national defense, often address environmental concerns, and frequently attempt to make markets more competitive. They also define and protect property rights, necessary for people to feel secure in making their plans. The federal government enforces antitrust laws and regulations to try to maintain effective levels of competition, but sometimes those laws reduce competition without meaning to (limits on or subsidies for certain items, such as dairy products). Citizens should vote for people who support or oppose various policies in accord with citizen wishes, but often potential voters don't bother to do so because they cannot see the economic importance.

Fiscal policy is the government's attempt to influence the economy through changes in taxes, or government spending. Governments pay for the goods and services they provide by taxing people, but those goods and services are generally available to all, not just to those who paid taxes (another example of **income distribution**). Most federal income comes from personal income and payroll taxes, while most of the spending is Social Security, defense, medical expenditures, and interest payments on the national debt. By contrast, most state and local governments get their money through sales and property taxes, and spend it on education, welfare, roads, and public safety.

Besides government, other significant financial institutions such as banks, labor unions, corporations, legal systems, and not-for-profit organizations are important to market economies. **Nonprofit institutions**, exempt from most taxes, include many private hospitals, schools, charities, and religious groups. **Corporations** generally limit liability and allow people to pool their investment resources through buying stocks, making it easier for people to invest. The arena in which stock is bought and sold is called the **stock market**, and it is a very important part of the marketplace in free-enterprise societies, reflecting through the rise and fall of prices on a daily basis how the economy is doing.

A nation's overall levels of income, employment, and prices are determined by spending and production decisions made by all households, companies, government agencies, and others in the economy. Conditions reported in the media (such as consumer confidence or predictions of recession) can influence decisions made by consumers, producers, and government policymakers. Abstract national changes can affect the individual's job opportunities (unemployment, for example, imposes costs on individuals and nations), as well as his or her earnings and prices he or she pays for goods and services. Unemployment can be made worse by tightening credit to lower inflation, which may also discourage economic activity. The rate of employment can sometimes be increased with looser credit, which may also have the effect of increasing inflation.

Gross domestic product (GDP) is a measure of a nation's economic output and income: the total market value of all goods and services produced in the economy for one year, divided by the number of people living in the country to get per capita GDP. Obviously, the higher the GDP, the higher the standard of living. With some exceptions, such as Japan or Singapore, the United States, Canada, and Western Europe generally have the highest GDP, because they are the most industrialized countries.

Inflation (a rise in both pay and prices, so a set amount of money doesn't buy as much) imposes costs on some people and benefits others because it reduces purchasing power (for example, it's good for people paying back mortgages with less valuable money but hard for the people who lent the more valuable money and are now getting back less valuable money, because they can't buy as much with the same amount of money as they could earlier). Additionally, when people's wages increase more slowly than the inflation rate, their purchasing power declines. Inflation, then, can reduce the rate of growth of national living standards. **"Stagflation"** occurs when inflation increases, but economic stagnation keeps the economy from growing.

Politicians disagree on how to deal with both inflation and unemployment. Federal budgetary policy and the U.S. Federal Reserve System's monetary policy of controlling the supply of both money and credit by raising or lowering the interest rate influence the overall levels of employment, output, and prices, affecting both inflation and employment levels. The federal government through the Federal Reserve System's macroeconomic policy decision affects both institutions and individuals, so there is much debate about the government's role and effectiveness in the goals of full employment, price stability, and economic growth.

Since voluntary exchange, in which all parties expect to gain, occurs only when all participating parties expect to gain, whether for trade among individuals, organizations, or nations, policies that alter trade barriers between nations, such as **tariffs** and **quotas**, have both benefits and costs. For example, if a country has high taxes on **imported** (brought in from another country) cars to protect the car industry, it may be harder to export (send to another country) cars if foreign countries put high taxes on imported cars, and it means that the price of cars for consumers stays high, since foreign cars will be more expensive. It also means most consumers will buy domestically built cars because they are cheaper, so the domestic car industry may raise its price because of the increased demand: every action has a reaction.

Additionally, some nations want trade barriers for national defense reasons or because some companies and workers are hurt by free trade: farmers in Florida do not like competing with Central American farmers in selling fruits and vegetables, just as many factory workers throughout the United States do not wish to compete with factory workers in Mexico, where wages are generally lower. But generally, when trading is easier, prices go down. International trade is also affected by the exchange rate, the value of one nation's money compared to another's.

CONSUMER CHOICES RELATED TO NEEDS AND WANTS

Economics is based on the needs and wants of humans for goods and services. But needs and wants are not necessarily the same, and, since consumers cannot have everything, much time and effort are spent on people making choices about which of their desires are actually needs and which are just wants. The only ways to narrow the gap between people's wants and what they can afford is for them to want less or produce more. When any choice is made, there are consequences of that choice: the person involved has decided that certain things are more important than other things, as something is gained and something is given up; hence, a logical person would choose food over a theater ticket, or shelter over an expensive dress, given a limited amount of money or resources. Most people would like more than a limited amount of money, so the amount of human effort given to obtaining money is called "human resources," while things like land, air, and minerals are "natural resources." Growing crops for food is a combination of human and natural resources.

Production is the use of resources to create things or services to satisfy wants. Capital goods go along with human and natural resources used for making other goods, and the humans involved in production are entrepreneurs (those who organize the economics activity) or labor (those who actually do the work). One way to produce more goods efficiently is through division of labor, which, combined with the Industrial Revolution (the invention of machinery that allows more goods to be more quickly produced), has made it possible for many people to have more goods than was typical in the past. One new issue that has arisen in recent years is the idea of over consumption of resources, particularly in the industrialized countries. There is, in fact, currently a strong movement toward voluntary reduction of individuals' carbon footprints and use of natural resources, i.e., smaller houses, more vegetarian diet, more efficient cars, solar power, etc.

No one has everything he or she wants, so "**scarcity**" affects value: the more people who want certain things, the scarcer those things are. Additionally, nothing is completely free: if the government or an individual or family supplies certain goods, the cost means that other goods, choices, or opportunities are limited. The limitations are difficult for societies as they try to figure out whether to spend money on schools or public health, law enforcement or rehabilitation, support for orphans or the elderly, or "guns or butter" (a shorthand phrase meaning spending money on defense or on luxuries for citizens).

Investment in factories, machinery, new technology, and the health, education, and training of people can raise future standards of living, so there are consequences to every investment decision made by individuals, businesses, and governments. **Interest rates** (the amount paid to borrow money), adjusted for inflation, rise and fall, thus affecting the allocation of scarce resources between present and future uses. People react to changes in interest rates depending on whether they are making or receiving interest payments. Higher interest rates encourage people to save more (because they will earn more on their savings) and borrow less (because it will cost them more). Lower rates do the opposite.

Riskier loans command higher interest rates than safer loans, because the chance of default is greater. Saving is the part of income not spent on taxes or consumption, and saving and investing can result in money for big items later, which require patience and sacrifice for now. Trade-offs come throughout life, and workers often can improve their human capital by improving skills and productivity, often through education. Standards of living generally increase as productivity increases, often driven by technological change.

ENTREPRENEURS AND WAGE-EARNERS

Entrepreneurs are people who take the risks of organizing productive resources to make goods and services, often to make new or improved products. Profit is an important incentive that leads entrepreneurs to accept the risks of business failure. For people to be entrepreneurs, they must accept the chance of failure weighed against the chance of profits that come with success, and many people are uncomfortable with that kind of risk, so prefer to work for others. Wages for workers depend on the entrepreneur's success, and public policies that affect the success affect the owner, the workers, and the public. Entrepreneurs have the pleasure of being self-employed and the satisfaction of creating or improving products, but they also work long hours, take much responsibility, and have stress from running the business. Conversely, workers have fewer of those worries but generally don't make as much money and must take direction from other people.

Income for most people is determined by the market value of the productive resources (generally labor) they sell. What workers earn depends, primarily, on the market value of what they produce and how productive they are, so people often predict future earnings based on education, training, and career options. Labor is a human resource used to produce goods and services. People earn income by exchanging their physical or mental labor or entrepreneurial talents for wages or profits, since employers or individuals expect to sell the goods and services those workers produce at prices high enough to cover the wages and/or other costs of production.

The wages paid for labor depend on the supply available and the demand for it. More productive or higher-skilled workers are of greater value and generally earn more, while those with few skills are more likely to earn less. Unions increase the negotiating power of workers against the power of a large employer, and fringe benefits and work rules may be as important as wages.

SUPPLY AND DEMAND

Free enterprise (also known as "capitalism" or a "**market economy**") is the system in which members of society are generally free to follow their own inclinations about how to deal with economic decisions. The consumer decides what he or she will buy, so the whole economics system is geared toward what the consumer wants and is willing to pay. Obviously, people who are consumers of some goods are producers of others, so self-interest makes people try to satisfy others so they themselves can make money and satisfy their own wants and needs. Prices, wages, production, profits, losses, and interest rates all indicate which parts of the market are thriving, which are attracting spending consumers, and which are failing.

Competition means that if there is a demand (resulting in a higher price), usually some producer will rush to fill it, but if too many people do so, the demand will lessen in relation to the quantity available. Then, the product will no longer be so desirable, resulting in a drop in price and, hence, less profit. The rush for the "hot" toy each Christmas (Bratz dolls, Pokemon, Tickle Me Elmo) that becomes more widely and cheaply available the following year, is an example of this principle. Another contemporary example is the change in the price of new electronic goods after they are introduced: for example, the prices of bread machines, DVD players personal computers and video gaming systems have dropped tremendously as a result of competition since they were first available.

This drop in price is wonderful for the consumer, but not so great for the producer, and since most consumers are also producers, there must be a balance in order for consumers to have money to spend; otherwise, a situation such as the **Great Depression** of the 1930s results, with cheap goods still unaffordable by unemployed and poverty-stricken consumers. Competition, therefore, forces each party to offer the most value for the least amount of money or to be ignored by the market, and it means that producers are constantly inventing, refining, and improving to attract consumers. All of this activity generally contributes to improving the material standard of living. It also means that on certain items, where there can be no more production (such as antiques or waterfront property) the price just keeps rising as demand goes up, with no consequent increase in production and drop in price.

In order for competition to succeed, consumers must have choices, information, and the ability to change to another producer (advertising frequently plays a role, for better or worse, in promoting choices and information, in the hope of getting new consumers or of promoting a move to a particular producer—the tobacco industry, in particular, has insisted that its advertising is aimed at getting current smokers to change brands, rather than at enticing nonsmokers to begin smoking, a claim somewhat weakened by the vast numbers of young people who continue to take up smoking). When the consumer is lacking those elements of choice, he or she is often victimized by the market, as in a situation when there is a monopoly (meaning one producer has the entire market). If there is only one store (or medical clinic or automobile dealer or lumberyard) in an area, it can charge high prices for poor goods and little service, but the consumer has no other choice available.

Even if a person makes an economic decision, there may come a point, known as the natural **law of diminishing returns**, when the benefit is outweighed by the cost (the fifteenth candy bar may not be as appealing as the first three, or the fifth pet dog may provide just as much work and expense but much less pleasure than the first dog), and so the person may change the decision. As it often does in public life, force may play a role in individual choice: parents or bullies may decide to allocate a resource for an individual, even for such simple items as concert tickets or cookies, or a theater's decision to take reservations, use a lottery, or distribute seats on a first-come, first-serve basis, may affect the individual's desire to consume entertainment.

People respond predictably to positive and negative **incentives**, monetary or nonmonetary, but because people have different value systems and usually pursue their self-interest, an incentive can influence them in different ways: a nondrinker is not going to buy more beer as the price becomes cheaper, but a drinker might well take advantage of the lower price.

When any good or service is distributed, there will be people who are unhappy with the method of allocation, since ethics, as well as economics, play a role in decisions: for example, should organ transplants be given to the sickest applicants or to those who have been waiting the longest or to those who can afford to pay the most for them? Should preference be given to those who were born with a bad liver over those whose lifestyle caused liver problems? Should music lessons, unaffordable to all children in a family, be given to just some? Should heating oil go only to those who can afford it, even if others are more frail? Those are questions that scarcity forces, and the answers are ones with which society and individuals wrestle.

Major scarcities facing the modern world are oil, water, and other nonrenewable resources. As the population of the world grows, and as formerly agricultural areas become industrialized and their standards of living rise, more and more people want more and more goods and services. For example, as the population of India and China not only grow but become more prosperous, wanting such conveniences as cars and air-conditioning, the price of oil keeps rising as the demand for oil rises. Therefore, the countries that are rich in this resource, many of them in the Middle East, as well as Russia, Argentina, the United States, and others, have become more and more politically important. Whether a country imports or exports oil has a great bearing on its prosperity and national security, although rising expectations of developing nations are increasing the demand for other natural resources and raw materials as well.

Western industrialized countries, especially the United States, tend to use a disproportionate amount of the world's resources, so a major challenge facing the world today is to create a source of renewable, nonpolluting energy, whether sun, wind, hydrogen, or some newer source. Many parts of the world, especially Europe, rely on nuclear power, but some countries are wary of nuclear power because of safety issues in the disposition of the radioactive waste. Even oil is controversial, as many scientists feel carbon emissions contribute to global warming, so countries are forced to balance their ecological concerns with their economic and national security concerns.

Economies can also be affected by the environment in other ways. The mildness or severity of weather and climate shape the prosperity of various regions, especially in the production of food and lumber, and the encouragment of tourism, a major world industry. The terrible disaster and loss of life from the December 2004 tsunami in Asia or the pain and dislocation caused by Hurricane Katrina in Mississippi and New Orleans, Louisiana affect whole economies as well as individual humans, as the population reacts in economic ways to many stimuli.

Economies also affect each other in many ways, so that one country's economic prosperity may rely on other countries' behavior in buying and selling. In the modern world, with increased speed in communication and transportation, countries are "closer," meaning less isolated and more influential on each other, than in the past. **"Globalization"** refers to the idea that all countries are intertwined, especially in an economic way, usually to the dismay of people who are losing jobs or markets for goods to other countries that pay workers less and/or are producing cheaper goods. Globalization affects quality of life, as some countries attempting to hold high standards of environmental or workers' rights compete with other countries that value those qualities less highly.

It is clear, then, that economics plays an intimate part in people's most private lives and in government's most public decisions. Knowing how the marketplace and the government work, and knowing that various policies have various results, can help the individual consumer be an active participant who is not victimized by lack of understanding and can make the best of his or her economic opportunities. No matter what the individual's income, conscious budgeting is important, because it can keep that individual aware of choices and decisions, making him or her a more informed, stronger participant in the marketplace.

Economics Resources

Getting Started Educationally

Calderwood. J. D., J. D. Lawrence, and J. E. Maher. *Economics in the Curriculum.* New York: Wiley, 1970.

"Economics in Elementary Schools" (theme issue). *Social Studies and the Young Learner.* November/December 1998.

National Content Standards in Economics. New York: National Council on Economic Education, 1997.

Economics Content for Teachers

Eggert, J. *What Is Economics?* New York: Kaufman, 1993.

Galibraith, John Kenneth. *The Age of Uncertainty: A History of Economic Ideas and Their Consequences.* Boston: Houghton Mifflin, 1977.

Heilbroner, Robert L. *The Worldly Philosophers: The Lives, Times and Ideas of the Great Economic Thinkers.* 6th ed. New York: Simon & Schuster, 1986.

Helibroner, R. and L. Thurow. *Economics Explained: Everything You Need to Know about How the Economy Works and Where It's Going.* New York: Touchstone, 1994.

Klein, Nacrni. *The Shock Doctrine: The Rise of Disaster Capitalism.* New York: Henry Hott, 2007.

Kourilsky, Marilyn L. *Understanding Economics: Overview for Teachers, Experiences for Students.* Menlo Park, Calif.: Addison-Wesley, 1983.

Maher, J. E. *What Is Economics?* New York: Wiley, 1969.

Slavin, Stephen L. *Economics: A Self-Teaching Guide.* New York: Wiley, 1988.

Economics Content for Students

Adler, David. *Prices Go Up, Prices Go Down.* Danubry, Conn.: Watts, 1984.

Anno, Mitsuma. *Anno's Flea Market.* New York: Philomel, 1984.

Caple, Kathy. *The Purse.* Boston: Houghton Mifflin, 1986.

Coleman, Penny. *Strike! The Bitter Struggle of American Workers from Colonial Times to the Present.* Millbrook, 1995.

Cordsen, Carol Fosket and Jones, Douglas. *Market Day.* New York: Dutton Children's Books, 2008.

D'Aluisio, Faith, and Menzel, Peter. *What The World Eats.* Berkeley, Ca.: Tricycle Press, 2008.

Garland, Sarah. *Going Shopping.* London: Frances Lincoln Children's Books, 2008.

Gibbons, Gail. *Department Store.* New York: Crowell, 1984.

Gibbons, Gail. *Corn.* New York: Holiday House, 2008.

Godfrey, Neale S. *The Kids' Money Book.* New York: Simon & Schuster, 1998.

Horowitz, Joshua. *Night Markets: Bringing Food to a City.* New York: Crowell, 1984.

Jeffers, Susan. *My Chincoteague Pony.* New York: Hyperion Books, 2008.

Levenson, George and Thaler, Samuel. *Bread Comes to Life: A Garden of Wheat and a loaf to Eat.* Berkeley, Ca.: Tricycle Press, 2008.

Lobel, Arnold. *On Market Street.* New York: Greenwillow, 1981.

Maestro, Betsy. *The Story of Money.* New York: Clarion, 1993.

Marsh, Carol. *The Teddy Bear Company. Economics for Kids.* Gallapade Carole Marsh Books, 1983.

Mitgutsch, Ali. *From Gold to Money*. Minneapolis: Carolrhoda, 1984.

Nakagawa, Chihiro, and Koyose Junji. *Who Made This Cake?* Honesdale, Pa.: Front Street (Boyds Mills Press), 2008.

Spier, Peter. The *Food Market*. New York: Doubleday, 1981.

Vila, Laura. *Building Manhattan*. New York: Viking, 2008.

Ziefert, Harriet. *A New Coat for Anna*. New York: Knopf, 1986.

Economics Websites

www.ncss.org (National Council for the Social Studies)

www.edhelper.com (Thousands of Lessons Plans, Including Economics)

www.nationalcouncil.org (National Council on Economic Education)

www.wsjclassroomedition.com (Classroom Edition of the Wall Street Journal)

www.ccee.net (Colorado Council of Economic Education K–12—Many Plans and Links to Other Sites)

http://www.frbsf.org (Federal Reserve Bank of San Francisco Lessons in Economic Education)

ecedweb.unomaha.edu/st-louis.htm (Economics Curriculum Materials)

cob.jmu.edu/econed/Elementary.htm (Economics Lessons for Elementary School)

cob.jmu.edu/econed/Middle.htm (Economics Lessons for Middle School)

http://www.montgomeryschoolsmd.org/curriculum/socialstd/Econ_Geog.html (Economics Lessons/Sources Related to Children's Literature)

harbaugh.uoregon.edu/children (Economic Behavior of Children)

www.econedlink.org/lessons/index.cfm (Economics Lessons)

http://ecedweb.unomaha.edu/home.cfm (UNO Center for Economic Education)

http://www.ncee.net/ (National Council on Economic Education)

http://www.econedlink.org/ (Economics Education Link)

http://www.frbsf.org/education/ (Federal Reserve Bank of San Francisco)

http://www.econed-in.org/ (Indiana Council for Economic Education)

http://fefe.arizona.edu/ (Family Economics & Financial Education)

http://business.fullerton.edu/Centers/econcenter/ (California State University, Fullerton)

http://www.kcee.wichita.edu/mainpage.htm (Kansas Council on Economic Education)

http://www.business.uc.edu/EconomicsCenter (Economics Center for Education and Research)

http://www.sjsu.edu/depts/economics/Educenter-econ.html (San Jose State University)

http://www.fffl.ncee.net/ (Financial Fitness for Life)

http://www.vcdh.virginia.edu/index.php?page=VCDH (The Virginia Center for Digital History at the University of Virginia)

http://www.ncee.net/ea/index.php (National Council on Economic Education)

http://ecedweb.unomaha.edu/K-12/home.cfm (Teaching K–12 Economics)

http://www.ncee.net/resources/lessons.php (National Council on Economic Educations Resources)

CHAPTER 5

Government*

THE PURPOSE OF GOVERNMENT

From the time people began living in permanent groups 6,000–7,000 years ago, conflicts between them needed resolving and cooperative efforts, such as defense and irrigation, needed coordinating, so gradually governments became part of their lives. Governments at various levels (most often local, state, and national in the United States) make and enforce laws. In early societies, and in some societies today, the power of government was simply seized by the strongest person or group, but generally an authority's power derives from custom (as in kings) or from the people (as in democratic societies in which the people vote). There are many forms of authority within government, including police, child welfare, environment, military, and education departments, all deriving their powers from various laws passed by the government.

Government can be both good and bad. **Anarchism** is the lack of government (either on purpose or through weakness or ineffectiveness), and, although some people dream of total freedom, it often ends up with weak people being preyed upon, with no defense against stronger people. Without any form of government, there would be no check on violence, greed, or aggression (aside from the acts of individuals), and no cooperation in such common areas as driving, parks, or national defense. Seventeenth-century political philosopher John Locke asserted that the purpose of government is to protect the right of its citizens, and if a government fails to do so, the people have a right to overthrow that government. By contrast, Thomas Hobbes argued that people act out of self-interest, so that strong government is needed, with citizens trading freedom for order in a "**social contract**." So government often works to defend the rights of individuals and of the greater society, but usually also limits certain rights (driving speed, pollution) and assigns certain responsibilities (paying taxes, serving in the army, obeying laws).

---

*Substantial portions of this chapter were adapted with permission. *National Standards for Civics and Government*. Copyright © 1994, Center for Civic Education, Calabasas, California. Used with permission.

Governments establish schools, provide health services, require licenses of competence in various areas in order to protect citizens' health and safety, build and maintain highways, regulate safety and sanitation, manage conflicts, and defend the nation. In nondemocratic countries, however, which are often dictatorial, communist, or **theocratic** (run by religious belief), government is more restrictive of than protective of individual rights.

In early societies, customs, traditions, and rules guided behavior and kept order, and in complex societies, laws (which in democratic societies apply to the lawmakers as well as to the people) do the same. Agreement upon the laws is essential for a society to function with order, predictability, and security, and in free societies, laws limit the rulers to protect the people. Without laws to secure lives, liberty, and property, **anarchy** (the lack of order in society) would prevail and the strong would quickly overpower the weak. But not all laws are good ones: laws should be clearly written for a specific purpose, possible to follow, designed to protect individual rights, unbiased against any group or person, and supportive of the common good, since individuals cannot, for example, provide effective highways or defense.

Laws are often very different, depending upon the kind of governments they reflect: in a **limited government** (most **constitutional democracies**), the laws apply equally to everyone and are designed to limit government power and protect the people, while in an **unlimited government** (**authoritarian** and **totalitarian** systems, such as Nazi Germany, Imperial Japan, Iraq and Iran, and some African countries, in which it is difficult to remove rulers), laws support the ruler's unlimited power and may be applied unevenly and arbitrarily. Limited governments depend upon the **"rule of law,"** the idea that society is governed according to accepted rules followed not only by the governed but also by those doing the governing. In limited governments, emphasis is placed on individual political participation and personal responsibility to the government and the laws.

Government may be more or less intrusive: if its purpose is just to protect the lives and property of citizens, there may be restrictions on the right of government to intrude into people's private lives; but if its purpose is to improve the moral character of the citizens, there may be laws regulating private behavior and beliefs. The United States (like Great Britain, Botswana, Japan, Israel, Chile, and most of Western Europe among others) is an example of a limited government, which protects the individual rights of the people as to privacy, association, religion, free expression, speech, and property, but it also has elements of moral concerns about private behavior, such as laws against drug use, certain sexual practices, and tobacco advertising, for example.

Civic life is the public life of the citizen concerned with the affairs of the community and nation (as opposed to private life and personal interests), while politics is the process through which people reach collective decisions that are enforced as common policy. Government is the institution (made up of individual people) with the authority to make and enforce laws, to manage resources, benefits and burdens, and to resolve conflict. School boards, city councils, state legislatures, courts, and Congress are examples of government bodies with legitimate authority, while gangs, military juntas, and dictatorships are examples of power without authority from the people.

VALUES OF AMERICAN DEMOCRACY

The fundamental values of American democracy are expressed in the **Declaration of Independence** ("All men [people] are created equal . . .") and the **U.S. Constitution** ("We the People of the United States, in order to form a more perfect union . . ."), supported by subsequent documents, including court cases, speeches, and so on. In particular, the first ten amendments to the Constitution, known as the **Bill of Rights**, were especially designed to protect individual rights and limit the power of the government. Important rights include the right to life, liberty, property, and the pursuit of happiness, the right to free speech and to freedom of religion, the right to equal protection under the law, and the right to bear arms. Ideally, Americans value the common good, justice, equality of opportunity, truth, diversity, and patriotism, and believe that respect for the law, education, work, and individual initiative are important. The principles of democracy support the ideas that the people are sovereign and are the source of the government's authority, that the power of government is limited by law, and that the people exercise their authority by voting directly or indirectly through their representatives. Power is the ability to make and implement changes in society. The framers of the Constitution attempted to limit power in two ways. First, the Constitution provides three branches of government that act as a system of **checks and balances** on each other. Second, the framers created a **federalist system** by allocating responsibilities and rights to the federal government, as well as to state and local governments.

The values, principles, and beliefs that Americans share are especially important since, unlike citizens of many other countries, Americans are not defined by ethnicity, race, or religion. Diverse in all those areas, they are united by their shared beliefs in freedom and individual rights, as expressed in such symbols as the flag, the Statue of Liberty, the national anthem, and such patriotic holidays as the Fourth of July, Presidents' Day, and Veterans' Day.

While American diversity has its benefits (variety of viewpoints, cultural and artistic traditions, and choices) and its costs (misunderstanding, conflict, and discrimination), it has always been a fundamental part of being American, since all Americans, including so-called Native Americans, immigrated from other parts of the world. Adhering to fundamental principles of justice and civil rights for all, including nondiscrimination, concern for the common good, and participation in government, can resolve much conflict raised by diversity, as can openness, communication, and common goals.

CONSTITUTIONAL GOVERNMENTS

A **constitution** is a set of written rules organizing government and allocating power (including spelling out the people's relationship to their government), but some countries, such as Great Britain, have constitutional government through unwritten tradition or "**common law**." More common are countries with so-called constitutions that do not limit government power, such as Nazi Germany, the former Soviet Union, or Iraq under Saddam Hussein, and in some countries the constitution is used to promote one group, class, party, or religion over another, as in China and Kenya. Ideally, the constitution limits government power and protects the rights of the individual, creating a state known as a true "constitutional government."

But a constitution is of little use if the people do not respect and adhere to it, so an educated and responsible citizenry that supports the principles of the constitution and insists that officials do the same is important to society. Just as there are different kinds of unlimited governments, there are different kinds of limited, or constitutional, governments. In the United States, powers are shared among three branches of government (legislative, judicial, and executive), while in Great Britain, for example, the **parliamentary system** provides for most power to be held by the legislature (Parliament), since the country's leader (the prime minister) is a member of Parliament chosen by the majority party, rather than directly elected by the people.

Additionally, the prime minister chooses members of the **cabinet** (important government officers) from the Parliament as well, and the government may be replaced by Parliament if a majority vote "no confidence" in the government. By contrast, in the United States, the president is elected separately from the legislators (senators and members of the House of Representatives), the cabinet members are never members of Congress, and elections are at fixed intervals of two (representatives), four (president), and six years (senators), depending upon the office.

Aware citizens examine other systems to help identify the strengths and weaknesses of their own system and how it may be improved (as with constitutional amendments in the United States), as well as understand events taking place in other countries. Aside from parliamentary systems, there are three major kinds of constitutional governments: under the **confederal system** (such as the United States under the Articles of Confederation, which predated the Constitution, or the Southern states as the Confederate States of America), strong states give only certain powers to the national government for specific purposes; under the **federal system**, power is divided and shared between the national and state governments (as currently in the United States); and under the **unitary system**, power is concentrated in a central government and local governments can exercise only those powers given to them by the central government (as currently the relationship between U.S. state and local governments).

THE U.S. CONSTITUTION

The Constitution is the main set of rules and laws that governs life in the United States. It is a remarkable written document and one of this country's greatest accomplishments. The values and principles contained in the Constitution are the bedrock of the country's purpose and beliefs. It states that the reason for government is to protect the rights of the individual and to protect the common good, and to further that end, it specifically limits the powers of the government and makes clear that government is the servant of the people, not their master. It also organizes the government into legislative, executive, and judicial branches. It is the supreme law of the land, and any law that contradicts it, even laws supported by Congress and/or the president, will be thrown out by the Supreme Court if that law is challenged. The Constitution gives people the right to choose their representatives and to change their government through voting, including even amending the Constitution itself.

The basis of American government is that the people are the sovereign, ultimate power and the government has limited power. The purposes of that government, stated in the Preamble to the Constitution are to form a "more perfect union," establish justice, insure domestic tranquility, provide for the common defense, promote the general welfare, and secure the blessings of liberty to ourselves and our posterity. The Constitution gives the government certain delegated or enumerated powers, such as taxing, making treaties, and settling controversies between states.

The limits on the government are ensured by a system of separation and sharing of powers among the executive, legislative, and judicial branches, and the system of checks and balances (requiring two-third legislative majorities for many actions, including overriding the president's veto and conviction in impeachment) ensures that the branches will review and restrain each other's actions.

The Bill of Rights (the first ten amendments to the Constitution, included at the time it was adopted) exists to reinforce individual rights and liberty and to guarantee limits on government power. Habeas corpus (people can't be seized and held without reason); trial by jury; ex post facto (an action cannot be made illegal after it is committed); freedom of religion, speech, press, and assembly; equal protection of the law; no cruel and unusual punishment; no search and seizure without due process of law; and the right to a lawyer are all vital elements of people's rights in the United States, which is quite remarkable among nations.

The unusual and fragile nature of liberty is very precious since, although some nations give their citizens similar rights, many more do not. The legal issues between citizens and government arise over interpreting these various rights. Where religious practice clashes with government policy, such as polygamy or using marijuana in religious ceremonies, which should prevail? Are pornographers protected by free speech laws? Is hate speech protected? Do advertisers have free speech rights? Should prayer be allowed in public schools? Is the death penalty cruel and unusual punishment? Is privacy imperiled by DNA banks, social security numbers, or national identification cards? These issues and many more are constantly being negotiated by the people and their government, usually via the courts, based on the Constitution, the Declaration of Independence, state constitutions and laws, federal laws, and civil rights legislation.

People do not always like the way legal decisions turn out, but one of the elements of democracy is respecting the law even while continuing to work to change it. A classic example is the Supreme Court's *Plessy v. Ferguson* decision of 1896, in which the court affirmed that "separate but equal" treatment of black citizens was constitutional; but by 1954, after years of legal challenges, the court reversed itself in the *Brown v. Board of Education* decision, which effectively outlawed legal segregation. Similarly, the states agreed to the amendment instituting Prohibition (the banning of alcohol) in 1920, but rescinded the ban in 1932, acknowledging the policy's failure.

According to the Constitution, the national (or federal) government is responsible for making, carrying out, and enforcing in a fair manner laws that protect individual rights (freedom of religion and expression, fair trials, the vote, equal opportunity) and promote the common good (national parks, defense, clean air, pure-food-and-drug laws). It is made up of three branches: the **legislative** (Congress, which makes laws), the **executive** (the president, who carries out and enforces laws), and the **judicial** (the Supreme Court, which makes decisions on the constitutionality of laws). The president, vice president, senators, and congresspeople in the House of Representatives are directly elected (the latter two together make up the Congress), although the Electoral College casts each state's vote for president, a major issue in the close election of 2000, in which one candidate, Democrat Al Gore, won the national popular vote and the other candidate, Republican George W. Bush, won the hotly disputed electoral vote and ascended to the presidency.

STATE AND LOCAL GOVERNMENT IN THE UNITED STATES

The states have constitutions as well, and each state has its own legislative (makes laws), executive (governor), and judicial branches. State governments usually concern themselves most with education, roads, health care, parks, public welfare, and law enforcement, as well as other important issues that may vary from state to state. High state officials are elected by the voters, and most state money comes from sales taxes, income taxes, and license-and-user fees.

Local governments provide many services, such as police and fire protection, utilities (water and/or sewer), education, public housing, zoning, licensing, libraries, museums, sports facilities, and transportation and roads. Most local government officials are elected by voters and may include mayors, city council members, school board members, and other officials; most local money comes from property taxes and sales taxes, and from the state and federal governments.

A citizen is represented by the president, the vice president, two senators, a congressman, a state senator, a state representative, and a mayor, city councilperson, or city or county commissioner, as well as a school board member and members of any other local governing bodies. It is important for citizens to know who represents them, how to contact their representatives, and which level of government is concerned with which issues and/or services.

The ordinary citizen has a role in the government as well: in a democracy, each citizen is a full and equal member of the community with equal rights under the law, not limited by gender or ethnicity. Although in the past the United States denied the vote to women and to slaves, male ex-slaves gained the vote after the Civil War and women gained it in 1920. Similarly, Native Americans often had limited rights in the past, but now may participate fully as members of their own tribal nations and/or as members of the general society. Citizenship means that the person is a legally recognized member of the nation and has equal rights and privileges under the law, as well as responsibilities (such as paying taxes). In return for their allegiance to the United States, citizens receive protection and other services from the government.

Noncitizens, called "aliens," have many of the same rights and responsibilities, but lack important rights such as the rights to vote, to serve on juries, and to hold elective office. In most cases, people born in the United States are automatically citizens, and others can become citizens through five years' residence, passing a test on the Constitution and the history and government of the United States, showing proof of good moral character, and taking an oath of allegiance. Their minor children become citizens when the parents are naturalized. Other countries have other citizenship requirements, and most countries control the number of immigrants and, hence, the eventual number of new citizens.

Since one of the most important elements of government is protecting individual rights, it is important for citizens to understand why those rights are so significant. Additionally, most are not absolute and some may be limited when they conflict with others. Personal rights include the right to association; to choose one's religion and neighborhood; and to travel freely, including leaving and returning to the United States and emigrating if so desired.

Political rights include the right to vote, speak freely and criticize the government, join organizations (including political parties), and run for and hold public office. Economic rights include the right to own property, start a business, change jobs, or join a union. Moral responsibility, self-discipline, respect for individual worth and human dignity, and compassion are important traits for individuals who wish to exercise their rights in a free society. Obviously many of these rights (including school prayer, welfare, equal pay for equal work, and fair housing practices) are political issues as well, as people argue over their application to individual lives.

In our very individualistic society, people sometimes forget that responsibilities are as important as rights. On a personal level, people are responsible for taking care of themselves and their families, accepting responsibility for their actions, and taking advantage of the opportunity to be educated. In the public arena, they have many responsibilities: obeying the law, respecting the rights of others, monitoring and communicating with their elected leaders, voting (locally, statewide, and nationally), paying taxes, serving on juries, and serving in the armed forces.

Individuals wishing to exercise civic responsibility should develop such important traits as civility (treating others with respect and not being insulting to them, even when disagreeing), respect for law, civic mindedness (concern for the well-being of one's community and nation), critical mindedness (questioning the truth of various positions, including one's own), persistence, and willingness to negotiate and compromise.

One of the elements that sets off a representative society from a dictatorship is the participation of the citizens, but in recent years, fewer and fewer people are participating in the political process through voting. This indifference is alienating, since if citizens want input, they must make themselves heard, including not only voting but also being informed, discussing public issues, contacting public officials, and joining interest groups and parties reflecting their views.

Political leadership and public service are vitally important, and, although people are increasingly cynical about politicians and the political process, they need to understand what politicians do and that political leadership is necessary, from the lowest local levels to the highest national levels. In order to best use their power of the vote, citizens should be able to analyze the qualities needed for responsible leaders in various positions and to evaluate candidates for those qualities to select competent and responsible persons to help run the government and the nation. Commitment to the values and principles of constitutional democracy, along with respect for the rights of others, are perhaps the most important public qualities, while needed personal qualities include the ability to work with others, reliability, courage, honesty, fairness, intelligence, the ability to work hard, and knowledge of issues.

It is important that citizens be knowledgeable about public affairs and about the underlying meaning, fragility, and relative rareness of democracy, in order that they may fully value and cherish the participatory system and explain and defend it to others. This awareness gives citizens the power to participate in, whether to reaffirm or to change, the government under which they live. Without the attention and participation of knowledgeable and caring citizens, democracy can wither and die.

THE UNITED STATES IN THE WORLD

Nearly all the various areas of the world are divided into independent nation-states, each of which uses some kind of law to administer its government, govern its citizens, make agreements, and conduct foreign policy. Although many nations belong to the international United Nations or other international organizations such as the Organization of American States or the European Community, all of which strive to settle disputes and promote such interests as human rights, economic development, and health issues, these organizations have little enforcement power compared to that of the nation-states themselves. Therefore, they are not always successful in preventing or settling local, regional, or worldwide wars.

In the international arena, nations deal with issues of trade, diplomacy, treaties, humanitarian aid, economic incentives and sanctions, and the uses of their militaries. They may have internal or external conflicts about national interests, ethnicity, religion, resources, territory, and power. The North American Treaty Organization (**NATO**), the World Court, and various regional organizations such as the Organization of Petroleum Exporting Countries (**OPEC**), help to organize and coordinate activities for groups of nations, but even within those groups, there is often dissent. Nongovernmental organizations, often nonprofit humanitarian groups such as the International Red Cross and Amnesty International, also have influence on the international scene.

But just as Japan withdrew from the League of Nations when it was sanctioned for aggression in Manchuria in 1931, any nation can leave any organization, and group actions are rarely binding: when the World Court faulted the United States for interference in Nicaragua in the 1980s, the United States ignored it. But although there is very little enforcement of group decisions, international organizations provide an important forum for exchange of various viewpoints, and, on occasion, do take decisive action. For example, the United Nations has intervened in war-torn areas around the world, such as Korea, Bosnia, and Kosovo, and many nations are more comfortable taking military action in concert with others rather than individually.

U.S. interaction with the rest of the world, or foreign policy, is carried out in many ways: Congress (the House and the Senate) has the power to declare war, raise and support armies, and provide a navy, and the Senate has the power to approve treaties. The president is also commander in chief of the armed forces and makes treaties and appoints ambassadors (official representatives) of the United States to various countries, regions, and/or organizations, such as the United Nations. The federal judiciary decides cases about ambassadors, treaties, and treason (turning against one's country, often involving spying to aid another country).

Sometimes issues become very confused, as in Vietnam, where the United States fought an undeclared war, or in Haiti, where U.S. troops are trying, not very successfully, to keep the peace and provide political stability. In many foreign policy situations, there is often disagreement about what actions are appropriate, and public opinion (often expressed in petitions, in the media, and in protests) frequently weighs as heavily as that of the experts: public opinion was a major factor during the Vietnam War, from which the United States finally pulled out because of public opposition.

While the American penchant for individualism and freedom has affected many countries around the world and thereby has encouraged democracy, the United States has also been affected by outside influences, from John Locke's early writings—so well-known to the founding fathers—to the United Nations' Universal Declaration of Human Rights. Because of the shrinking of the world due to improved communications and transportation, American influences have spread greatly, often in areas where local order has broken down and people are looking for a system to emulate.

Conversely, international events (demographic, environmental, economic, or political) often affect the United States, such as Haiti's and Central America's unrest that brought thousands of refugees to the United States, or Canada's complaints about the effects of U.S. air pollution, or the effect on American wages in relation to those in Mexico as a result of the North America Free Trade Agreement, or American military and humanitarian involvement in the Balkans as a result of the breakup of Yugoslavia.

In 2003, the United States took a new approach to spreading its influence. Without direct military provocation, and against the advice of United Nations inspectors and many U.S. allies, the United States invaded Iraq, erroneously convinced the country was developing "weapons of mass destruction," and helped remove its leader Saddam Hussein. Then, with no exit strategy militarily or politically in place, the U.S. military stayed in Iraq, in part to keep the country from imploding, as multiple factions fought each other and the United States. The method of withdrawal from Iraq was a major theme in the campaigns for the U.S. presidency in 2008. Although Saddam Hussein was a tyrant and a dictator, this preemptive action dramatically diminished the standing of the United States in the international community.

As population growth has leveled in the United States, the issues of population growth in other countries and subsequent increased numbers of immigrants and refugees to the United States for economic/political reasons (many, Russians, for example, fled their destabilized country after the fall of communism) have come to the forefront. The depletion of natural resources and the spread of pollution often have put the United States, which, like many other industrialized countries, has a low birthrate but consumes a disproportionate share of the world's resources in maintaining its citizens' lifestyles, at odds with poorer countries.

The United States is a member of many international organizations and was one of the founders of the United Nations, headquartered in New York City. The United States continues to be a major influence on the rest of the world, both because of its superpower status and because of its political tradition (as expressed in the Declaration of Independence, the Constitution, and the Bill of Rights). American ideals have clearly influenced much of the world from the French Revolution to the democracy movements in Eastern Europe, Latin America, South Africa, and even the People's Republic of China.

Resources on Government

Getting Started Educationally

Abraham, K. "Political Thinking in the Elementary Years: An Empirical Study." *Elementary School Journal.* November 1983: 221–231.

Bonar, D., A. Francis, and R. Hendricks. "Encouraging Law-Related Education at the Elementary Level." *The Social Studies.* July/August 1989: 151–152.

Cotton, Kathleen. *Educating for Citizenship.* Portland, Ore.: Northwest Regional Educational Laboratory, 1996

Drisko, J. "The Responsibilities of Schools in Civic Education." *Journal of Education.* 175,1, 1993: 105–119.

Hickey, M. "Mock Trials for Children." *Social Education.* January 1990: 43–44.

National Standards for Civic and Government. Calabasas, Calif. Center for Civic Education, 1994.

Parker, W. C. "Participatory Citizenship: Civics in the Story Sense." *Social Education.* October 1989: 353–354.

Parker, W. C., M. Mueller, and L. Wendling. "Critical Reasoning on Civic Issues." *Theory and Research in Social Education.* 12,1, 1989: 7–32.

"Social Studies and the Community" (theme issue). *Social Studies and the Young Learner.* September/October 1990.

Government Content for Teachers

Bachman, Steve. *U.S. Constitution for Beginners.* New York: Writers and Readers Publishing, 1987.

Bailyn, Bernard, ed. *The Debate on the Constitution.* Library of America, 1993.

Becker; Carl Lotus. *The Declaration of Independence: A Study in the* History *of Political Ideas.* New York: Random House, 1958.

Bowen, Catherine Drinker. *Miracle at Philadephia: The Story of the Constitutional Convention May to September 1787.* Boston: Little Brown, 1966, 1986.

Engle, Shirley H. and Anna S. Ochoa. *Education for Democratic Citizenship.* New York: Teachers College Press, 1988.

Heineman, R., S. Peterson, and T. Rasmussen. *American Government.* New York: McGraw-Hill, 1995.

Government Content for Students

Decisions, Decisions 5.0 (software). Watertown, Mass.: Tom Snyder Productions, 2008.

Decisions, Decisions: Current Issues (software). Watertown, Mass.: Tom Snyder productions, 2008.

Fine, Anne. *The Road of Bones.* New York: Farrar, Straus and Giroux, 2007.

Fritz, Jean. *Shh! We're Writing the Constitution.* New York: Putnam, 1987.

Our Town Meeting: A Lesson in Civic Responsibility, (software). Watertown, Mass.: Tom Snyder Productions. 1987.

Sim City (and the rest of the series that allows students to deal with government in creating a town or city).

Sis, Peter. *The Wall: Growing Up Behind the Iron Curtain.* New York: Farrar, Straus and Giroux, 2007.

Spier, Peter. *We the People: The Constitution of the United States of America.* New York: Doubleday, 1987.

States and Traits (software). Design Ware, 1984.

Thomas, Garen. *Yes, We Can: A Biography of Barack Obama.* New York: Feiwel & Friends, 2008.

Unlocking the Map Code (software for map skills). Rand McNally.

Government Websites

www.whitehouse.gov (White House and Inhabitants)

www.fedworld.gov (U.S. Government Information)

www.fbi.gov (FBI Files under Freedom of Information Act)

www.fair.org (Examines Bias in the Media)

www.ncss.org (National Council for the Social Studies)

www.socialstudies.org/resources (Government and Politics from the National Council for the Social Studies)

www.edhelper.com (Thousands of Lessons Plans, Including Civics)

www.ecedweb.unomaha.edu/lessons/fecga.htm (Economic Functions of Government)

www.nytimes.com/learning (*New York Times* for Grades 3–12)

lcweb2.loc.gov/ammem/today/today.html (Today in History)

www.blackfacts.com (Black Facts Online)

www.mountvernon.org (Mount Vernon)

www.library.georgetown.edu/dept/speccoll/amposter.htm (U.S. World War I Propaganda Posters)

www.library.georgetown.edu/dept/speccoll/britpost/britpost.htm (British World War I Propaganda Posters) *www.si.edu* (Smithsonian Museum)

http://www.civiced.org/ (Center for Civic Education)

http://www.cived.net/ (National Alliance for Civic Education)

http://www.sog.unc.edu/programs/civiced/index. php (University of North Carolina School of Government)

http://www.justicelearning.org/ (New York Times Learning Network)

http://www.civnet.org/ (CIVITAS)

http://www.emsc.nysed.gov/ciai/civics.html (New York State Education Department)

http://www.earthday.net/~earthday/civicseducation (Earthday)

http://www.educationatlas.com/civics-education.html (EducationAtlas.com)

http://www.hvcp.org/index.php?ltemid=27&id= 36&option=com_content&task=view (Hudson Valley/Catskill Partnership)

http://www.cyfc.umn.edu/ (Children Youth Family Consortium)

http://www.generationioshua.org/dnn/Education (Home School Legal Defense Association)

http://www.speakout.com/index.html (Politics, Activism, Political Issues, Government, and Elections)

http://www.unicef.org/ (Website devoted to worldwide childhood issues)

http://www.abanet.org/publiced/schoolshome.html (Teachers and Students ABA Division of Public Education)

http://www.ilo.org/global/lang—en/index.htm (International Labour Organization)

http://www.ohchr.org/EN/Pages/WelcomePage .aspx (Office of the High Commission for Human Rights)

http://www.un.org/Pubs/CyberSchoolBus/index. shtml (United Nations Cyberschoolbus)

http://videocast.nih.gov/sla/NARA/dsh/index.html (Democracy Starts Here)

http://www.civicyouth.org/ (The Center for Information & Research on Civic Learning and Engagement)

A FINAL WORD

This book may help give teachers the impetus and the confidence to encourage their students' interest in social studies content, and to teach the lessons that so often go untaught in the social studies at the elementary level. Whether the reason for the widespread neglect of the social studies is lack of knowledge or interest on the teacher's part, or simply the pervasive time constraints of language arts, math, and "specials," the social studies should be a part of the curriculum and every child should have the opportunity to develop his or her knowledge of the nation and the world, in history, geography, government, and basic economic concepts.

Clearly, there are omissions here even in the second edition, some deliberate because of space constraints, some inadvertent. The resource guide may help those who would like to pursue overlooked areas of study or further to enrich the above-mentioned areas. It will, of course, be dated by the time this book is published, but one of the joys of the social studies is the wonderful torrent of new and continuous information. With the attention on the study of the humanities, or human endeavor, that began in the Renaissance, the social studies (unknown at the time by that name) began to thrive. Through the years, the accumulation of writings in the humanities has covered several of the areas of most concern to humankind: history (including religion, art, literature, and science), geography (including culture and climate), economics (including how resources are allotted and how the haves and have-nots treat each other), and government (with its intimate relationship to all of the above).

In one sense, almost all of life is social studies, as it relates to society and to the individual's time and place within his or her society. This book aspires to help open that remarkable accumulation of knowledge to pique the interest and encourage the knowledge of the teacher, and through the teacher, to give the student the great gift of being a thinking participant in his or her world.

GENERAL RESOURCES
FOR THE TEACHER

Note: specific content resources can be found at the end of each chapter

There are many thousands of books, articles, and various other resources, including software and websites. From the plethora available, here are some idiosyncratic favorites the teacher may deem helpful, many classics in their field, others recent and valuable, some traditional and others revisionist, but he or she will undoubtedly find many good selections well beyond this list, particularly in the mushrooming websites, the constant flow of new children's literature, and the field of multicultural education. There are also many good biographies easily found in libraries and media centers by particular subject name (so they are not listed here for most well-known individuals). In addition to the following general resources, specific suggestions are given at the ends of each chapter.

The National Council for the Social Studies (NCSS) (3501 Newark Street, NW, Washington, D.C. 20016 and on the Web at socialstudies.org) publishes, the teacher-oriented journals *Social-Studies and the Young Learner* and *Social Education*, which contain individual helpful articles each month on teaching various social studies content. *Social Education*'s list of "Notable Children's Trade Books in the Field of Social Studies" appears each year in the April/May issue. In addition to selling the various National Standards, NCSS also publishes and sells many valuable individual books and support materials that the teacher may find helpful. *The Social Studies* (Heldref Publications, 4000 Albemarle Street NW, Washington, D.C. 20016) is another journal with articles on innovative ways of teaching social studies content to elementary students.

The elementary and/or middle school teacher who cares about content will find a classroom encyclopedia, either electronic or hard copy, indispensable for answering the inevitable student questions on far flung social studies material. He or she may also wish to acquire high-school-level textbooks as resources in the various content areas from the district school book depositories.

Dover Books (31 East 2nd Street, Mineola. N.Y. 11501 or store.doverpublications.com) and Bellerophon Books (36 Anacapa Street, Santa Barbara, CA 93101 or www.bellerophonbooks. com/shopsys) are particularly fine resources for social studies-related coloring books, paper dolls, and other similar materials.

Tom Snyder Productions (80 Coolidge Hill Road, Watertown. MA 02172 or http://www .tomsnyder.com) are among the leaders in producing social studies software. Social Studies School Service (10200 Jefferson Boulevard, P.O. Box 802. Culver City. CA 90232, http://www .socialstudies.com) produces an annual catalogue selling social studies books. DVDs, videos, kits, software, masters, and so on.

Comprehensive, descriptive, and analytical sources for children's literature, much of it relevant to social studies, are the 7th edition of Donna Norton's *Through the Eyes of a Child: An Introduction to Children's Literature* (Upper Saddle River, NJ and Columbus. Ohio: Merrill Prentice-Hall, 2006), especially the chapters on Historical Fiction, Multicultural Literature, and Nonfiction: Biographies and Information Books; and Carl M. Tomlinson and Carol Lynch-Brown's *Essentials of Children's Literature*, 6th edition (Needham Heights, MA: Allyn & Bacon, 2007), especially the chapters on Historical Fiction. Nonfiction: Biography and Informational Books, and Multicultural and International Literature, with their attached lists of children's books.

A good general overview of social studies content and expectations can be found in *Expectations of Excellence: Curriculum Standards for Social Studies.* Washington, DC: National Council for the Social Studies. 1994 [not undated since].

Detailed, helpful state standards for social studies are available online through the each state's department of education.

INDEX

A

Abernathy, Ralph, 54
Abnaki, 32
Abolition and abolitionists, 20, 34, 38
Aborigines, 84
Absolute monarchy and divine right of kings, 10
Abu Bakari II, 19
Act of Settlement, 10
Adams, Abigail, 34
Adams, John, 33, 35
Adams, Sam, 33
Addams, Jane, 37
Adolphus, King Gustavus, 9
Aeschylus, 4
Affirmative action, 54
Affonso, King, 20
Afghanistan, 14, 15, 56, 73
Africa and Africans, 3, 4, 5, 19–21, 25, 30, 39, 42, 45, 50, 52, 65, 66, 67, 68, 72, 74, 75, 80, 81, 89
African animals, 75
Age of Disunity, 17
Age of Exploration, 65
Age of Reason, 9
Age of the Country at War (Japan), 18
AIDS, 55, 75
Akbar, 15
Alaska, 29, 36, 76, 77
Albanians, 6
Aleuts, 29
Alexander the Great, 4, 15
Alexandria, 4, 74
Algeria and Algerians, 20, 52, 58, 75
Ali, Sunni, 19
Alien and Sedition Acts, 35
Allen, Ethan, 35
Allies, 14, 19, 41, 42, 48, 49, 50
Alps, 4, 83
Al Qaeda, 56
Alsace-Lorraine, 42
Amazon River, 66, 79
American Indians. *See* Native Americans and Indians
American Revolution, 10, 26
Americans, 14, 21, 25, 29, 31, 33, 34, 38, 41, 42, 48, 49, 50, 53
Americas, the, 1, 20, 21, 24, 29, 30, 31
Amnesty International, 108
Amundsen, Roald, 81
Anarchism and anarchy, 101, 102
Anasazi, 22
Andes Mountains, 79
André, John, 34

Anglican, 10
Anglo Saxons, 6
Angola, 52, 75
Anguilla, 78
Animism, 75
Anschluss, 47
Antarctic animals, 81
Antarctic Circle, 71, 79
Antarctic Ocean, 66
Antarctica, 65, 67, 68, 80–81
Anthony, Susan B., 38
Anthropology, 3
Antietam, 38
Antigua, 78
Apache, 22
Apartheid, 52
Appalachians, 32, 34, 38, 77
Appeasement, 47
Appomattox, 38
Arabs and Arabian Peninsula, 6, 13, 14, 19, 20, 42, 44, 65, 66, 73, 74
Arafat, Yasir, 14
Aral Sea, 73
Arapaho, 23
Arawaks, 23, 30
Archaeology, 3
Archangel, 42
Archimedes, 4
Archipelagos, 72
Arctic, the, 22, 29, 42, 80, 81, 82
Arctic Circle, 71, 72, 82
Arctic Ocean, 29, 76
Argentina, 40, 56, 79, 80
Aristarchus, 4, 70
Aristophanes, 4
Aristotle, 4
Arkansas, 37, 54
Armenia and/or Armenians, 39, 45, 73
Armistice Day, 42
Arnold, Benedict, 34
Arthur, King, 5
Articles of Confederation, 35
Aruba, 79
Aryans, 15
Ashanti, 20
Ashikaga, 18
Asia and/or Asians, 3, 13–19, 39, 42, 45, 50, 52, 65, 66, 67, 72–73, 75, 82
Asoka, 15
Atahualpa, 24
Athens, 4
Atlantic Ocean, 66, 74, 76, 79, 82
Atomic bomb, 49, 50
Attucks, Crispus, 32
Aurangzeb, 15

Australia, 29, 39, 49, 52, 67, 80, 81, 82
Australian animals, 84
Austria and/or Austrians, 9, 10, 11, 12, 14, 36, 40, 41, 42, 43, 44, 47, 83, 84
Austro-Hungarian Empire, 40, 83
Axis, 47
Axum, 19
Azerbeijan, 73
Azores, 24
Aztecs, 21, 22, 24, 31

B

Baber, 15
Bach, Johannes Sebastian, 9
Bacon, Francis, 9
Bacon, Roger, 6
Bacon's Rebellion, 31
Bahamas, 52, 78
Bahrain, 14
Baker, Josephine, 45
Balboa, Vasco Núñez de, 23
Balfour Declaration (letter), 14, 45
Balkans, 40, 109
Baltics, 47
Baltimore, Lord, 27, 28
Bangladesh, 16
Banneker, Benjamin, 30–31
Bantu, 19
Barbados, 78
Barbuda, 78
Barter, 89
Barton, Clara, 39
Barundi, 75
Bastille, 11
Batista, Fulgencio, 53
Battle of the Nations, 11
Bay of Pigs, 53
Beethoven, Ludwig van, 9
Belgium, 20, 47
Belize, 76
Bell, Alexander Graham, 39
Bengal, 16
Benin, 20
Bentham, Jeremy, 91
Bering, Vitus Jonassen, 29
Bering Sea, 29
Berlin Conference, 20
Berlin Wall, 50
Bernstein, Carl, 55
Bible, 7, 28, 30
Bill of Rights, 35, 103, 105, 109
Bin Laden, Osama, 56
Birmingham bus strike, 54
Bismarck, Otto von, 12
Black Americans, 30, 31, 38, 39, 34
Black Legend, 29

Black Muslims, 54
Black Panthers, 54
Black Sea, 73, 82
Blank check, 40, 43
Blitz, 48
Blitzkreig, 47
Block, Adriaen, 25
Blum, Leon, 44
Bodies of water (definitions), 67
Boer War, 20, 40
Bolívar, Simón, 36
Bolivia, 80
Bonaparte, Napoleon, 11
Boone, Daniel, 34
Booth, John Wilkes, 39
Borneo, 49
Bosnia-Herzegovina, 40, 57, 108
Boston Massacre, 32
Boston Tea Party, 32
Botswana, 75
Bourbons, 9
Boxer Rebellion, 17
Bradford, William, 26
Bradstreet, Anne, 26
Brahe, Tycho, 9
Brahmins, 15
Brant, Molly, 28
Brazil, 25, 36, 74, 79, 80
"Bread March of the Women", 11
Brent, Margaret, 28
Bresk-Litovsk, Treaty of, 42
Breugel Pieter, 7
Britain and British. *See* Great
    Britain
British Columbia, 77
British Empire, 16, 39
British Guiana, 80
Brontë, Emily, 12
Brown, John, 38
Brown, Willa, 45
Brown v. Board of Education, 53, 105
Bubonic plague ("black death"), 6
Buddha, Gautama, 15
Buddhists and Buddhism, 18, 73
Bulgaria, 42, 50
Bulge, Battle of the, 49
Bunker Hill, 33, 34
Burma, 49
Burton, Sir Richard, 20
Burundi, 52
Bush, George W., 57, 106
Byzantine Empire, 5, 13

C

Cabinet, 104
Cabot, John, 24
Caesar, Augustus, 4
Caesar, Julius, 4
Calhoun, John C., 37
California, 37
Calvin, John, 8
Cambodia (Kampuchea), 51, 73

Canada, 25, 28, 29, 32, 34, 52, 53,
    76, 77, 78, 109
Canberra, 84
Cannae, 4
Capital and capitalism, 90
Caribbean (area), 78
Caribbean Sea, 76
Carnegie, Andrew, 39
Carthage, 4, 74
Cartier, Jacques, 28
Caspian Sea, 73
Castro, Fidel, 53
Catherine the Great, 11, 12
Catholic Church, 6, 7, 9, 11, 13,
    29, 44
Catholics and Catholicism, 8, 24,
    28, 33, 77, 80, 83
Cayuga, 23
Central Powers, 14, 41, 42
Central America, 76, 77, 78, 109
Chad, 75
Chamberlain, Neville, 47
Champlain, Samuel, 28
Chandragupta Maurya, 15
Charlemagne, 5
Charles I, King, 10
Charles II, King, 10, 27, 28
Charles V, King, 8
Chateau Thierry, 42
Checks and balances, 35, 105
Cherokee, 23, 30
Cheyenne, 37
Chiang Kai-shek, 17, 45, 51
Chicago, 77
Chickasaw, 23
Chief Joseph, 37
Chile, 79, 80
Ch'in, 16
China and Chinese, 3, 16–18, 23,
    45, 51, 67, 73, 89, 90, 91, 109
Chinook, 22
Choctaw, 23
Chopin, Frederic, 12
Chou, 16
Christ, 5
Christians and Christianity, 5, 7,
    73, 75, 77, 83. *See also* Catholics
    and Catholicism; Protestants
    and Protestantism
"Chunnel", 57
Churchill, Winston, 48
Cinqo de Mayo, 36
Civilian Conservation Corps, 46
Civil Disobedience, 16
Civil rights, 54
Civil War, 38–39, 106
Clark, George Rogers, 34
Cleaver, Eldridge, 54
Clemenceau, Georges, 43
Clinton, Hillary, 57
Clinton, William Jefferson, 57
Clive, Robert, 16

Clay, Henry, 37
Code Napoleon, 11
Colbert, Jean Baptiste, 90
Cold War, 50, 52
Colombia, 78
Columbus, Christopher, 8, 23
Comanche, 23
Committees of Correspondence,
    32
Common Era, 5
Common law, 103
Common Market, 57
"Common Sense", 33
Communications inventions, 58
Communism and communists, 17,
    42, 50, 91
Compass rose, 69
Competition, 89, 97
Compromise of 1850, 37
Concentration camps, 49
Concord, 33
Confederal system, 104
Confederates, 38
Confucius, 16
Congo (Zaire), 20, 52, 75
Congo River, 19, 66
Congress (U.S.), 35, 43
Congress of Vienna, 12
Connecticut Compromise, 35
Conspicuous consumption, 91
Constantine, 5
Constantinople, 13
Constitution, 35, 103, 104–106, 109
Constitutional Convention, 35
Constitutional government, 35,
    102, 104–106
Continental Congress, 33, 34, 35
Contra scandal, 57
Cook, James, 29
Cooper, James Fenimore, 36
Copernicus, 9, 70
Coral Sea, 49
Corbin, Margaret, 34
Cortes, Hernando, 24, 31
Costa Rica, 76
Counter-Reformation, 8
Cowpens, 34
Crazy Horse, 37
Creek Confederacy, 23
Crimean War, 12, 41
Crimes against humanity, 50
Croatia, 57
Cromwell, Oiver, 10, 31
Cromwell, Richard, 10
Crucible, The, 27
Crusades, 6, 65
Crust (Earth's), 67
Cuba, 25, 53, 78
Cuban missile crisis, 53
Cultural Revolution, 17, 55
Custer, George, 37
Custer's Last Stand, 37

Czar, 43
Czechoslovakia, 42, 47, 50, 57, 83

D

D-Day, 49
Da Gama, Vasco, 8, 24
Da Vinci, Leonardo, 7
Darfur, 75
Dahomey, 20
Daladier, Edouard, 47
Danube River, 5, 66, 83
Dare, Virginia, 25
Dark Ages, 5
Darwin, Charles, 79
Davis, Angela, 54
Davis, Benjamin O. Jr., 38
Davis, Jefferson, 38
Dawes, William, 33
Dawes Act of 1887, 37
Day, Thomas, 31
D' Este family, 7
De Gaulle, Charles, 48
De Gouges, Olympe, 11
De Las Casas, Bartolomé, 29
De León, Ponce, 23
De Coronado, Francisco, 24
De Soto, Hernando, 24
Declaration of Independence, 33,
    103, 105, 109
Degrees, 70
Deficit spending, 91
Delaware, 25, 27
Denmark, 47, 78
Depression. *See* Great Depression
Descartes, Rene, 9
Dias, Bartholomeu, 8
Dickinson, Emily, 36
Dieppe, 49
Diet (legislature), 18
Directory, 11
Domenica, 78
Dominican Republic, 78
Douglas, Marjorie Stoneman, 55
Douglass, Frederick, 38
Drake, Francis, 29
Dred Scott Decision, 37–38
Duke of York, 27
Dunkirk, 48
Dunston, Hannah, 32
Dust Bowl, 46
Dutch., 18, 25, 26. *Also see*
    Netherlands
Dutch Guiana, 80
Duvaliers, the, 91

E

Earhart, Amelia, 45
Earth, 65, 66, 81
Earthquakes, 68
East India Company, 16
Easter Rebellion, 41
Eastern Europe, 11, 50, 83, 109

Eastern Front, 49
Eastern Orthodox Church, 13
Economics, 88–99
Ecuador, 76, 79, 80
Edict of Nantes, 8, 10
Edison, Thomas, 12, 39
Edward VIII, King, 44
Edwards, Jonathan, 28
Egypt and/or Egyptians, 4, 19, 75
Eisenhower, Dwight, 48
El Salvador, 78
Elba, 11
Eleanor of Aquitaine, 6
Electoral College, 106
Elevation, 68
Elizabeth I (Tudor), Queen, 8, 25
Elizabethan Age, 8
Emancipation Proclamation, 38
Emerson, Ralph Waldo, 36
Enclosures, 13
Engels, Friedrich, 91
England and/or the English, 5, 6,
    7, 8, 9, 10, 44, 46, 47, 57, 92. *See
    also* Great Britain
English Bill of Rights, 10
Enlightenment, 6, 9–12, 13
Entrepreneurs, 96
Equator, 69, 74, 79, 80, 81
Equiano, Olaudah, 20
Equilibrium price, 89
Equinox, 71
Erasmus, 7
Eratosthenes, 4, 66
Eskimos, 22
Estates General, 6, 10
Estonia, 42, 47, 50
Ethiopia and/or Ethiopians, 19, 47,
    75
Ethnic cleansing (genocide), 57
Etruscans, 4
Euclid, 4
Euphrates, 3, 66
Euripides, 4
Europe and/or Europeans, 4–13,
    39, 46, 48, 50, 65, 67, 72, 74, 76,
    80, 81, 82–83, 98
European Community, 108
European Union, 57, 83
Everest, Mount, 67

F

Falkland Islands (Malvinas), 56,
    79, 80
Fascism, 44, 91
Federal government, 104
Federal Reserve, 94
Federalist Papers, The, 35
Feminine Mystique, The, 54
Ferdinand, King, 23
Ferdinand, Franz and Sophie, 40
Feudalism, 5, 11
"Final solution", 46

Finland and/or Finns, 25, 42, 47
Fiscal Policy, 93
Fitzgerald, F. Scott, 45
Five (Six) Nations, 25
Florida, 35, 36, 37
Flu epidemic, 42
Ford, Gerald, 55
Ford, Henry, 39, 45
Ford's Theatre, 39
Fourteen Points, 43
France and/or French, 4, 6, 7, 8, 9,
    10, 11, 12, 14, 28, 29, 34, 36, 40,
    41, 43, 44, 47, 48, 52, 57, 83, 92
Franco, Francisco, 44
Franco Prussian War, 12
Frankenstein, 12
Franklin, Ben, 33
Franks, 5
Free French, 48
Freedom March, 54
French and Indian War, 28
French Guiana, 80
French Indochina, 49
French Revolution, 10, 35, 109
Friedan, Betty, 54
Friedman, Milton, 91
Frontenac, Count, 32
Fugitive Slave Act, 37
Fuller, Margaret, 36
Fuller, Thomas, 30
Fundamental Orders of
    Connecticut, 27

G

Galapagos Islands, 79
Galbraith, John Kenneth, 91
Galileo (Galilei), 9, 70
Gallipoli, 41
Gandhi, Mohandas, 16, 36, 54
Ganges River, 66, 72
Garibaldi, Giuseppe, 12
Garvey, Marcus, 20
Gates, Horatio, 34
Gatling, Richard, 41
Gaul, 4
Gay rights, 54
Geneva, 8
Geography, 65–87
George I, King, 10
George III, King, 33
Georgia, 27, 28
Georgia (in the former Soviet
    Union), 73
Germany and Germans, 6, 9, 12,
    39, 40, 41, 42, 43, 44, 46, 47, 48,
    49, 50, 57, 83, 91, 92
Geronimo, 37
Gettysburg, 38
Ghana, 19
GI Bill, 50
Gilded Age, 39
Global Positioning System, 65

Global Warming, 71, 81
Globalization, 98
Globe (characteristics of), 66, 68–71
Glorious Revolution, 10
Gobi Desert, 73
Golden Age, 4
Golden Mean, 4
Goods and services, 95
Gore, Al, 57, 72, 106
Government, 101–109
Grand Banks, 25
Grand Canyon, 24
Grant, Ulysses S., 38
Gravity and motion, laws of, 9
Gray Panthers, 55
Great Awakening, 28
Great Britain, 14, 17, 20, 32, 35, 36, 40, 48, 50, 52, 56, 80, 81, 84
Great Depression, 44, 45–46, 52, 89, 92, 97
Great Lakes, 77
Great Rift Valley, 3
Great Schism, 7
Great Wall of China, 16, 17
Great Zimbabwe, 19
Greater Antilles, 78
Greece and Greeks, 4, 5, 7, 65
Green Mountain Boys, 33
Greene, Nathanael, 34
Greenland, 78
Greenwich, 70
Grenadines, 78
Grey, Edward, 41
Gross Domestic Product, 94
Guadeloupe, 78
Guam, 36
Guantanamo Bay, 56
Guarani, 21
Guatemala, 76, 78
Guilford Court House, 34
Gulf of Mexico, 76
Gulf Stream, 82
Gulf War, 56
Gutenberg, Johannes, 7
Guyana, 80

H

Habsburgs, 9
Haiti, 36, 78, 91, 108, 109
Hale, Nathan, 34
Hamilton, Alexander, 35
Han, 17
Han Wu Ti, 17
Hancock, John, 33
Hannibal, 4
Harappa, 15
Harlem Renaissance, 45
Harvey, William, 9
Hat Act, 32
Hawaii, 29, 36, 48, 77. *See also* Pearl Harbor
Hawkins, John, 24

Hawthorne, Nathaniel, 36
Hemingway, Ernest, 45
Hemispheres, 69, 70, 71
Henry, Patrick, 33
Henry VII, King, 7
Henry VIII, King, 8
Henry of Navarre, 8
Henry the Navigator, 8
Hesse, 33
Heyerdahl, Thor, 23
Heyn, Piet, 29
Hideyoshi, 18
Himalayas, 73
Hindenburg, Paul von, 44
Hindus and Hinduism, 15, 73
Hippocrates, 4
Hiroshima, 49
Hiss, Alger, 51
Historical man, 1
Hitler, Adolf, 46, 47, 50
Hittites, 3
Ho Chi Minh, 51
Hobbes, Thomas, 9, 101
Holbein, Hans, 7
Holocaust, 14, 47, 49, 83
Holy Roman Empire, 6, 8, 9, 10
Homer, 4
Honduras, 76, 78
Hooker, Thomas, 27
Hoover, Herbert, 46
Hopewell, 22
Hopi, 22
House of Burgesses, 26
Hsia, 16
Hsun-tzu, 16
Huang Ho River, 16
Hudson, Henry, 25
Hudson Bay, 25
Hudson River School, 36
Hudson River Valley, 25
Huguenots, 8
Human resources/capital, 95
Hume, Allen O., 16
Hundred Days' Reform, 17
Hundred Years' War, 7
Hungary, 12, 42, 50, 57
Huns, 5
Hurricane Katrina, 98
Huss, John, 7
Hussein, Saddam, 56, 109
Hutchinson, Anne, 26
Hyksos, 3

I

Ice Age, 21
Iliad, The, 4
Immigrants and immigration, 36, 40, 57, 78
Incas, 22, 24, 80
Incentives, 97
Income (and redistribution), 93

Indentured servants, 31
Independence movements, 21
India, 15-16, 45, 52, 72, 73
Indian Ocean, 66, 72, 74, 81, 84
Indians (Native Americans), 21–26, 28, 29, 30, 31–32, 37
Indochina, 51
Indonesia, 72, 73
Indulgences, 7
Indus River, 3, 66, 73
Industrial Revolution, 12, 20, 39, 41, 83
Inflation, 95
Inquisitions, 8
Interest rates, 95
Intergovernmental Panel on Climate Change, 72
International Date Line, 69
Intifada, 14
Inuit, 22
Iran (Persia) and Iranians, 14, 56, 73
Irangate, 57
Iraq, 3, 14, 56, 73, 108
Ireland and/or Irish, 37, 41
Iron Act, 32
Iron Curtain, 83
Iroquois and Iroquois League, 23, 25, 28
Isabella, Queen, 23
Islam., 13, 73, 75. *Also see* Muslims
Islamic fundamentalist, 14, 55
Israel, 14, 15, 47, 73
Isthmus, 67
Italy and/or Italians, 4, 6, 12, 39, 41, 42, 47, 48, 49, 91
Ivan the Great, 11
Ivan the Terrible, 11

J

Jackson, Andrew, 37
Jackson, Jesse, 54
Jackson, Stonewall, 38
Jacobins, 11
Jamaica, 78
James I, King, 10
James II, King, 10, 27
Jamestown, 25
Japan and/or Japanese, 18–19, 40, 45, 48, 49, 50, 73, 108
Java, 49
Jay, John, 35
Jefferson, Thomas, 33, 35
Jemison, Mary, 32
Jews and/or Judaism, 3, 5, 6, 8, 26, 36, 45, 46, 47, 49–50, 73, 83
John (Lackland), King, 6
Johnson, Andrew, 39
Johnson, Lyndon, 51
Joliet, Louis, 28
Jordan, 73
Joyce, James, 45
Juan Carlos, King, 44

Justinian, 13
Jutland, Battle of, 41

K

Kalahari Desert, 75
Kansas Nebraska Act, 37
Katyn Forest, 47
Kemal, Mustafa (Ataturk), 14
Kennedy, John F., 54
Kennedy, Robert F., 54
Kenya, 52
Kepler, Johannes, 9
Kerensky, Alexander, 43
Key, 69
Keynes, John Maynard, 91
Khan, Genghis, 13
Khan, Kublai, 13
Khmer Rouge, 51
Khoisan, 20
Khomeini, Ayatollah, 55
King, Martin Luther, Jr., 16, 36, 54
King William's War, 32
King Philip's War, 31
King's Mountain, 34
Knox, John, 8
Kociuszko, Tadeusz, 12, 34
Kongo, 19
Koran, 13
Korea, 51, 73, 108
Korean War, 51
Kornilov, General, 43
Kosovo, 57, 108
Kristallnacht, 46
Kush, 19
Kuwait, 56, 73

L

Labour government, 50
Lafayette, Marquis de, 34
Laissez-faire economics, 90
Lao-tse, 16
Laos, 51
Latimer, Louis, 39
Latin America, 24, 36, 39, 53, 76, 109
Latitude and longitude (and minutes, seconds and degrees), 69
Latvia, 42, 47, 50
Law of diminishing returns, 97
Lawrence, T. E., 44
League of Nations, 43, 108
Leakey, Louis, 3
Lebanon, 14, 73
Lee, Henry "Light-Horse Harry", 34
Lee, Richard Henry, 33
Lee, Robert E., 38
Legalists, 16
Legend, 69
Leibniz, 9
Lenape Indians, 27
Lend-lease, 48

Lenin, Vladimir, 42, 43
Lesser Antilles, 78
Leviathan, 9
Lexington, 33
Liberia, 20
Limited government, 102
Lincoln, Abraham, 38, 39
Lincoln, Benjamin, 34
Lindbergh, Charles, 45
Linnaeus, Carolus, 9
Lithosphere, 67
Lithuania, 42, 47, 50
Little Bighorn, 37
Livingston, David Dr., 20
Local government, 106
Locke, John, 9, 101, 108
Long March, 17, 45
Longfellow, Henry W., 33
Louis XIV, King, 10
Louis XV, King, 11
Louis XVI, King, 10, 11
Louisiana Purchase, 36
Louisiana Territory, 36
L'Overture, Touissaint, 36
Luba, 19
Lusitania, 41, 45
Luther, Martin, 7–8
Luxembourg, 47
Lydians, 80

M

Macedonia, 57
Machiavelli, Niccolò, 7
Machu Picchu, 80
Macroeconomics, 88
Madagascar, 75
Madison, James, 35
Magellan, Ferdinand, 8, 23–24
Maginot Line, 47
Magna Carta, 6
Magnus, Albertus, 6
Magyars, 6
Maine, 27, 37
Malcolm X, 54
Mali, 19, 75
Malinche, 24
Malthus, Thomas, 90
Manchuria, 108
Manchus, 17
Mandela, Nelson, 52
Mandingo, 19, 20
Mansu Musa, 19
Mao Tse-tung, 17, 45
Marbury v. Madison, 36
Marco Polo, 6, 17, 89
Marcos, Ferdinand, 91
Maria Theresa, 12
Marianas Trench, 68
Marie Antoinette, Queen, 11
Marion, Francis, 34
Market economy, 96
Markham, Beryl, 45

Marne, 41
Marshall, George, 50
Marshall, John, 36
Marshall, Thurgood, 53
Marshall Plan, 50
Martel, Charles, 6
Martinique, 78
Marx, Karl, 91
Marxists, 43
Mary I (Tudor), 8
Maryland, 28
Massachusetts, 26, 27, 34
Massachusetts Bay Colony, 26
Matzeliger, Jan, 39
Mauritania, 75
Maximilian, Archduke, 36
Maya, 21
Mazarin, Cardinal, 10
Mazzini, Giuseppe, 12
McArthur, Douglas, 50
McCain, John, 57
McCarthy, Joseph, 51
McClellan, George, 38
McCoy, Elijah, 39
Meade, George S., 38
Medicaid, 92
Medicare, 92
Mediterranean Sea, 65, 66, 72, 74
Meiji, 18
Mekong River, 73
Melanesia, 84
Melbourne, 84
Melville, Herman, 36
Memphis, 38
Mencius, 16
Mensheviks, 43
Mercantilism, 90
Mercator projection, 68
Mesopotamians, 3
Mestizo, 24, 80
Mexican War, 16
Mexico, 32, 36, 76, 77, 78, 109
Mexico City, 78
Michaelangelo (Buonarroti), 7
Michigan, 37
Microeconomics, 88
Micronesia, 84
Middle Ages, 5–7
Middle East, 3, 6, 15, 39, 44, 48, 73, 74, 75
Middle Kingdom, 16
Midway, 49
Mill, John Stuart, 91
Miller, Arthur, 27
Ming, 17
Minoans, 4
Minutes, 70
Mississippi River, 38, 66, 77
Missouri, 37, 77
Missouri Compromise, 37
Moguls, 13
Mohammed, 13

Mohawk, 23
Mohenjo-Daro, 15
Money, 89, 90
Mongolia, 73
Mongols, 11, 13, 15, 17, 18
Monopoly, 92
Monroe, James, 36, 53
Monserrat, 78
Montcalm, General, 28
Montezuma, 24
Montgomery, Bernard, 48
Montreal, 77
Moody, Deborah, 25
More, Thomas, 7
Morgan, Daniel, 34
Morgan, Garrett, 39
Moroccans, 19, 75
Morse, Samuel, 39
Mound builders, 22
Mount Everest, 67, 73
Mozambique, 52, 75
Mozart, 9
Muhammad, Elijah, 54
Muir, John, 36
Munich, 47
Murmansk, 42
Muslims and Islam, 6, 8, 13, 14, 15,
    16, 19, 54, 55, 56, 73, 74, 75, 77,
    83
Mussolini, Benito, 47, 49
Myanmar (Burma), 73
Mycenaeans, 4

N

NAACP, 53
NAFTA, 78
Nagasaki, 49
Namibia, 75
Napoleon, 11, 12, 41
National Assembly, 11
National health insurance, 93
Nationalism, 12, 47, 55, 57
Nationalist Chinese, 17, 45
Native Americans, 21, 23, 37.
    See also Pre-Columbian
    Indians; *individual groups*
NATO, 110
Natural resources, 96, 99
Navajo, 22
Nazi Germany and Nazis, 44, 49,
    54, 104, 105
Needs and wants, 96
Nehru, Jawaharlal, 16
Netherlands and/or Dutch, 8, 9,
    10, 18, 20, 24, 25, 26, 27, 29, 30,
    34, 40, 47, 51, 79, 80
Netherlands Antilles, 79
New Amsterdam, 25
New Deal, 92
New England, 27, 30, 31
New Guinea, 84
New Hampshire, 27

New Jersey, 27, 33, 34
New Netherland, 27
New Orleans, 38, 70, 71
New Sweden, 25
New World, 8, 9, 20, 23, 24, 25, 28,
    29, 30, 32, 36, 40
New York (state), 14, 25, 27,
    33, 41
New York City, 34, 36, 50, 55, 56,
    111
New Zealand, 29, 81, 84
Newfoundland, 24
Newton, Huey, 54
Newton, Isaac, 9
Nez Perce, 37
Nicaragua, 53, 58, 76, 78, 110
Nietzsche, Friedrich, 1
Niger, 75
Nigeria, 19, 52, 75
Nightingale, Florence, 12
Nile River, 4
Nixon, Richard, 51, 54, 55
Nobel Peace Prize, 40
Nobunaga, Oda, 18
Noh plays, 18
Nonaggression treaty, 47
Nonprofit institutions, 94
Nootka, 22
North America, 9, 22, 24, 25, 26,
    28, 29, 32, 40, 67, 68, 76, 77, 78,
    79, 80
North Carolina, 25, 31, 33, 34
North Sea, 82
Northern Ireland, 41
Northwest Territory, 35
Norway and Norwegians, 47
Nova Scotia, 28

O

Obama, Barack, 57
Occupied France, 49
Oceania, 84
October War, 14
Odyssey, The, 4
Oglethorpe, James, 28
Ohio, 35
Oil embargo, 19
Okinawa, 49
Old Masters, 7
Oligopoly, 93
Oliver Cromwell, 10, 31
Olmecs, 22
Olympics, 4
Oman, 14, 67, 73
Oneida, 23
Onondaga, 23
OPEC, 55, 110
Operation Barbarossa, 48
Operation Torch, 48
Opium War, 17
Opportunity cost, 89
Oregon Territory, 36

Organization of American States,
    110
Ottawa, 77
Otto the Great, 6
Ottoman (Turkish) Empire, Turkey
    and Turks, 12, 13, 14, 39, 40,
    41, 42, 44, 45, 73, 83
Owen, Robert, 92
Oyo, 20

P

Pacific Ocean, 23, 25, 26, 29, 30, 42,
    45, 49, 50, 68, 69, 72, 76, 79, 84
Paine, Thomas, 33
Painting, 7, 17, 45
Pakistan, 16, 52, 73
Palestine, 14
Palladio, Andrea, 7
Panama, 23, 67, 76, 78
Panama Canal, 67, 78
Pangea, 67
Paraguay and Paraguayans, 21, 80
Paris, 29, 47
Parks, Rosa, 54
Parliament, 10, 32, 33, 45, 106
Parliamentary system, 106
Patricians, 4
Pawnee, 23
Pearl Harbor, 19, 40, 48, 49
Peasant rebellions, 6
Peasants, 11, 30, 43
Peloponnesian Wars, 4
Penal colony, 84
Peninsula, 67, 73
Penn, William, 27
Pennsylvania, 15, 27, 33, 34, 35, 56
Pericles, 4
Perma Frost, 71
Perry, Matthew, 18
Pershing, John, 42
Persia and Persians. *See* Iran
Personal responsibilites, 104
Personal rights, 109
Peru and Peruvians, 21, 22, 80
Peter the Great, 11
Petrarch, 7
Philadelphia, 27, 35
Philip's War, King, 31
Philip of Macedonia, 4
Philippines, 8, 23, 36, 39, 48, 49, 53,
    73, 92
Phoenicians, 3
"Phoney war", 47
Physiocrats, 91
Pickett, George E., 38
Pilgrims, 26
Piracy, 29
Pitcher, Molly, 34
Pizarro, 24, 31
Plains of Abraham, 28
Plains Indians, 23
Plantations, 8, 20, 25, 28, 30

Plate tectonics, 68
Plato, 4, 91
Plebians, 4
Plessy v. Ferguson, 53, 107
Plymouth, 26
Plymouth Rock, 26
Pocahontas, 26
Poems on Various Subjects, 33
Pol Pot, 51
Poland and Poles, 12, 34, 42, 43, 47, 49, 50
Polish Corridor, 47
Polish partitions, 12
Political influence, 94
Political leadership, 109
Political rights, 109
Pollution, 77, 81, 103, 111
Polo, Marco, 6, 17
Polynesia, 84
Poor, Salem, 34
Pope, the, 5, 6, 8, 24, 80
Port Arthur, 40
Port Hudson, 38
Portugal and the Portuguese, 8, 9, 15, 18, 19, 20, 23, 24, 25, 36, 40, 44, 48, 52, 76, 80, 92
Pound, Ezra, 45
Powhatans, 26
Preamble, 107
Pre-Columbian Indians, 31
Prehistory, 1
President, 72, 77, 78, 84, 106, 107, 108, 110
Prices, 90, 91, 94, 95, 96, 97, 98
Prime Meridian, 69, 70
Prime Minister, 10, 48, 56, 77, 106
Prince Henry the Navigator, 8
Princeton, 36
Principe, Gavrilo, 40
Printing press, 7, 17, 24
Privateering, 29
Production, 91, 92, 94, 96, 97, 98
Productive resources, 97
Productivity, 97
Profit, 90, 97, 98
Progressive Era, 39
Prohibition, 45, 107
Property rights, 94
Protestant Reformation, 7, 26
Protestants and Protestantism, 7, 8, 9, 10, 28, 77, 80
Provincetown, 26
Provisional government, 43
Prussia, 11, 12, 34
Public health, 93, 96
Public safety, 94
Public Works Administration, 46
Puebla, 36
Pueblos, 22
Puerto Rico, 23, 25, 36, 39, 53, 78
Pulaski, Kazimierz, 34
Punic Wars, 4

Purchasing power, 95
Pure competition, 93
Purges, 43
Puritans, 25, 26, 32
Putnam, Israel, 34
PWA, 46
Pythagoras, 4

Q
Qatar, 14, 73
Quakers. *See* Society of Friends
Quebec, 28, 29, 33, 52, 53
Quebec Act, 33
Quebec City, 28
Quechua, 21
Quito, Ecuador, 80
Quotas, 94, 95

R
Rainforests, 73, 77
Raleigh, Walter, 25
Rape of Nanking, 49
Raphael (Santi), 7
Rasputin, 43
Reagan, Ronald, 56
Recession, 55, 92, 95
Reconstruction, 39
Red Army, 43
Red Cross, International, 39, 110
Red Sea, 48
Reforms, health and safety, 13, 39
Regulation, 91, 93, 94
Reichstag, 44
Reign of Terror, 11
Relative price, 90
Religion, 3, 4, 5, 7, 9, 57. *See also individual religions*
Religious freedom, 25, 26 *See also* Freedom of religion/toleration
Religious fundamentalism, 14
Renaissance, 6, 7, 8, 13, 70
Rent control, 93
Reparations, 27, 43
Representation, 6, 11, 13, 32, 35
Representatives, 105, 106, 107
Restitution, 49
Revere, Paul, 33
Revolutionary War (American), 31, 32
Rhine River, 43
Rhineland, 47
Rhode Island, 26, 34
Rhodesia. *See* Zimbabwe
Ricardo, David, 91
Richelieu, Cardinal, 8
Richmond, 38
Rift Valley, Great, 3
Rights of Man and Citizen, 11
Ring of Fire, 68
Risk, 97
River of Grass, 55
Roanoke Island, 25

Roaring Twenties, 45
"Robber barons", 39
Robespierre, 11
Robin Hood, 5
Rockefeller, John D., 39
Rockwell, George Lincoln, 54
Rolfe, John, 26
Roman Empire, 5, 6, 13
Romania, 44, 50
Romanov, Michael, 11
Romanovs, 11, 43
Romanticsm, 12
Rome and Romans, 4, 5, 6, 7, 13, 47, 65, 73, 74
Rommel, Erwin, 48
Roosevelt, Eleanor, 46
Roosevelt, Franklin, 46, 48
Roosevelt, Theodore, 36, 40
Roosevelt Corollary, 53
Ross, Betsy, 34
Royal Air Force, 48
Royal Observatory, 69
Russia and Russians, 11, 12, 13, 19, 29, 30, 36, 40, 41, 42, 43, 44, 45, 47, 48, 49, 50, 53, 57, 58, 72, 73, 82, 83, 92, 99, 111 See *also* Soviet Union
Russian Orthodox Church, 43
Russian Revolution, 43
Russo-Japanese War, 40
Rwanda, 52, 75

S
Safety net (economic), 92
Safety regulations, 93
Sahara Desert, 75
Salazar, Antonio, 44
Salem, Peter, 34
Salem witch trials, 27
Sampson, Deborah, 34
Samurai, 18
San Martin, José de, 36
San Andreas Fault, 68
Santo Domingo, 78
Sappho, 4
Sarajevo, 40
Saratoga, 34
Saudi, 15, 56
Saudi Arabia, 14, 73
Savannah, 75
Saving, 96, 97
Savings and loan scandal, 57
Scandinavia and Scandinavians, 6, 23, 82
Scarcity, 89, 96, 99
Schlieffen Plan, 41
Schuyler, Philip, 34
Scotland, 8, 10, 32, 92
Scott, Robert, 81
Seale, Bobby, 54
Seasons, 71, 80
Second Continental Congress, 33

Segregation, 52, 53, 107
Senate, 4, 35, 57, 110
Seneca, 23
Seneca Falls Convention, 38
Senegal, 33
"Separate but equal", 107
Separation of powers, 35
Separatists, 26
Sepoy Rebellion, 16
Serbia, 40, 57
Serfdom, 91
Serfs, 5, 12
Seven Years' War, 12, 29
Sex scandal, 57
Shah of Iran, 14
Shakespeare, William, 7
Shang, 16
Shawnee, 32
Shays' Rebellion, 35
Shelley, Mary, 12
Sherman, William, 38
Shikibu, Murasaki, 18
Shiloh, 38
Shinto, 18
Shogun, 18
Siberia, 21, 29, 73
Sierra Leone, 20, 52
Silent Spring, 55
Silent barter, 19
Sinai Peninsula, 14
Singapore, 73, 95
Sino-Japanese War, 17
Sioux, 23, 37
Sitting Bull, 37
Six Day War of, 1967 14
Slaves and slavery, 4, 5, 9, 19, 20,
    22, 24, 25, 27, 28, 29, 30, 31, 33,
    34, 35, 36, 37, 38, 75, 77, 78, 80,
    91, 108
Slavic countries, 13
Slovenia, 57
Smith, Adam, 91
Smith, John, 26
Social Security, 46, 92, 93, 94
Socialism, 44, 92
Socialists, 44
Society of Friends (Quakers), 27
Socrates, 4
Solomon Islands, 84
Solstice, 71
Somalia, 75
Songhai, 19
Soninke, 19
Sons and Daughters of Liberty, 32
Sophocles, 4
Sumter, Fort, 38
South Africa, 20, 40, 52, 74, 75, 111
South America, 21, 22, 23, 24, 25,
    29, 30, 36, 39, 52, 66, 67, 68, 76,
    77, 78, 79, 80, 81
South Carolina, 28, 38
South China Sea, 66

South Dakota, 37
South Pacific (area), 23, 30
South Pacific Ocean, 72
South Pole, 68, 71, 81
Southern Ocean, 81
Soviet Union, 31, 32, 50, 57, 72, 73,
    83, 105 *See also* Russia
Spain and/or Spanish, 4, 6, 8, 9, 10,
    12, 13, 20, 22, 23, 24, 25, 26, 28,
    29, 30, 31, 34, 35, 36, 39, 40, 44,
    48, 51, 76, 77, 80, 83, 92
Spanish American War, 36, 39
Spanish Armada, 9
Spanish Civil War, 44
Spanish Sahara, 39
Sparta, 4
Sputnik, 50
Squanto, 26
Sri Lanka (Ceylon), 67, 73
St. Brendan, 23
St. Helena, 11
St. Kitts and Nevis, 78
St. Lawrence River, 28
St. Lucia, 78
St. Peter's Cathedral, 7
St. Vincent, 78
Stagflation, 95
Stalin, Joseph, 43, 49
Stalingrad, 48
Stamp Act, 32
Standard of living, 95, 98
Stanley, Henry, 20
Stanton, Elizabeth Cady, 38
Star Chamber, 10
State and local government, 94,
    105, 106, 108
States' rights, 36, 38
Steuben, Baron von, 34
Stock market, 94
Stonewall riots, 54
Stowe, Harriet Beecher, 38
Stuart, J.E.B., 38
Stuarts, 10
Stuyvesant, Peter, 25
Subsidies, 92, 93, 94
Sudan and/or Sudanese, 20, 70, 75
Sudetenland, 47
Suez Canal, 14, 48, 67
Sugar Act, 32
Sui, 17
Suleiman the Magnificent, 13
Sumatra, 49
Sumerians, 3
Sun, 70, 71, 81
Sun Yat-sen, 17, 45
Sundiata, 19
Sung, 17
Supply and demand, 90, 97
Supreme Court (U.S.), 35, 36, 37,
    53, 56, 57, 106, 107
Surendranath Banerjea, 16
Suriname, 80

Swahili, 19
Sweden and/or Swedes, 9, 25, 29,
    48
Switzerland, 8, 48, 83
Sydney, 84
Syria, 14, 73

T

Tahiti, 29
Taiping Rebellion, 17
Taiwan (Formosa), 51, 73
Taj Mahal, 15
Tajikistan, 73
Tale of Genji, 18
Taliban, 14, 15, 55, 56
Tamerlane, 13
Tanganyika, 52
Tannenberg, 41
Tanzania and/or Tanzanians, 3, 20,
    75
Taoists and Taoism, 16, 73
Tariffs, 38, 94, 95
Tasmania, 84
Taxes, 5, 6, 10, 21, 32, 56, 94, 95, 97
Teach, Edward ("Blackbeard"), 29
Tecumseh, 37
Ten Commandments, 3
Tennessee, 38, 46
Tenochtitlán, 22
Teotihuacán, 22
Texas, 36, 37, 54
Thailand, 49, 67, 73
Thatcher, Margaret, 56
Theodora, 13
Third World, 52, 57
Third Estate, 10
Thirty Years' War, 8, 9
Thoreau, Henry David, 16, 36, 54
Tibet, 73
Ticonderoga, 33
Tigris-Euphrates River, 3
Timbuktu, 19
Time of Troubles, 11
Time zones, 71
Titanic, 45
Tobacco, 94, 98
Tobago, 79
Tokugawa, 18
Toleration Act, 28
Toronto, 77
Tours, 6, 13
Townshend Acts, 32
Trade, 90, 91, 95, 96
Trail of Tears, 37
Transcendentalists, 36
Treaty of Brest-Litovsk, 42
Treaty of Paris (1763), 29
Treaty of Paris (1783), 34
Treaty of Tordesillas, 24, 80
Treaty of Versailles, 43
Trenton, 33
Trinidad, 79

Triple Entente, 40
Trojan War, 4
Tropic of Cancer, 71
Tropic of Capricorn, 71, 74
Trotsky, Leon, 43
Truman, Harry, 49, 53
Truth, Sojourner, 38
Tsunami, 67
Tubman, Harriet, 38
Tunisia, 74
Turkey. *See* Ottoman Empire
Turkmenistan, 73
Tuscarora, 23
Tuskegee Airmen, 38, 45
TVA, 46
Twain, Mark, 36
Twentieth Century, 39–58
Tyrol, 42
Tz'u-hsi, Dowager Empress, 17

U

Uganda, 52, 75
Ukraine, 43
Uncle Tom's Cabin, 38
Underground Railroad, 38
Unemployment, 91, 92, 95
Unions, 94, 97
Unitary system, 106
United Arab Emirates, 14, 73
United Nations, 110, 111
United Nations Universal
    Declaration of Human Rights,
    111
United States, 13, 15, 18, 19, 20, 24,
    29, 30, 35, 36, 39, 40, 41, 43, 45,
    46, 49, 50, 51, 53, 54, 55, 56, 57,
    65, 67, 68, 74, 76, 77, 78, 82, 90,
    92, 93, 95, 99, 103, 104, 105,
    106, 107, 108, 109, 110, 111, 112
Universities, 6, 24
Upanishads, 15
Ural Mountains, 72, 82
Uruguay, 80
U.S. Constitution, 35
U.S. Treasury, 89
Utilitarianism, 92
Utopian Socialists, 92
Uzbekistan, 73

V

Valley Forge, 33
Van Eyck, Jan, 7
Van Leeuwenhoek, Antonie, 9
Vancouver, 77

Vandals, 5
Vanderbilt, Cornelius, 39
Veblen, Thorstein, 92
Vedas, 15
Venezuela, 79, 80
Vermeer, Jan, 7
Verrazano, Giovanni da, 28
Versailles, 11, 43, 44, 47
Vesalius, Andreas, 9
Veterans' Day, 42
Viceroys, 24
Vichy, 49
Vicksburg, 38
Victoria, Queen, 40
Vietnam, 51, 54, 73, 77, 92,
    110
Vietnam War, 51, 54
Vikings, 5, 23
Virgin Islands, 78
"Virgin Queen", 25
Virginia, 15, 25, 26, 28, 31, 33, 34,
    38, 56, 77
Virtual representation, 32
Visigoths, 5
Volcanoes, 68
Volga River, 67, 83
Voluntary exchange, 95
Voters, 94
Voting Rights Act, 53

W

Wages, 91, 95, 97
Wales, 32
Wallace, George, 54
Walloon, 83
War, 108, 110
War of 1812, 36
War on poverty, 54
Wars of the Roses, 7
Washington, George, 33, 35
Washington (state), 77
Washington, D.C., 15, 31, 39, 46,
    54, 56, 77
Washington Post, 55
Watergate, 55
Waterloo, 11
Wayne, Anthony, 34
Wealth of Nations, 91
Webster, Daniel, 37
Wegener, Alfred, 67
Weimar Republic, 44
Welfare, 54, 94
Wesley, John, 28
West Bank, 14
West Indies, 28, 31

Western culture, 14
Western Europe, 93, 95, 104
Western Front, 41, 42
Western hemisphere, 80
Wethersfield, 27
Wheatley, Phillis, 33
Whiskey Rebellion, 35
Whitefield, George, 28
Whitman, Walt, 36
Whitney, Eli, 35
Wilhelm II, Kaiser, 44
William of Orange, 10
William the Conqueror, 6
Williams, Roger, 26
Wilson, Woodrow, 43
Windsor, 27
Winthrop, John, 26
Wisconsin, 35, 37, 51
Wittenburg, 7
Wolfe, General, 28
Women's rights, 14, 38, 55
Woods, Granville T., 39
Woodward, Bob, 55
Workers, 92, 93, 94, 95, 97, 99
World Court, 110
World War I, 12, 13, 14, 16, 40, 41,
    42, 43, 44, 45, 46, 47, 49, 52, 83
World War II, 14, 16, 17, 19, 21, 38,
    39, 40, 41, 43, 44, 45, 46, 47, 48,
    50, 51, 52, 53, 75, 83, 84, 92
Wounded Knee, 37
WPA, 46
Wright, Orville, 13, 39
Wright, Wilbur, 13, 39
Writing system, 73
Wu Hou, 17
Wuthering Heights, 12

Y

Yangtze River, 73
Yemen, 73
Yorktown, 34
Young Turks, 44
Yprés, 41
Yugoslavia, 42, 48, 50, 57, 83, 111

Z

Zaire. *See* Congo
Zambia, 52, 75
Zanzibar, 20
Zhukov, Georgi, 48
Zimbabwe, 19, 52, 75
Zimmerman telegram, 42
Zionists, 14
Zulu, 20